Dear Adrienne —
Here's to some wonderful
memories —

Lessons from the Hoghouse

Love,

Elizabeth Clark
Sept 2013

Lessons *from the*
HOGHOUSE

One Woman's Guide to Building Her Country
Dream in a World of Ghosts, Manure,
Metal Men, and Groundhog Hunters

A Barnyard Memoir

ELIZABETH CLARK

Free Spirit Books

An imprint of

American History Press

Franklin, Tennessee
Staunton, Virginia
(888) 521-1789
Visit us on the Internet at:
www.Americanhistorypress.com

ISBN 13: 978-1-939995-01-8
Library of Congress Control Number: 2013946989

September 2013

Table of Contents

Foreword

*"Some place where there isn't any trouble. Do you suppose
there is such a place, Toto?"*

- Dorothy Gale in *The Wizard of Oz*

That place in my youth was a ten acre patch of land, a small island of country life in a sea of split-level and two-story modern colonial houses set primly on quarter acre lots in a neighborhood in the Philadelphia suburbs. It was a small farm hidden behind ancient towering arborvitae bushes, hedgerows of multiflora roses and thick patches of elderberries. Most people in the neighborhood didn't even know it existed. But we did. My sisters and I stumbled onto it one afternoon while looking for a lost kitten. Populated with goats, ducks, dogs, cats and a small herd of brown Jersey cows, Flower Hill Farm was a welcoming playground for the neighborhood urchins.

The couple who owned the farm, Max and Phyllis Feidler, were in their seventies and childless. They loved us all like the grandchildren they never had. In the days before lawsuits, limited liability partnerships, signed releases and parental supervision dominated all childhood activities; we played in the hayloft, rode the more tolerant of the cows (fervently wishing they were horses), drank still-warm milk squeezed fresh from mostly clean udders and swam in the pond with the ducks. Somehow we all survived and even thrived in an environment of freedom where the only rule was that we stay out of the bull's pasture.

When I was eleven, my family moved to New Jersey, away from my beloved Flower Hill Farm. I mourned the loss, but moved on, as we all do. I spent the next thirty-something years growing up, going to college, getting a job, car, apartment, boyfriend, better job, bigger house, better boyfriend. You know. Doing all the things that we think that people think we ought to do. But in the back of my mind, I always dreamed of returning to that little patch of peace and safety called Flower Hill Farm.

FOREWORD

This book began as a series of e-mail newsletters sent to family and friends to chronicle the events surrounding my purchase of a fixer-upper farm in Bernville, Berks County, Pennsylvania. Much of it was written late at night, when I was far past exhaustion, yet trying to convince those who knew me that I was alive and well and still clinging to a thread of sanity. These letters allowed me to see the wonder in overcoming challenges both large and small, to laugh at myself and enjoy the journey. When I took them out and re-read them I realized that I had finally found the love of my life, my very own Flower Hill Farm.

Acknowledgements

Special thanks go out to my friend, Sue Lange, who led me every step of the way and when I got bogged down demanded that I "...just get over yourself and write the darn thing." Thanks also to the members of the Saturday Scribbler's writers critique group, whose diplomatic commentary has kept me on track: Marilyn Klimcho and Lou Rushing for the edits and advice, Clem Page for prayers and encouragement and Gayle Cooper for believing that anything is possible as long as you're willing to work for it.

Dedication

This book is dedicated to my father, Charles, who always said I was not one to let the truth get in the way of a good story and to my friend and mentor, Wissie, whose courage, zest for life, love of horses and belief in me never wavered.

WANTED: Woman with great vision and poor eyesight to refurbish old farm. Stubborn animals, resident ghosts and local characters included. Wit and humor required.

Invest in Your Dreams

The decision to buy an old farmhouse in Pennsylvania was a sudden one. Most people who take on the work, expense, and frustration of an old "fixer-upper" report that, although they may have thought about it for years, the decision, when it transforms from the whimsical someday-maybe kind of fantasy into the concrete reality of the here and now, is based purely on impulse. Just like with enlightenment, finding your soul mate, or deciding to quit drinking, many first-time farm buyers can remember exactly where they were and what they were doing the moment they decided to take The Plunge.

For my "come to Jesus moment" I was with my friend Gayle and her husband Bill. Newlyweds (again) who had recently bought a farm, their mission was to find cheap, working farm implements at auction prices. I was taking a break from an over-controlling entrepreneurial boyfriend and was glad for the excuse to join them at the auction rather than go through yet one more Saturday night of making *hors d'oerves* and mixing martinis for his prospective clients. A critical review of the merchandise revealed a darling antique oak washstand which would be a perfect "finishing touch" for my late-1800s, totally restored, Victorian-style rented home, so I was excited to join them.

Although I didn't realize it at the time, I was enjoying my last six months of living the sheer bliss of perfectly finished woodwork, working appliances, a leakless roof and easy access to a supermarket that sells fresh sushi.

Flower Hill Farm thus had its beginnings at a used furniture and antique auction gallery, a "We Buy Old Furniture, We Sell Antiques" kind of place. The Saturday night auction is a great Pennsylvania tradition. While America's suburban citizens may be headed for the symphony, a five-star restaurant, or the multiplex cinema, the folks from the country are gathering at the local auction house.

A typical public sale attracts a crowd of two hundred people or so. Like all tribal rituals, the event has its own cultural norms. Amish farmers sit to the far left of the auctioneer, or lean against the back wall. The ladies from the Grange gather in a close-knit cluster just right of center. (They never actually buy anything; auctions just provide a convenient forum for trading canning recipes). Nouveau antique dealers are about three rows back from the front; the more seasoned ones are in the back row next to the auctioneer's son so that they can see when he is bidding up the merchandise. First timers find comfort by sitting near the food table.

Pennsylvania auction food is integral to the experience. Typical offerings include creamed corn chowder, perogies (sautéed in butter and onion), haluski (egg noodles and cabbage sautéed in butter and seasoned with anise), halupkies (ground meat wrapped in cabbage leaves and boiled for hours in stewed tomatoes), bratwurst with sauerkraut, waffles with ice cream and bake sale items used to raise money for the local 4-H Bovine Club. This is all washed down with ample amounts of diet soda. The food may not be made by Mom, but it is lovingly and very abundantly prepared by the Ladies Auxiliary of the North Penn Rod and Gun Club.

On this night the auctioneer had assembled a collection of Victorian furniture, farm implements, music memorabilia from the sixties and seventies, and surplus candy from a bankrupt novelty shop.

The crowd was getting restless after forty-five minutes of sheer torture as the auctioneer tried to rid himself of eighty cases of Halloween candy from the novelty shop dispersal. He informed the exasperated and increasingly agitated mob that he would not move on until all glow-in-the-dark Gummy Worms were sold. Desperate, the attendees formed an ad hoc alliance, the kind that usually happens during floods, earthquakes and tornados. People quickly put their own self-interest aside and worked to achieve a common goal: within minutes everyone with a bidder's number had a box of Gummy Worms stowed among their auction purchases.

From there we moved on to the Elvis Presley collection. At first, only the auctioneer noticed the two Elvis fans squirming with anticipation in rows three and six. Although sitting separately, these two women were cut from the same cloth. One had blond hair bleached almost to ivory with only the slightest hint of dark roots around the part in the middle. The other had dark-chestnut-to-ebony-black hair that gave the illusion of having purple highlights when the florescent lights hit it at just the right angle.

They were sizable people, the type I sometimes privately refer to as "fluffy Americans." Their black Spandex stirrup pants were stretched taut around derrieres that migrated across two of the red metal-framed folding chairs (the type with the wooden seats). The blond was wearing a flowing blouse with a peasant-style neckline in bright magenta. The brunette had on what appeared to be its cherry red twin. Each had artificial nails painted to match their blouses, with faces adorned with pancake makeup and a lot of eyeliner and mascara. These were certainly not traditional Amish women, unless they had formed their own sect. Next to each was a diminutive, yet dedicated spouse at the ready to bring drinks, food, empty boxes, newspaper or whatever was required to support their endeavor. The auctioneer held up the first of the Elvis items, the "Jailhouse Rock Commemorative Plate," one of a collection. Both women immediately began to cry.

From then on, it was an auctioneer's dream come true. He spoke only to the two women, espousing the virtues and value of each and every of the Elvis items. His voice took on a sing-song and mesmerizing quality as he slowly lured them in as if they were the only three people in the room. Everyone else became a bystander in the midst of a sacred ritual of give and take.

The blonde clearly had an edge both financially and in bidding strategy. As the prices increased, she became more aggressive, periodically turning around to glare at the brunette who started out guns-a-blazing and then pulled back just a moment before victory. (Or at least when, in the consensus of the crowd, the blonde was about to cave in).

They worked through the commemorative painted plates (six for the blonde and three for the brunette), and split one and one on the right and left profile "acrylic on black velvet" Rhinestone Elvis paintings framed in white lacquer. By this time their emotions had gotten the best of them, and both women were dabbing their mascara-streaked faces with lace-trimmed hankies.

Then came the "Love me Tender" lamp. It was an eighteen-inch-high glowing bust of Elvis, leather jacket collar turned up around his face, lips pursed in his famous pout. It was crowned with a red velvet fedora-shaped lampshade trimmed with gold tassels. There was only one.

This was going to get ugly.

I looked nervously over at Gayle. We were women of the world. Although we came from different backgrounds, we had both been around enough college fraternities, biker bars, and office Christmas parties to know the five telltale signs that tell you when it's time to make a quick exit. First, when you hear breaking glass, second, when the police show up, third, when a jealous boyfriend storms out, fourth, when you look around and the host, hostess and/or the bartenders are gone and fifth, when livestock get off the elevator.

But now we added a sixth: when a quarter ton of women start bidding for the only "Love Me Tender" lamp ever offered for public sale in Eastern Pennsylvania. We grabbed a couple of brownies from the Bovine Bake Sale and some Diet Pepsis and headed for the relative safety of the parking lot.

It was one of those cool, starlit late summer nights in September when the crickets were still out and the breeze wasn't quite cold yet. It's was no longer still and sticky, but rather the time of year when a light sweater would do. A couple of farmers were standing in their denim overalls chewing tobacco and discussing tractors in a sing-song language. It was Pennsylvania Dutch, a language that contains no Dutch words, has a few English undertones and sports several key phrases that sound rather Yiddish. Although it is ostensibly German, it has become regionalized to the point that no one from the Fatherland would understand a word of it. It is spoken by the Amish and some older "Dutchie" farmers, but the language constructs have invaded the local English dialect such that folks in these parts are known to "Toss the baby from the wagon a flower" or "Throw your father down the stairs his hat."

While the battle raged on in the auction hall, I began reciting my mantra about how someday I was going to have a horse farm with an old stone house on thirty acres, surrounded with a wrap-around porch, a porch swing, fragrant herb gardens, and a picturesque barn.

The dream was so vivid that I could easily visualize the traditional Pennsylvania stone-and-wood-sided "bank barn." For the thousandth time I explained to my patient friends that post and beam bank barns were the greatest architectural achievement of the eighteenth century. The barns were built into the side of a hill so that horses could pull the hay wagons up to the second story. The first level, the livestock level, being partially underground, was cool in the summer and warm in the winter. My fantasy farm had a stream and was partially wooded, but with plenty of pasture and not too much swamp. It was....

Gayle stopped me and said, none to gently, "You will never have your farm."

Shocked, hurt and taken aback by my best friend's lack of faith in The Dream, I said, "What do you mean by that?"

Gayle answered, "You have been talking about this farm nonstop for two years but have not made a single, solitary move toward it. You will never have it until you commit to it."

"I'm very committed," was my petulant reply. In truth, I was offended. How could Gayle not see that I had all the herbs picked out for the garden and had named each goat that scampered about in my active imagination?

"Then go buy one."

"I don't have the money, but I've been saving up. Besides, now isn't the right time what with the economy and all. My job is a little uncertain, and I don't know how things are going to work out with Curtis."

My own words sounded hollow and whining even to me. I tried to end the conversation with "The bottom line is that I can't afford it."

"Can you afford a pitch fork?" Gayle persisted.

"What does that have to do with anything?" Our exchange was getting bizarre, even on this particular evening.

"Well, if you are going to farm, you are going to have animals. Animals eat hay. Animals produce manure. In order to move hay from outside the stall to inside the stall and to move manure from inside the stall to outside the stall, you will need a pitchfork. Therefore, if you are going to farm, you need to invest in a pitchfork. Then you need to make a tangible investment every week until you actually OWN a farm. Dreams without investment can never happen."

Normally, I would have written this off as New Age talk, "name it and claim it" preachy psycho-babble, except for one thing: I knew that ten years ago, Gayle had spent a month hiding in the attics, garages and hay lofts of the few friends willing to run the risk while she was stalked by an abusive and dangerous ex-husband. When she finally returned to her small house in a small town, she found it stripped. All of her clothes, household goods and appliances, right down to the contents of the garden shed, were cleaned out and sold. All the money and belongings were just gone.

Through sheer determination, she had managed to hang onto her house. Every day had then become a struggle for survival. Some nights it was so cold that she used a hair dryer to warm her son's bed so that he could get to sleep. The oil company stopped deliveries, but luckily the electric company couldn't shut off power during the winter. She had survived.

Like Scarlett O'Hara groveling in the turnip patch, Gayle vowed, as God as her witness, she would never go hungry again. Through wit, grit, hard work, and guile, Gayle now had a college degree, a new husband, a twenty-five acre farm and a son enrolled in private school. So I couldn't ignore the fact that she knew a little something about making dreams come true.

Before I could answer, we became aware of an eerie silence in the auction hall, the kind of stillness that occurs after a pitched battle. The carnage was over. We returned to see the blonde carefully wrapping the "Love Me Tender" lamp in an "Elvis in Vegas" hand-woven lap robe. Her face glowed with absolute and total victory. Three rows back, the brunette sat in her chair weeping softly. Her husband, his arm reaching half way around her back to give her comfort, whispered, "It's okay, Buttercup, you'll find another one someday." Indeed.

In that very moment, in the surreal glow of the fluorescent light of the auction hall The Cold Hard Truth hit me like a bucket of iced Gatorade. That woman was NEVER going to own a "Love Me Tender" lamp. Even if she read every auction notice in the *Lancaster Farming* newspaper and found another such treasure for sale, she would still, at the last moment, the Moment of Truth, back away from her dream. She would let someone else with more fire, more desire, more commitment, INVEST in their dream and steal it away from her with a winning bid

I bought a used pitchfork for fifty cents that night. The next week I bought a wheelbarrow and a used (more like "serviceably sound") pickup truck. Six months later I found myself standing on my own farm, complete with a manure-filled bank barn, a broken-down eighteenth century home, an outdoor wine cellar, and a ramshackle hoghouse, wondering if I should have been more selective about the dream I chose to follow.

Kissing Toads

They say you have to kiss a lot of toads before you find your Prince Charming. Well, the same goes for farm buying, especially when the dream is large and the bank account small. Who can resist the fantasy of living in the country, harvesting nature's bounty, brewing teas from wildflowers, healing with herbs, whipping together a garlic poultice when needed, and dashing through the snow in a one-horse open sleigh? These thoughts run through the mind of many an eight-year-old. But some people never outgrow them.

It is true that I have the underdeveloped life goals of an eight-year-old. I also enjoy an eclectic, yet moderately successful career as an engineer, project manager, strategic planner and health care consultant. As part of my strategy for finding my farm, I relied on some vague knowledge of market segmentation. I divided the real estate market for the would-be gentlewoman farmer into four segments, each of which was primarily based on price and level of property distress.

The first, Category One, is the true country estate. Category Ones conjure up the image of Thoroughbred horses grazing in lush green pastures while the master relaxes with a glass of tawny port by a roaring fire after a brisk ride to the hounds, with a brindle Mastiff lying contently at his feet.

The house is a tasteful blend of natural woodwork, stone, pocket doors, fireplaces that don't smoke and plumbing that actually works. The walls scream for antique paintings of hunt scenes and stoic family portraits.

These houses, like good antiques, are generally inherited, not sold; so there's not much point in looking for them in the multi-listings. They make great bed and breakfasts for the well-funded entrepreneur, but without access to a trust fund, indentured servants or a brindle Mastiff, I felt compelled to pass on Category Ones.

Category Twos include the recently renovated farmhouse and the new house on acreage. They are a short cut to the simple life and exude the charm of indoor plumbing. They generally have access to electricity, cable and phone, and even have a working septic. The drawback with Category Twos is price and a shared dream with the previous owner who ran out of funds, got divorced or otherwise tanked. You are buying the product "as is." If it is a restoration, prepare for the sentimental inflation factor. Sellers who put this much time and talent into a project, and install this many flea market treasures while fixing up their own version of nirvana are just not capable of thinking clearly at selling time.

Category Twos can come under the "too good to be true" axiom. Above all else the key words are "Buyer Beware." One remarkably low priced Category Two that I considered was a brand new three-bedroom ranch house on twelve acres which had never been occupied. It was built with every "extra" and upgrade imaginable. But a close inspection revealed a major flaw. Apparently there were some irreconcilable differences between the builder and the owner.

Throughout the project, the owner, an outsider from New Jersey, insisted that the builder provide upgrades at no extra cost. He was pushy about it, constantly waving the contract in the builder's face, relentlessly demanding that he get what was due to him. The builder retaliated by finishing every detail in the house as the owner specified. But the owner forgot to specify a septic system, so the builder never provided one. Owner tried to sue. Builder's Cousin Fred was the district judge. Owner tried to get another contractor. Builder's Uncle Henry was in charge of septic system permits. Owner was shit out of luck. I passed on this one. Bad Karma.

The final segments are: Category Three, "partially renovated," and Category Four, "totally trashed." As I am lower on the financial totem pole, these were the waters in which I had to fish.

There is a fine line between the Threes and the Fours, but an experienced farm shopper can generally sense their differences by the liberal use of creativity in their respective real estate descriptions. "New roof and recently renovated kitchen, new barn and fence, relocation forces sale" (No doubt a Category Three. Interpretation: May not have indoor bathroom facilities, and the relocation is more than likely due to a divorce, since fixer-uppers are hard on relationships.) "Gentleman's farm, beautiful views, modern kitchen (read indoor plumbing), upgraded electrical service" (Falls right into Category Three). "Wanted: Buyer with great Vision and poor eyesight," (Category Four, but you have to give the listing agent points for honesty and a touch of humor). "A few finishing touches will make this your dream property, hunting and fishing on your own acreage" This reeks of Category Four. It's a trick question. The finishing touches are a roof and foundation and "hunting and fishing" is real estate agent code for land that has either a two-hundred-foot drop to a stream below or is located squarely on the Susquehanna River flood plain.

The "drive-by" is a great time saver, or at least it is for the real estate agent. When an agent is willing to give directions to a property and suggests a drive-by, it means that they don't want to waste their valuable time showing some starry-eyed cheapskate with a pipe dream a property that is hopelessly unsellable. It can also be fun and educational, like a "Where's Waldo" puzzle, to figure out just what the intractable flaw is that makes it so.

Some are obvious, like the beautiful clapboard house I noticed in the multi-list photograph. The text read: "Fully restored home on twelve acres, with two stocked ponds and a three stall barn, conveniently located to major transportation routes." It met my miserly price range criteria so, full of hope and promise, I called the agent and greedily scribbled down the drive-by directions. He also faxed me a plot map, and I couldn't help but notice that the property was exceptionally long and thin for a twelve acre farm. It was easy to find. It sat on the median strip that separated Interstate 78 from "old Route 22." The trucks flew by the back deck at eighty miles per hour on their way west to Harrisburg on Route 78 and zoomed past the front porch on the way east to Allentown on Route 22. Scratch that one off the list.

Sometimes it pays not to follow the real estate agents instructions to the letter. One agent had given me very specific (emphatically specific was more like it) drive-by directions for a lovely, totally refinished nineteenth century farmhouse and bank barn. As I am directionally challenged, I carefully drove out to the farm following the agent's instructions and was not disappointed. The buildings were in fine shape and the property had obviously been tended with great care. I could have bought it on the spot. In my excitement I became so lost in the fantasy of moving in and buying a flock of chickens that I made a wrong turn going out of the driveway. As I drove down the road bordering the farm I saw a sign that said, "Future Home of Hazardous Waste Disposal Facility—Partners in Progress." Where's Waldo?

Once the drive-by phase is over, the property showing becomes a dangerous time for the urban pioneer. The Category Threes can be dressed up, a la the Big Bad Wolf, to appear a lot more finished and less scary than they really are. When the realtor opens the door to that country kitchen with the herbs hanging from a beam ceiling, and the cinnamon scent of snicker-doodles or hot apple pie fills the air, it's easy to be swept away in the moment. (The scent actually comes in a spray can. It's used just before company arrives. It handily masks the smell of cat urine.) Add in some placid sheep, spring flowers, and a puppy or two frolicking on the lawn and you are certain to miss some salient details, but then again that is the idea.

I looked at many such places. One farmhouse seemed to be the perfect fit. The land was charming. It had a small pond, a chicken house, a cute three-stall barn, and was nestled in a valley that was clearly God's Country. I was trying not to be too picky as my price range did not allow for many choices, but I was a little disappointed with some of the remodeling. The workmanship was poor, and some of the doorways and windows didn't look quite straight. The house had a couple of other minor problems, like the chimney sloped away from the house to the point where it had pulled about six inches from the roofline. I asked a friend who did house inspections and repairs to take a look at it and give me an idea of what it would cost to fix the chimney. He looked at it for about ten seconds and burst out laughing. It turned out that the chimney was not pulling away from the house, but rather the house was pulling away from the chimney. Where's Waldo?

Category Four properties have a raw and brutally honest character about them. They are the Clint Eastwood of properties, presented without excuse or apology. They are trashed. They are totaled. They have nothing to hide. Everything is negotiable. They are fraught with their own set of dangers.

The worst house I encountered while bottom fishing for property was a huge brick Victorian Center Hall Colonial on eight acres. It had been majestic in its time. One could easily imagine a crystal chandelier gleaming in the front hall where one bare light bulb now swung from a wire. Luckily, the electricity had been turned off, probably to keep the place from burning down. The previous tenants had hastily abandoned the house, leaving a trail of shoes, clothes and personal hygiene items leading down the stairs, through the central hall, and out the front door to the circular driveway.

A young couple looking at the house was headed upstairs when I arrived with my real estate agent, Ann. This was the first day that the house was on the market. The listing agent standing in the doorway looked pale and a bit horrified, almost embarrassed. Apparently she had not done a pre-listing inspection. The owner, an out-of-town nephew of the deceased couple who had owned the house, had gotten word that the tenant had moved out and had asked the agent to sell the property quickly to settle the estate. He also had no clue as to the condition of the house.

As I peered past the agent through the front door, I could see that the downstairs rooms, although in disarray with significant damage to the plaster, were large and had some great architectural features. The front hall staircase had a beautiful curved shape and although every third banister or so was missing, shades of its former elegance still shown through. I faded into fantasy mode, picturing myself in a long, velvet, tailored deep green gown, standing third-step-up with a glass of Chardonnay in one hand with the other poised on a richly-polished mahogany railing, a silver and gold Christmas corsage carefully pinned above my left breast. There I would welcome my guests with a sweeping gesture toward the perfectly-trimmed fir tree in the corner of the parlor stretching toward the ceiling next to a fireplace with a roaring Yule log.

The listing agent "ahemmed" to snap me back from my trance and suggested to Ann and I that we visit the barn while the other couple finished touring the house. We walked over and opened the barn door. The interior was dark with low ceilings, and the stench of something large and very dead was overpowering. Without going in, we closed the door and turned around just in time to see the other couple slamming their car doors and leaving in a cloud of dust. A menacing sign, but since we had come this far, we decided to at least look through the house itself. The listing agent had composed herself somewhat by this time, and was in rare form, the ultimate saleswoman. She looked at us with her best straight face and said, "Of course, the house and barn will be "broom swept clean" at the time of closing." After adjusting a wisp of hair that had strayed from her perfectly-coiffed upsweep she continued. "This property could easily be restored to its former grandeur with patience and a bit of investment."

The basement foretells the difference between a restoration project and a tear down in the world of Category Four houses. Electrical system, plumbing and heating, foundation, and floor joists are all there, with the possibility of attendant termites, powder post beetles, and mold problems, all of which are easily identifiable to the trained eye. Since it would be getting dark soon, I asked to see the basement before going upstairs. The listing agent pointed to a door at the far end of the dark narrow hallway that led to the kitchen. I opened the door and, while talking to Ann over my shoulder, started to walk through it. Ann, anticipating her commission in the last gasps of sudden death, grabbed my arm and pulled me back with such force that we landed in a heap on the ripped linoleum kitchen floor. She scrambled to her feet, mumbling "Sorry..." as I lay bewildered on the floor. "...but I noticed that the basement stairs were gone." They were indeed absent, leaving a sheer drop into a dark and sinister abyss. Perhaps a perfect setting for a horror film, but not for me.

Now, those who have never seen a Category Four property are probably wondering why anyone would have remained at this point. Hope springs eternal in the bosom of the ignorant and underfunded.

"Stairs are not a problem to install," I thought optimistically, "Home Depot has them pre-cut and ready to go." Cautious, but uncowed, we resumed our tour, ascending the fairly intact front hall staircase to the second floor. The wide windowsills and tall ceilings gave the rooms a quality of airiness. Some of the original wooden shutters were still in place and a couple of large mirrors hung over fireplaces in large sitting rooms. The bathrooms were all a total wreck, but it looked like recent damage. Not a problem, bathrooms always have to be replaced in Category Fours.

Somewhat encouraged, we continued climbing, this time up a narrower staircase to yet a third floor. Here the rooms were smaller, probably originally designed as servant's quarters. We opened the door to the second room down the hall, and stopped dead in our tracks. We both stood stunned, the proverbial deer in the headlights. With one motion and without a shared word, we turned and sprinted down two flights of stairs, past the startled listing agent, and into the parked car. Ann fired up the engine and peeled out in a cloud of dust. After driving for about a mile in shocked silence, she finally pulled up at a stop sign. She turned to me and said, "Should we call the police?"

"And tell them what?" I said, more angry than afraid at this point. "That the third floor has a room with child toys, burned candles, and baby clothes all arranged around a pentagram made of braided human hair?"

"Maybe I'll just let the listing agent handle that," replied Ann vaguely, her hopes for a commission quickly fading into oblivion.

Category Fours are not for the faint-hearted.

Nothing worth having comes easily. And the universe will extract its "pound of flesh" before any great dream can be realized. The timid falter and the strong succeed. By this time I was definitely feeling faint-hearted, but some dreams are just too overpowering to ignore. In one last attempt, one last hurrah, I donned my most comfortable sweatpants, poured a glass of Chardonnay and turned to the internet.

The internet is a unique tool to use in the search for "handy woman's specials." After inputting your desired zip code one can check a few "key feature" boxes, set a ridiculously low price range, specify your acreage, and seamlessly enter the virtual world of distressed properties.

The listing photo for Berks County listing #7723 didn't look too bad. It was a simple brick Pennsylvania farmhouse with a large wrap around porch, bank barn, and several outbuildings, all nested on thirty-six acres. The price was higher than budget, but the image looked like it was taken in the spring and it was late February now, so I might be able to bank on its having had too long of a shelf life. The truth was I was now obsessed. I had found the ONE, the real estate equivalent of a soul mate. I called Ann, who did not return my call right away since she was still in therapy from the Victorian Center Hall Colonial showing.

Hysterical and fearful that this farm that had gone totally unnoticed for ten months would suddenly be discovered and snatched away, I sent urgent emails and left messages with Ann's secretary. Nothing in this world can get a real estate agent through therapy faster than a hysterical buyer. They know that indeed a sucker is born every minute. She agreed to show it the following day.

That morning Ann showed up in an impeccable maroon ultra-suede jacket with matching gloves and business suit. Her hair was perfectly coiffed. She wore faux fur-lined ankle boots with three-inch heels.

We walked down the broken-brick pathway to the kitchen door, stepping gingerly over partially-empty cat food cans, Christmas lights that had burned their brightest maybe ten years ago, and dog droppings. The back door was covered with dirt and "gook," as my mother would say. Ann gingerly opened the lock box and let us inside. The walls throughout the house were a dark walnut shade of 1970s paneling (except in the areas here and there where a sheet was missing). The drop ceilings had some nasty looking stains on them and most rooms had large chunks of the wall and or ceiling missing. The bodies of a couple of dead bats were visible through the plastic covers over the fluorescent lights in the kitchen. Half the doors were missing on the kitchen cabinets. The temperature in the living room was a balmy forty degrees. Sleeping bags lay crumpled on the living room floor.

The basement tour was not quite so depressing: beams were solid, plumbing was copper and not lead, and only minor rewiring would be required. The electric box needed to be replaced and the junction to the main breaker was a splice about the size of a person's fist with wire wrapped in white adhesive tape. It was a miracle that the place hadn't burned to the ground.

The second floor provided no additional encouragement. Small piles of gray snow had collected on the floors under the cracked bedroom windows providing testament that the living room was by far the warmest room in the house. That explained the sleeping bags. The doors, which had been used by an earlier owner as partitions to keep the sows separated in the hoghouse, were propped into the door frames or dangling on a single hinge. The hemlock floors had holes in them and the bathroom wall was unfinished, providing convenient access to the closet in the front bedroom. Interestingly, all the closets were lined with cedar. The cast iron claw foot bathtub only had hot water going to it. Obviously cold water was unnecessary as one simply had to wait for the water to cool to the right temperature in order to take a bath. The outdoor garden spigot only provided hot water, no doubt allowing the efficient gardener to both water the garden and blanch vegetables at the same time.

When we approached the attic, Ann said, "Do you mind if I wait here, I'm a little afraid to go up there." No stranger to discovering unpleasant surprises in basements and attics and cognizant of Ann's sensitive state post-therapy; I tried to compel her with logic, "What are the odds of two houses having pentagons in the attic?"

"What about vermin?"

"Well, if anything was living in the attic, it's probably taken up winter residence somewhere in the lower part of the house since the heating system was clearly marginal and the attic was too cold for anything creepy to winter over."

Unconvinced, Ann decided against the climb; I forged on alone.

The attic was filled to beyond capacity with the remnants of one-hundred-thirty years of tenants. Various-sized boxes, the requisite old fashioned "dress form," old clothes, books, paint cans, a black Remington typewriter and odd building materials were shoved into every available space. No water stains were evident, a sign indicating that the roof was in good shape. Satisfied that no pentagrams or human braids were to be found, but acutely aware of the cold creepiness of the space, I returned to the second floor where Ann was waiting patiently. What I failed to notice in my haste to descend the dark, narrow steps were the ample piles of bat guano that covered the floor.

At this point I was confident that the farm was well beyond my capabilities and out of my price range given the amount of work it needed. I was not interested in taking on a house in this condition. But I decided to be polite and at least finish the showing since we had come this far.

We headed to the barn. Ann opened the door and a pony's head instantly appeared in the open doorway. Startled, Ann shrieked and fell backwards into a snow bank, leaving her little fur-lined ankle boots the only part of her clearly visible. I pulled her out and dusted her off as best I could and told her that she was welcome to wait in the car while I toured the barn. In for a penny, in for a pound, Ann hung in there like a trooper, or at least like an agent in a "down market" with bills to pay.

The barn was a typical Pennsylvania bank barn. It had once been a cow barn, but somewhere along the way it had been updated with horse stalls. It now housed one elderly pony mare and some sheep, whose manure removal had not been a priority for some time past. The combination of sheep and horse manure had accumulated to more than five feet deep in some areas, creating some headroom problems for the pony.

Our sudden arrival combined with Ann's scream had startled the thirty or so resident chickens roosting in feed tubs in the stalls, and they suddenly began a mass poultry panic. Chickens were everywhere, flinging themselves against the bars of the stalls, falling to the ground and running in circles in a state of blind hysteria, feathers flying everywhere. Soon the air was thick with toxic clouds of horse, sheep and chicken manure. Ann continued to exhibit the kind of brave composure that comes from years of working on a straight commission business. The little maroon suede suit no doubt had a future at the local dry cleaners; the fate of the little ankle boots was indeterminate. I looked at Ann's hair, now sporting a few feathers and a sprinkling of chicken shit and hoped, for her sake, that this was her last showing for the day.

We trudged out and through the snow to the upper part of the barn, slid the heavy wooden doors open, and stepped into the hayloft. The structure had been built over two harvest seasons between 1772 and 1774. It had a large interior, with two "threshing floors" in the center for winnowing wheat and two large cribs on either end for storing hay. Its large beams were made entirely of American chestnut, a tall, majestic tree that once dominated American forests. Many of them had trunks several feet in diameter and grew so large that they shaded out all the forest undergrowth so that one could easily ride through the forest on horseback. These trees became virtually extinct when a similar species of Asiatic chestnut was imported to America in the late 1800s. The native American chestnut was not resistant to a blight carried by the newly introduced tree, so by the 1930s most of the American chestnut trees had vanished. Vanity had changed the face of the forest forever. Here we were standing in a barn built entirely of this piece of Americana, moving toward decay and disinterest, or destined to be dismantled and reconstructed as beam and glass "barn built" houses that have become the current passion of the well-heeled. This barn, this house, this homestead had to be preserved. I felt a kind of giddiness, and my jaw dropped open and I fell totally and irreversibly in love. I had found my dream. "Wanted: Someone with poor eyesight and great vision." Waldo or no, welcome home.

LESSON 3

Way-finding

I made an offer that was a full-third lower than the already reduced asking price and boldly informed Ann, "This is a take it or leave it offer and I won't respond to a counter offer." I also added "manure" clauses to every page of the contract requiring that all manure be removed from the barn, house, hoghouse and other outbuildings. Ann interpreted these inclusions as surprisingly tough negotiation tactics. In retrospect, what I was really doing was making one last ditch effort to preserve my relatively easy "meet you at happy hour at Viva's and sure we can go to the beach this weekend" kind of carefree lifestyle. A part of me clung to the "drop everything and go for sushi" high power executive world while the eight-year-old child within clamored for Lassie and Flicka. I left it to the Fates. If the sellers took the offer, fine, I was getting a good deal. If not, I was off the hook.

They jumped at it.

The jaws of the trap clamped shut. The property was now "Under Agreement."

"Under Agreement." Sounds so happy and carefree, brimming with goodwill, promise, and opportunity. Putting a house "Under Agreement" is not unlike the dating period of a new relationship. Everyone's doing their best to look good. They're shaving their legs, following advice from Ms. Post, and making sure nothing inappropriate is showing. Oh, there were a few things to check before signing the "pre-nup," but I was already in love and no one, not family, friends nor legal or financial advisors, was going to talk me out of it.

The pre-purchase inspection went surprisingly well. Fearing rejection from the mortgage company, the inspector received strict instructions from both Ann and me to ignore "cosmetic" issues and focus only on deal breakers (like the house falling away from the chimney, absent septic systems or large, unstable sinkholes in the basement). Ann drove me out to meet the inspector on the appointed day. The tenants were not home, but the key was in the lock box. They had left three potentially rabid dogs loose in the house, but Ann, not to be dissuaded and ever-mindful of her commission, grabbed a the nearest weapon she could find. Parked by the back door was a fluorescent orange skate board with one set of wheels missing. Ann picked it up and, brandishing it like a shield, entered the house ahead of us. She drove back the two leaping and snarling Jack Russell Terriers like a skilled Kung Fu fighter. The third dog, a Springer Spaniel, shook uncontrollably and promptly pissed on the floor. The inspectors report was short and to the point. "I am willing to certify that the primary residence, barn and hoghouse will probably not fall down within the next year barring any unforeseen natural or man-made calamity." The bank bought his story. On to closing day. March the thirty-first.

If being "Under Agreement" is the dating portion of buying a new house, the "Closing" is the consummation of the marriage. After the closing there's no going back. You're stuck with him whether he farts under the blanket or not.

I arrived at the closing directly from work, ironically dressed bride-like in a "winter-white" wool suit. Ann was her usual impeccable self, wearing a powder blue ensemble with matching leather pumps. She was looking much less pale, and even seemed to have a young glow about her. The prospect of walking off with probably her hardest won commission check had put the bloom back on the rose.

We entered the sterile, efficient conference room. The sellers were seated at opposite ends of the long mahogany conference table, each facing the opposite walls, backs to the table. They wore cutoff denim shorts and tank tops. Both were doughy and round with dour faces and arms tightly crossed against their chests looking like a pair of comical bookends.

The mortgage representative sat on the near side with all the documents in order before him, with a bottle of local wine on the table next to him. Just beyond the wine were the coveted house keys and an electric garage door opener with duct tape over the battery compartment.

Opposite sat a small bald-headed man in an expensive but ill-fitted suit. He had very pointy features and sharp beady eyes. He looked to be about eighty. "I am Attorney Heffelfinger." he proclaimed, with what I interpreted as a pompous lilt to his voice. "And what might your role be here today?"

"I am the buyer. " I replied. "My role is to provide the check."

"You may sit down." He gestured to the chair beside the mortgage agent. "Where is your husband?"

"Still searching for his soul mate." I said. Attorney Heffelfinger didn't get the joke. "I'm single, never been married," I said with a saccharine smile. "That explains why you look so happy," interjected the soon-to-be-ex-husband of the seller team.

Attorney Heffelfinger eyed me suspiciously but continued, "I am the attorney for the sellers. I will clarify; I am the attorney for the wife. I will be representing her interests and I will also be reviewing the terms of the divorce agreement that I have drawn up." I was not really listening; instead I was absent mindedly counting the number of times he used the word "I." When all other words were filtered out, he sounded like an Indian chanting in one of those 1960s western movies, "Aye, aye, aye, aye."

The word "divorce" initiated an instant reaction not unlike a bell ringing to start a boxing round, or perhaps a red flag waving in front of a bull. The sellers wheeled about in their chairs screaming to beat the band. Accusations were hurled across the room, with each accusing the other of infidelity, infertility, immorality, impotence, ignorance, illegitimacy, illiteracy, incompetence, incontinence and insensitivity. Strangely, they would pause periodically, as in a soliloquy or *Roadrunner* cartoon, and turn to me to say, "Oh you will love the apples. Those trees are over one hundred years old, heirloom apples, they make great apple pie!" Or "If you need anything, just ask Mitch, he farms the fields and is just the nicest man!" Then back to the fray. It was deafening, at times even frightening.

I shouted to the title agent who was trying to read the pertinent terms of the mortgage agreement to me as required by Pennsylvania law. "I can't hear you. Can we go somewhere else quieter? Perhaps the tailgate of my truck? It's parked next to the highway." "What?" he replied. I gestured toward the door and mouthed "Let's get out!" The title agent nodded gratefully and we exited to a quiet conference room. Ann watched after us longingly, but decided that it was probably her role to remain with the sellers. I completed the buyer's portion of the business with the title agent and tentatively approached the door to the original conference room.

The glass in the door vibrated with the volume of the relentless shouting. I sighed, but the keys were on that table and the only way out of this was through it. After two hours of weeping and gnashing of teeth an agreement was reached on back child support, ongoing health insurance for the wife and kids, disposition of two car titles and the sale of a small farm tractor to someone's brother-in-law. I received far too much personal information, keys to the house, the duct-taped-over garage door opener, the bottle of locally-bottled Pennsylvania wine and a mortgage that would keep me working until I was of a ripe old age.

The next day, the first day of true property ownership, was an unseasonably warm April Fools Day. Starry-eyed, optimistic and still on that adrenaline high that comes from cashing in your life savings on a dream, I set out on this April first full of hope and promise, determined to convert the Bootleg Road property to my very own little piece of heaven.

The first challenge was to find the place I had just bought. I had only been out to the farm twice before, and both times I had tagged along with the real estate agent. This was to be my first experience with Bernville geography.

Please permit a digression for geographic reference. Since Bernville is close to the Middle of Nowhere, strangers often find it difficult to navigate from one place to another in the area. It is true today that in the big modern world none of this should make a difference. It's simply a matter of plugging an endpoint into a Geographic Positioning Device, and letting the GPS take the guesswork out of everything. No more getting lost, no more stopping at gas stations for directions or flagging down a terrified bicyclist wearing a T-shirt from the local high school proudly proclaiming her to be a Tulpehockin Terrapin, who, once she is assured that you are not going to kidnap her, tells you that she's "Not from around here." Yes, in the big modern world all that is true, but not in radio-free Bernville. Satellite signals do not function here, unreliably or otherwise. So geography is important in Berks County; you actually have to know what is where.

Skull Hill is an outcropping of land just northwest of Flower Hill Farm. The origin of the name is unknown. Perhaps it's because the hill is shaped like a skull, or because, according to legend, an Indian massacre occurred there in the 1700s. Realistically, and much less romantically, it's more likely that someone with the surname Skull once owned the land.

The hill is bounded by Bootleg Road (named for a past bootlegging operation), Skull Hill Loop Road (that, yes, loops around it, originality not being a particularly strong suit in some local naming patterns), Irish Creek Road (that runs, surprise, along Irish Creek) and Molasses Hill Road (That received its moniker sometime in the early nineteenth century when a four-mule team got spooked just as they were nearing the top of the hill with a wagon load of molasses barrels. The wagon tipped over, and the road was a sticky mess for months, which gave new meaning to the expression, "slow as molasses in January." At least the locals remember it like that). Blottadahl Road is a short stretch of single lane road which apparently encompasses the Village of Blottadahl. The boundaries for the Village of Blottadahl are a bit vague and they don't appear on any map, nor is there an actual village there. Its population appears to be mostly bovine with a smattering of *Homo sapiens*. A painted sign erected in a cow pasture just behind two strands of barbed wire fence proudly memorializes Blottadahl's most famous son. He left the safety of the Bernville suburbs for the wilds of California and had the distinction of being Ronald Reagan's mail carrier for three years.

Most other roads in, near, or around Bernville are eponymously named Bernville Road. Route 183 is called Bernville Road. The Penn-Bernville Road, Robesonia-Bernville Road and Heidelberg-Bernville Road are all known as Bernville Road. Old Bernville Road runs parallel to Shartlesville-Bernville road and also connects Shartlesville to Bernville. Irish Creek Road is also known as Bernville Road at the point that it intersects with Main Street in Centerport by the fork in the road near the Camel Inn. It's a literal fork in the road: eight-feet tall, cut from a single piece of sheet metal, it has four tines and is shaped like a dinner fork. Despite extensive research (I asked the bartender at the Camel Inn) no one knows exactly how it got there. Rumor has it that is was put there to make it easier for the more literal out-of-town relatives to find the Moon Family Reunion, "Just bear right at the Fork In The Road." Go figure.

Recognizing that back road navigation may be difficult for the out-of-town traveler, the state of Pennsylvania has attempted to make things easy by naming all major highways around Bernville either Route 222, 322, 422 or 22. One exception is Route 78, which also masquerades as Route 22 for several mile-long stretches at a clip, and a small section of highway connecting Route 222 to Route 422 which lacks any signage or identifiers and is known by all the locals as "the road to nowhere." It used to go nowhere because of a lack of construction funding, but now, thanks to a new administration in the governor's mansion, the highway is finished and it goes somewhere, but is still called "the road to nowhere." Routes 322 and 422 are also the same road for a short stretch, as are 222 North (which runs, you guessed it, east) and 422 West (which goes north). For each of these there is a corresponding "old route" and a bypass with the same numerical designation, but not necessarily close to, or running in the same direction as, the "real" Routes 222, 322, 422 or 22. At one time there was a Route 122 that connected 22 and 222 but that was changed to Route 61, apparently as a feint-hearted attempt to "stop the road madness."

As if this were all not bad enough, whenever a new governor is elected the main highway exit signs are re-numbered using a different basis for the numbering system. For clarification, the "old" exit numbers are then posted below the "new" exit numbers reaching back at least three exit number generations.

All of this is supposed to either support clear navigation or, much more likely, prevent further migration of people from New Jersey to Eastern Pennsylvania.

Another challenge to way-finding in Berks County are creatures called "Fire Police." They are not actually police, nor are they firemen. The qualifications needed to become a Fire Police Person are unclear; there doesn't seem to be a sign-up anywhere or an annual drive or anything of the sort. Fire Police positions may be inherited. Not being a native Berks-countian, I am not at all sure of the intricacies of the thing, but it probably goes something like this: Once someone is appointed, anointed, or assigned to be a Fire Police they are issued a Day-Glo green vest with a hot pink X in the middle of it, a yellow rain slicker with reflector tape around the sleeves, six orange cones, a flashlight with an orange "saber" light cover, and a round blue light for the family pick up truck. From then on, anytime there is an emergency of merit anywhere in the confines of Berks County a special signal goes out to all the Fire Police radios. They immediately don their vests, leap into their pickup trucks, and, with blue light flashing, drive to the nearest intersection and place the six cones across one of the roads to block the flow of traffic. It doesn't matter where the problem is (the Fire Police themselves often don't know). They just close off the road and stand there for hours waving their saber light and telling every motorist in the nicest and most polite and concerned way, "Road's closed, you'll have to go round."

Now, the county roads are merely paved-over dirt roads that used to be wagon tracks that were initially worn footpaths that, before that, were deer trails. So "going around" could easily mean a twenty mile jaunt where one is totally at the mercy of the migratory patterns of white-tailed deer that lived in the seventeenth century. Interestingly, although Fire Police appear to come from the ranks of fourth generation Berks-countians, none of them are able to provide alternate directions as to how one might get to where one was going before some mishap somewhere caused all the roads to be closed. Fire Police are worthy of admiration for their dogged stick-to-it-tive-ness. Once installed at an intersection, a Fire Police Person will not abandon his/her post or open the road unless specifically directed to do so by the Fire Marshall or deputized designee. They are loyal as Rottweilers. Many a Fire Marshall has gone to bed after a late night fire only to awake with a start six hours later and remember that he left Floyd at the corner of Bellman's Church Road and Irish Creek Road and forget to tell him to stand down.

I got lost, detoured and misdirected, but finally arrived at my new home by way of God Knows Where four hours later than planned.

Following the written-in-stone rules for new fixer-uppers that I've learned to make up on the fly, my naive goal for the first weekend of home ownership was to get one bedroom not only habitable, but downright comfortable.

Having one room completed in the midst of chaos is important to personal stability. This would allow me to go inside, close the door so that only the freshly-painted back side showed, and pretend that the rest of the house looked this nice. I could even install the phone in here so that I could call my friends and lie to them about how well the house was coming along. Life is short. Use denial as a coping mechanism.

This lofty goal meant propping up the sagging ceiling, painting the peeling walls, and nailing the loose woodwork together. I was thrilled to find beautiful cherry molding, already cut and mitered, leaning against the closet wall ready to be nailed onto the door and window frames. Apparently some previous owner had both good taste and great visions of home restoration, but they had left before they got far into the project.

My first thought was to paint all the upstairs rooms and use the existing carpets as drop cloths, since the floor coverings were a few years past totally shot. Whatever their original colors, they had faded to a grayish-yellow with deep, dark, ominous stains. Judging from the smell, a previous owner's dogs (or hogs?) apparently had some serious house-training issues. The carpets had to go and the sooner the better.

I wandered from room to room in a daze trying to prioritize my efforts into some kind of a list, or at least select the least trashed room to fix up first. I wandered in ever decreasing circles for about half-an-hour and was slowly pivoting around on one leg in the living room when my friend Patty appeared at the kitchen door. It was a shock to see her as the directions I'd given her were the same ones I had used to get myself four hours worth of lost.

In spite of all the perils, there was Miss Patty as big as life.

"How did you find it?" I asked.

"Good guessing," Patty said. "And I stopped at the fire hall. Some guy with a beer belly and a Yuengling gave me directions. He said he was the Fire Marshall."

Patty, like me, was forty-something, independent, and had been single most of her life. She was "sportin' a new beau" and was keen to show him off. Glenn was tall with salt and pepper hair, a twinkle in his eye, was cute as they come, had a great body, and was head-over-heals over Patty. His gig was home remodeling and had been since the age of eleven. After years of working for other people, Glenn was trying to start his own business.

It was the beginning of great friendship between Glenn and me. He took a self-guided tour of the house while Patty and I caught up on things. After completing his look-see Glenn met us in the upstairs bedroom. He was too polite to mention it, but the urine smell in the carpet was making his eyes water. "Is there anything I can do to help?" he asked hopefully.

I was unable to believe my good fortune. On my first day of Category Four ownership, here was a healthy male with upper body strength and construction skills standing in my bedroom. A brief fantasy passed before my eyes before I remembered Patty was my best friend. Some lines just don't get crossed.

"I could use a hand getting these carpets out," I partially fibbed.

Glenn was all over that. He whipped a carpet knife out of his seemingly permanently attached tool belt and started slicing the offending carpets into sections for easy removal. We rolled the first rotten, slimy section up and shoved it through the open second-story window. Out went the carpet, and out went the window. THUD. CRASH. The three of us stared out of the gaping rectangular opening at the pile of splintered wood, twisted aluminum, broken glass and stained carpet on the lawn below.

"Glenn installs windows," Patty said quietly.

LESSON 4

Ghosts Don't Care

With only the slightest nod from me, Glenn started measuring and figuring and taking notes on a yellow pad. He came up with a good estimate, and, more important, an immediate start date. As he and Patty stood downstairs in the driveway before leaving, Glenn remembered that he had left the carpet knife in one of the bedrooms. We traipsed back upstairs, but the knife was nowhere to be found.

"I'm sure it will turn up. I'll keep looking," I said.

It was mid-afternoon by now, and a thunderstorm was coming up over Skull Hill. As the sky grew darker and darker, I frantically began covering the gaping hole in the wall left by the fallen window with a roll of duct tape and some plastic garbage bags. Not that it would matter, since all the other windows had at least one-inch gaps between the window frame and the walls. As the rising wind blew through the house it produced soft musical noises that at times sounded like voices conversing in the downstairs parlor.

As the storm drew closer, I felt a crawly feeling on the back of my neck, and the hair on my arms stood up. I jumped as I heard the kitchen door slam shut. I was certain that I closed it after Patty and Glenn left. In the same instant the telephone rang.

"Oh good," I thought, naively. The local phone company had reported that they couldn't start service until Monday, but they must be calling to notify me that they were able to do the work ahead of time. I picked up the phone and heard background static, as if someone was on the line but not speaking. "Hello? Hello?" I asked. No one was there. I hung up and clicked the receiver a couple of times to try to get a dial tone. Nothing. The phone was dead as a doornail. It hadn't been turned on at all.

"Must have been a surge in the line from the electrical storm," my logical engineering mind concluded.

I returned to my remodeling efforts, patching a few large nail holes in the plaster walls in one of the upstairs bedrooms. The previous owners were not much on art, but they had hung a lot of crucifixes and horseshoes over the doors, windows, and beds, creating holes which now needed spackling. This should have been my first clue.

Over the next several weekends there was great progress made on the house. Glenn did a wonderful job installing the windows, and friends came out in shifts to help with plastering, painting, cleaning out and cleaning up. Nine trash bags filled with cat food cans were removed from under the bushes by the front porch. The holes and broken boards in the hemlock floor upstairs were repaired using a clever remodeler's trick of cutting wood from the attic floor. The "new" boards would be from the same material and age as the floor to be fixed. Afterwards the newly-patched floors were sanded and varnished. They were perfect, with honey and caramel tones coming through the beautiful natural grain of the wood. They shone like new money, and made the old walls, ceilings and door look like hell.

Gayle (the friend from the auction who was responsible for initiating and encouraging this adventure) showed up and took on the vile job of cleaning the toilets. They were black from years of mineral deposits and God-knows-what-else, so this was a huge gift. I'm not the housekeeper of the year, but I had tried every chemical available to get them clean and finally resolved that they would have to be replaced. Another unbudgeted expense on an already over-budget project.

"I know how to fix this," said Gayle, while draining the water out of a toilet and donning a pair of elbow-length rubber gloves. "Get me a brick." The disciples never questioned Jesus when he asked for stuff while he was working his miracles. Jugs of water, fishes, loaves, get whatever she needs, there is a miracle to perform here! Besides, I readily acknowledge that I have limited knowledge of these things, so I was ready to try anything to avoid replacing those toilets. I ran and got a brick from the broken sidewalk. Gayle hit it with a hammer and knocked a chunk off. Using this as a scrubber she went to work. Softer than porcelain and harder than the scale, the brick worked wonders. It took a couple hours but the toilets looked as good as new in the end.

That evening, after all the workers had left for the day, I realized that I was tired past the point of exhaustion. I was just easing myself into bed when I received a call from Gayle.

"Liz, you have many friends who have been good enough to help at your farm. If we are going to spend more time there at least you owe us full disclosure"

"Disclosure of what? The hazards all seem pretty obvious."

"You didn't tell us about the ghosts."

"What ghosts?"

"If I have the story right, you own one of the most haunted houses in Berks County."

Gayle had left the farm around mid-afternoon. She explained that while stopping at Centerton Nursery to pick up some plants she ran into a friend she hadn't seen for awhile.

"I've just come from my friend's farm over near Bernville. It's an old brick farmhouse on Bootleg Road, and boy does it need a lot of work!" Gayle explained.

"It's not the old Schock place, is it?" her friend had asked, somewhat ominously.

"How did you know? There's an engraved stone on the 'new' part of the house that says, 'Jesse and Rebecca Schock, 1865.'"

"That place is haunted. It's even written up in one of Charlie Adams's books. In fact, it has its own chapter!"

Charles Adams III is a bit of a local legend. He writes books about hauntings up and down the East Coast in places as varied as New York, Cape May, and Gettysburg. He is originally from Berks County, so this area is featured in many of his books. My Bootleg Road property is mentioned in "Haunted Houses of Berks County, Book III," specifically in the chapter titled "The Little Boy in the Closet."

A woman in the aisle next to Gayle looked up from the flats of annuals and broke in, "Is that the farm with the brick house on one side of the road and a big barn on the other side? We used to take the school bus through there when we were kids. We'd tell each other scary stories about the Woman in White who is sometimes seen by the pond below the house. They say she's looking for her dead children."

An older gentleman nearby was selecting some tomato plants. He chimed in, "My dad lived out in that area when he was a kid in the 1920s. He said the place was abandoned and really run down. One day, a couple of his buddies said they were going to break into the house and check it out. He was late getting there on account of having to finish his chores, see. As he was riding his bicycle up the hill toward the house, he saw his two buddies scramble out of the second-floor window, jump off the porch roof, grab their bicycles and fly down the road right past him. They were pale as ghosts themselves. They never, ever told him what happened in there, but none of them went past that place again."

Gayle said, "Who knows how many other stories there are? Those three were the only other customers in the place!"

Only a few states have real estate laws requiring the seller to disclose paranormal activity to a prospective buyer, and Pennsylvania is not one of them. So ghosts were the farthest thing from my mind when I purchased the property. Termites, bats, rodents, and powder post beetles were at the top of my list; ghosts were not even on the radar screen. Ghosts! What recourse is there? Best to check the fine print in the title insurance policy.

As a person pretty much ruled by logic and cause and affect, I put together a rational explanation. The house was, after all, on Bootleg Road. The Reading area, and Bernville in particular, was a well-known supplier of bootleg alcohol to Allentown, New York, New Jersey and Philadelphia during Prohibition. And the property does show some evidence of having been such an operation. In the small bedroom above the kitchen, as I discovered after tearing down three ceilings, were about thirty mason jars filled with sticky amber residue. No one was brave enough to open the jars or sample the contents, botulism being a particularly nasty concern. More jars and a few jugs were found out in the woods in block bunkers dug into the banks near the stream. Seems like not all the corn was reserved for cattle fodder in the Roaring Twenties. The neighbors said there had been a second barn on Bootleg Road. If you believe the local legend, it burned down after a still exploded inside. Its stone foundation is still visible under a tangle of vines and scrub bushes in the woods.

It was all very simple. Very logical. If I were in the bootlegging business, I would try to keep people from coming around. It would make perfect sense to spread some very scary stories around the neighborhood. Not only would they keep people away, but they would also explain strange noises or lights in the woods late at night. Ghosts would be the perfect disguise for illegal activities. Satisfied, I tucked the thought of ghosts neatly away and continued to sleep like a baby.

When it comes right down to it, ghosts don't really care whether you believe in them or not.

In the ensuing months, I continued to work on the house to try to get it in a livable state. At first I was commuting over an hour and doing the work on evenings and weekends. The goal was to be in by the end of June. As always happens when great need arises, I was amazed at the many talents my friends possessed. Bonnie was a treasure. Her husband owned a plumbing business, and when she was young and in love, she used to go to work with him and help him install the baseboard covers in customers' homes. This is one of those atypical skills that should never be taken lightly.

For some reason the baseboard heat pipes installed throughout the house were completely void of radiator covers. It may have been a misguided attempt to improve the efficiency of the heating system or some strange ritual, but the baseboard covers and their assorted pieces were scattered about the property.

Lucky to have Bonnie's skillset and level of patience, I cheerfully wandered the garage, milk house, hayloft, swamp, back pasture and the hoghouse collecting radiator pieces for Bonnie. She then figured out which room and to which radiator they belonged. With the patience of Job she hammered them straight and fit the tops and the bottoms, vent pieces, clips and the end pieces all together into a workable arrangement. As there were nine rooms to be fitted up, this took her quite a few evenings.

Surprisingly, every time we returned to the house, there seemed to be more radiator cover pieces than what we remembered collecting. These new pieces were invariably piled on the back porch. I thought that I had them all out of the garage, or another outbuilding, but on the next trip out I would find another two or three pieces on the back porch.

I chalked it up to either workmen or neighbors kind enough to bring the parts over for us to use. In retrospect, it probably doesn't make a lot of sense that un-introduced neighbors would momentarily pause their busy lives and think, "Oh, we have a new neighbor, we should really go over there and find some radiator parts in the woods or in the swamp and leave them on her back porch. No need to leave a note as we are just being neighborly."

Truth was, between a full-time job, working evenings and weekends to get the house ready to move in to, and then the packing required for the move, I was too exhausted to look a gift radiator part in the mouth.

Some of the evening sessions ran very late. Usually by the time Bonnie and I decided to call it quits for the night we were too tired to go out and find something to eat. St. Bonnie once again came to the rescue with a small, portable "dorm room" sized refrigerator. On the last evening of radiator reconstruction, we unceremoniously plopped it into the middle of the kitchen floor and plugged it in. We tossed in some sandwiches and sodas and went to work.

Three hours later, we finally had found and fixed almost every missing piece on the property. All nine rooms had complete sets of radiator covers. Only one end cap in the living room set was missing. "Not a show stopper," I declared. "I can live without it."

Giddy with success, we danced around the living room yahooing and high fiving. Just as we were prepared to leave out the kitchen door, we abruptly stopped. There, on top of the small refrigerator, was the last radiator end cap. Lying next to it was Glenn's missing carpet knife. Do...do...do...do.

Not willing to deal with the consequences of these stranger-than-life happenings at my new-found farm, I developed another logical explanation. Perhaps some as yet un-introduced neighbor had stopped in while we were upstairs fixing the radiators and set the items on the refrigerator. Happens all the time. Just good old fashioned Bernville neighborliness. Can't wait to meet all these helpful folks.

After I finally moved into the house permanently, I began experiencing strange, repeating patterns. For example, one Saturday afternoon, I was sorting laundry in the upstairs guestroom. A thunderstorm could be heard approaching in the distance, and suddenly the hair on my arms stood up. I heard the kitchen door slam, although I was sure I had closed it, and the phone immediately rang. Once again no one was there, only static. This sequence of events still goes on today, repeating itself two or three times a year. Especially in early April. Even after the kitchen door was replaced with a new one, the sound of the *old* door slamming reverberates in the house whenever a thunderstorm approaches. I blame it on the wind, but every once in a while I swear I can hear voices coming from the downstairs parlor.

There are also a few issues with home maintenance. No matter how many times certain repairs or renovations are made, the change won't "stick." Plumbing in the upstairs bathroom has been replaced four times in five years, each time by a master plumber and each time with a stronger, more durable material. The pipes fail whenever I go away for a weekend. Even with a live-in house sitter it still happens. Recently, at my wits end, I was able to get a great deal on some nuclear-grade steam piping from a cancelled nuclear plant. Perhaps now I can leave for a weekend without having to replace the dining room ceiling. On the bright side, my overhead drywall taping and spackling skills have become the envy of my peers. Three different electricians have replaced the light fixture and all associated wiring to the ceiling light in the second floor landing. Everything is new, from the electrical box in the basement up to the light fixture. Nevertheless, it continues to blink off for a half-hour between 10:15 and 10:45 each and every night.

The windows in the upstairs guest bedroom crack at ninety-day intervals. The room is unoccupied, and the windows are unmoved. The crack in the inside pane arcs across the top half of the window. One window every three months, like clockwork. The first time, the window company honored the warranty claim, but blamed the installer, the second time they blamed the manufacturer. The third time they were plumb out of answers. "Must be ghosts," quipped the window company rep after the fourth replacement. I just smiled weakly and thanked him for his time. I finally gave up on replacing them and now live with the cracks. It's only one room after all.

If there are ghosts, and that is a very, very big IF, I haven't experienced any hostility from them. Most friends who visit, even the "sensitive" ones, claim that the property is peaceful and restful.

However, there is one exception: the small matter of the white cat by the hoghouse. The first time I ran over it was a few months after I had moved into the farm. I was driving home at about 10:00 p.m. one evening when suddenly, out of the corner of my eye, I saw a large, white, long-haired Persian-looking cat dart out from behind the hoghouse and run in front of the car, or more precisely, run under the car. Too late to even react, I heard and felt the sickening thud of the cat hitting the undercarriage. I stopped the car, heart racing, and jumped out to look underneath, fully expecting to see a dead or at least a very injured cat. Nothing. I crawled under the car and looked at the undercarriage with a flashlight. Nothing. I looked on both sides of the road and drove up and down looking for the injured cat. Nothing. Shaken, and not knowing any of the neighbors well enough to ask who may have owned the animal, I went to bed feeling guilty and miserable.

A few months later, I was enjoying a rare evening of social life. Some out-of-town friends were visiting the Reading area and had come up to share a bottle of wine and some Chinese takeout. The couple left around ten in the evening. A few minutes later, as I was getting ready for bed and reveling in memories of an evening with stimulating conversation about topics other than drywall, I heard them frantically knocking at the front door.

"Liz, we're so sorry, we were going past the hoghouse and your cat ran in front of the car. We had no time to stop. I'm sure we hit it; we heard a thud as it hit the underside of the car. We looked and couldn't find it. We are so sorry...." my guest said with tears in her eyes.

"What did it look like?" I asked, hurriedly putting on my coat and "muck boots," trying to remember the emergency number for the small animal vet and thinking about when I last saw the black and orange tortoise shell barn cat.

"It was your white Persian cat. I'm so, so sorry."

The next morning I called Gayle to tell her the story. After a long moment of silence Gayle said weakly, "Liz, I ran over a white cat near your place about a month ago. I didn't say anything because I didn't want to upset you...."

The truth is that local people are afraid of the place. Neighbors walking on the road pick up their pace as they pass by the farmhouse. It may have had something to do with the large number of shotgun shells found under the windows in the upstairs bedrooms, or it could be that a prior owner had a pack of vicious dogs who used to run out and bite people as they walked along the road. But it also may be a fear of ghosts.

For example, one night during my first Christmas at the farm, I had a fire going in the fireplace and Christmas carols playing on the stereo. I was happily trimming the fresh-cut Christmas tree and enjoying a mug of hot cider. The fact that it was seven degrees outside made the fire seem even more cozy and inviting. It was a Norman Rockwell moment to be sure. Suddenly, there was a knock on the door. One of the neighbor's kids had run out of gas and asked if he could use the phone to call his mom.

"Sure, come on in," I said, happy for the company and a chance to get to know one of the locals.

He quickly called his mother and begged her to come and get him. As he hung up the phone, I asked, "Would you like some hot cider?"

"No thanks, I'll just wait here," he said nervously, his ski-gloved hand clasped on the kitchen door knob for a quick escape.

"Okay, I'm just trimming the tree, make yourself at home."

He was very quiet. His eyes darted around the kitchen and living room, and he jumped every time one of the dogs moved. He finally got up the courage to say, "I've heard that this house has ghosts."

"I've heard that too, but I'm not really sure about that." I replied, casually picking up a crystal ornament and gently hanging it on the tree.

"Have you had anything strange happen?"

I reflected for a few moments. I didn't know how to respond. The things I'd experienced all had logical explanations, so there was no sense feeding the neighborhood rumor mill. "No, nothing very out of the ordinary." I said.

"You haven't had your keys float through the air or seen strange lights by the pond or in the barn or had glass break for no reason or heard footsteps on the stairs or seen the little boy in the closet?" he fired off in one long breath.

"Are you sure you wouldn't like some hot cider?" I replied, turning to hang another ornament on the tree. "And by the way, do you know anyone around here who owns a long-haired white cat?"

I looked up in time to see the kitchen door slam shut.

Dismissive of the ghost stories, but curious about the property, I eventually turned to the internet to look up some of the area history. I clicked on a link for the Berks County Historical Society, and was redirected to a website for the Berks County Paranormal Society. "Why not ask?" I thought while sending off an email inquiring if they had any background on my property on Bootleg Road.

The response from Tom, the President of the Paranormal Society, was almost instantaneous. "All we have is what is in the Charlie Adams books," he said. "Have you had any contact with ghosts? Are you experiencing any paranormal activity? May we come out and do an investigation?"

At this point, my entire life was pretty much paranormal, but I knew what he meant. "What would an investigation entail?" I wrote back. It is so easy to get sucked into things on the internet.

"We do a background check and history of the property before we come. The day of the investigation we arrive around 10:00 p.m. and usually finish by about 1:30 or 2:00 in the morning. We take digital photos and look for 'orbs' or balls of energy. We take thermal readings to find 'cold spots.' We may also videotape sections of the house. We just got this terrific new equipment for taking EVP's (electronic voice profiles) of ghosts." (Apparently, and this is according to the experts, ghosts prefer to use frequencies that are either too low or two high to be heard, leaving the audible ones for the living.) Tom continued, "If we find any paranormal activity you will receive a certificate stating that fact, suitable for framing."

"I'm not sure I believe in ghosts," I replied. "But I do know that I'm not interested in stirring anything up that isn't already here. I have to ask that your investigation not include candles, séances, Ouija boards, or large women in India-print mumu's swooning into trances. Levitation should also be avoided, no one's head should rotate 360-degrees, no one should puke up green pea soup and please, don't bring any pentagons made of braided human hair. If you don't find any ghosts may I have a certificate stating that my house is ghost-free, suitable for framing?" Not sure what else to ask I added, "Do you have any references?"

Tom gave the Topton Hotel, site of a recent investigation, as a reference. The society also had a gig going with the Discovery Channel and a local educational channel. Tom was professional and quite serious about the society's study of the paranormal, although none of the members claimed to be psychic or to possess supernatural powers. He assured me that they hadn't broken anything in any prior home investigations. Good enough. I agreed to meet with them in a month once the document search was completed. Yes, I pondered, a Certificate of Normalcy was just what this place needed. That would straighten everything out on many levels.

Tom and two other Paranormals arrived right on schedule on a Saturday night. They started with a review of the property history. One of the team, Amy, was a history buff and had spent several hours in the county courthouse doing a tedious deed search.

Amy traced the deeds back to when John Himmelberger bought the property in the early 1800s. At that point the farm already had a one room stone house (the current kitchen) and at least one barn. Deeds before that were difficult to read since they were all handwritten, obviously by the same guy who copied the Declaration of Independence, in that small flowing script that constituted the "fine print" in legal documents of Colonial times.

John Himmelberger's daughter, Rebecca, married Jesse Shock in the late 1850s. They had two daughters and a son named Emerson. Jesse soon became a widower, but later married a second Rebecca with whom he built the front part of the house (the documents implied that the second Mrs. Schock financed the construction). In 1905 the farm was sold at a sheriff sale ordered to settle a lawsuit between stepson Emerson and a woman named Molly. For the next three transfers of the property, each deed contained a stipulation that a dower's payment be made to Jesse's widow, Rebecca, on April first of each year. The property was not a prosperous one. It changed hands frequently between 1905 and 1924. Most of the transactions were by forced sheriff sale. Finally, it had achieved some stability in the 1940s and 50s.

Amy's survey hadn't found any evidence of violent or sudden deaths in the house, but records from the 1800s are sketchy at best. According to some old church records, Jesse Schock's final resting place was in a cemetery in downtown Bernville.

"The only unusual events I could find in the area were an Indian massacre somewhere over near Skull Hill, and somewhere near Bernville a barn that was being used to make bootleg liquor exploded, killing the bootlegger's wife and five children. Not sure where that is though."

I felt a slight chill thinking of the ruined barn foundation at the edge of the woods. "Stay calm, stay cool, you are one night away from getting your Certificate of Normalcy," I said to myself, putting on my best "poker face."

The Paranormals held a mini-meeting in the kitchen. First, since it was a regular meeting of the society in addition to being an investigation, they reviewed results from a previous investigation in a row house in Reading. They passed around "confirmed" orb pictures and a photograph of a ghostly face in a mirror. In addition they reviewed some of the EVPs collected from a nearby cemetery rumored to be haunted by one of Berks County's most notorious murderers. The voice recording sounded like "eveeermmnopstropsometag." Somehow the Paranormals interpreted that to mean, "I've been waiting for you to come." The next was "umberganderslugmenderfort" which was helpfully translated to say, "this one is mine." It sounded like gobbledy-gook to me, but everyone else seemed so excited that I decided to nod agreeably and go along with the rest of the crowd.

The evening's game plan was to set up a video camera in the upstairs closet to record anything that might be happening among my "will definitely fit when I'm ten pounds thinner" wardrobe that was hanging there. They then spent the next three hours moving from room to room taking digital photos, recording temperatures with a laser device and looking for stray electromagnetic currents. During the EVP searching phase, everyone had to be very quiet while Tom asked the furniture questions such as, "How old are you, how did you die, and why are you still here?"

Nothing happened. Nada, rien, nothing, total uneventfulness. Not even an orb or a temperature change or a rustling of the curtains. All indications were negative. Not a ghost to be found.

"Well, that's a shame. Can I have that Certificate of Normalcy?" I asked hopefully.

"We'd like to come back next week and check out the outbuildings if that's okay. Outside investigations generally start just before sunset."

Nothing worth having comes easily. I resigned myself to waiting another week for the certificate.

The next Saturday, the investigators arrived with the previous week's report. None of the EVP recordings detected anything out of the norm. A re-review of the digital photographs all came out negative. One of the team members had actually watched an entire ninety minutes of video of my "thin clothes" looking for paranormal evidence. With nothing more racy than a black drop-back Christmas gown with a rhinestone buckle in a size ten to look at, it must have been a torturous hour-and-a-half. The only oddity that the team noted was that the camera set on the tripod pointed at the closet kept refocusing on its own. Amy took it to a camera shop for a tune up and lens cleaning just to be sure.

The Paranormals started the outside investigation in the barn by taking digital photographs. This process involved taking as many pictures as possible of nothing in particular in the hope that something will somehow appear out of nowhere. Amy, being a seasoned team member, took about three hundred shots in a twenty minute time frame. Everybody then convened in the kitchen to develop a game plan.

"We have unconfirmed anecdotal evidence from past residents of paranormal activity in the house," Tom reported. "However, our visit last week showed no evidence of any paranormal activity despite intensive investigation. Tonight we will continue our investigation of the property including the major outbuildings in an effort to confirm or deny the presence of ghosts."

"Deny, Deny, Deny," I rooted quietly to myself.

Just then Amy, who had been clicking through the photos on the digital camera, whispered, "I think I've got something." Tom took the camera and began reviewing the images himself.

"This may be an orb, or it could just be dust. No, in the next image it appears to have moved laterally across the barn aisle. It may be an orb, it may be dust, it could be an orb, it may be an orb. I think it's an orb!"

The group let out a collective gasp. They were clearly thrilled. They packed all their equipment up and headed over to the hayloft to continue the investigation. On the way over to the barn Paul, another member of the team, turned back toward the house and pointed his laser temperature detector to record temperatures across the front of the structure. While scanning the upstairs bedrooms from left to right he announced the temperature readings. As the laser crossed the first bedroom window he read out the temperatures "seventy, sixty-eight, sixty-eight, sixty-eight." As the beam crossed to the second bedroom, he suddenly called out, "Whoa, forty-five degrees! A cold spot!"

Tom immediately ordered everyone to a halt and said, "I need to get an independent temperature verification using our calibrated equipment." His laser read a constant temperature of sixty-eight degrees across the front of the house. Tom's authority as leader was absolute: I was thankfully still in the running for the Certificate of Normalcy.

The Paranormals assembled on the threshing floor of the second story of the barn. The sun was setting so I turned on the lights in the hayloft. These consisted of two incandescent light bulbs over the large sliding wooden barn doors, each sheathed in quart-sized mason jars to protect them from breakage and the barn from fire. Not much light, but enough to see clearly. The video camera was set up on its tripod in the middle of the threshing floor and turned on to record whatever significant events might occur.

"Complete silence is essential," Tom ordered. "The EVP recorder is very sensitive. No talking. Remain completely still and be as quiet as you can. I'm going to ask a series of questions and wait for a response."

"What is your name?" he asked the bales of hay. Fifteen full seconds of silence.

"How old are you?" Another fifteen seconds of uncomfortable silence.

"How did you die?" Twenty seconds of silence. The bystanders were starting to get a little restless.

"Is anyone here with us?" *Instantly*, the lights in the hayloft dimmed to nothing and came back on again.

"It's the well pump coming on," I nodded to myself. "Must be creating a little power drain."

Unfazed, the leader of the Paranormals continued. "Who is the President of the United States?"

It did occur to me that this question could be confusing to a ghost living in the barn. It could even be construed as a trick question. The structure was built between 1772 and 1774. If the ghost was one of the builders, he/she would not know what a President of the United States even was. But not being familiar with the rules of spiritual "tweeners," I wasn't sure if they were up to date on current events. I kept silent; after all, what did I know?

The interrogation continued for about ten more minutes. With nothing remarkable happening, the crowd was now quite tired of standing still and being quiet.

"Are you still here?' Tom asked.

BANG. The lights dimmed to total darkness, stayed off a few seconds, and then came back on. It was long enough to shut down the Dusk to Dawn lights in the barnyard so that the entire barn area was momentarily plunged into total darkness. (Once shut off, Dusk to Dawn lights take about five minutes to come back to full brightness).

"Did you see that?" said two of the Paranormals simultaneously.

"Hold it! Don't say a word!" Tom admonished. He took the three-part Citing of Paranormal Activity Interview Questionnaire NCR form out of his metal clipboard. "You two have to be interviewed separately for the investigation to be legitimate."

Each described the exact same thing. A blue orb, or ball of light, moved from the beams over the barn door toward the left side of the barn. It then traveled along the crossbeam to the back of the barn and disappeared. I missed the whole orb movement because I was mesmerized by the video camera on the tripod. Without the help of a human hand, it managed to turn itself off, then on, then off, then on again.

Everyone was in a dither. Paul, who was new to the team, had never experienced anything quite this real and became a little bit freaked out, no doubt wondering whether he had made the right choice for a hobby.

"This is very exciting," said Tom. "Paranormal activity comes in several forms. Most are 'holographic' ghosts. These are the 'faces in the mirror' or the spirit walking down the hall oblivious to the observer. Another is sequential events that may be triggered by something where the same sequence of activities plays over and over, like footsteps on the stairs, doors slamming, telephones ringing, etc. The third, and most unusual, is the interactive haunting. These spirits are aware of the living and are able to interact with them. You have an interactive haunting! This is so terrific!"

My hopes for a Certificate of Normalcy slowly faded to a wisp of nothingness.

"What about breaking glass and moving tools?" I asked.

"That's either a poltergeist, or sometimes a prankster, usually a ghost of a younger person. They can be a pain in the neck."

Inspired by the evening's success, the team decided to have another go at finding ghosts back at the house. They gathered in the upstairs guest bedroom and sat themselves quietly on the floor and the bed. Tom set up the EVP computer on a small desk by the notorious closet. The screen glowed in the darkened room. It looked like an EKG screen. The EVP computer does real time identification of ghost voices. Tom began the interview. As he asked each question the flat green line on the screen became agitated, reflecting his spoken voice. Between questions the line flattened in the silence of the room. The group held its collective breath. No one wanted to appear the cad and interrupt when the ghost began to speak. The first four questions were answered by a flat green line. After the fifth question a small, barely perceptible squiggle appeared. It was a potential EVP! Tom started clicking away on the computer, attempting to develop and amplify the faint squiggle. He replayed the voice, now amplified so the group could hear.

I was prepared for the same garbled syllables I'd heard from the Paranormals' previous investigations. This time, however, a small child's voice said something that sounded for all the world like the words, "I love you."

Amy broke the silence. "That sounds like a little boy saying, "I love you!"

"And that is where this investigation ends," I said definitively. If I had to live in this house along with paranormal activity that said, "I love you" I didn't want to have to deal with whatever else the little fellow had to say.

The next week I got a call from Tom. "We found some interesting things on the barn sound recording. We'll be out on Friday with our final report."

The team arrived Friday evening and sat around the coffee table in the living room. They reviewed the investigation report including ambient temperatures, lunar phases, and sunspot activity on the nights of the investigation. The final report, which was to be posted on their website, was thorough and professional. Descriptions of the location and property were kept sufficiently vague as to allow the property and its owner to remain anonymous. Tom set the laptop computer on the coffee table and played the barn EVPs. Other people's ghosts may mumble, but the Flower Hill Farm residents spoke clearly and articulately.

In response to the question, "How old are you?" a voice of an elderly man responded, "I'm seventy." Two additional EVPs were recorded. Each corresponded with the timing of the blinking lights. The first said, "Help me." And the second, and more urgent sounding recording said, "Listen!" I took all this information in stride. Including the "suitable for framing" certificate that proclaimed: *Let it be known that from this time forth this residence and associated outbuildings are official places of paranormal activity, as determined and evidenced through rigorous examination, scientific testing, and independent review.*

I thanked the Paranormal team for their investigation of the property and for the professional way they conducted their work.

For several days afterward I wondered what my personal responsibilities were with regard to the spirits that may or may not be in the barn and the house. I briefly considered asking an opinion from my church, but I am an Episcopalian. Since the church is going through a rough patch and has a tough time providing definitive direction on much of anything these days, I thought it best not put them to the test.

Was I supposed to guide the ghosts toward the light? Was that a little presumptuous? What was the protocol for dealing with hauntings?

Logic prevailed. EVPs could be anything. Power outages were more than common out in the country. Orbs could have been a reflection from the Dusk to Dawns going out. Tools get misplaced, phones ring for no reason. Radiator parts can show up anywhere at any time. If you start looking for something, you'll probably find it. Anyone can string together coincidences. All perfectly explainable.

About a week after receiving the Certificate of Paranormal Activity, I was getting ready for bed. I had just gone into the guestroom to get something out of the "thin clothes" closet. As I turned to go out the door into my bedroom I shut off the light and, tongue in cheek, said to the closet, "Good night, Little Boy, I love you!" Immediately the house and barn plunged into total darkness. The house lights flickered on after a couple seconds, but the barn stayed dark until the Dusk to Dawns recovered.

Memo to self: Do not speak to the ghosts unless it is absolutely necessary.

Unfortunately I discovered that every once in a while, it becomes absolutely necessary.

The next project on the list was the barn restoration. Once again I turned to my good friend Glenn to do the work. He didn't even blink when I instructed him in my rudimentary understanding of ghost etiquette at the start of the job.

"One little thing about doing work in the barn," I began, clearly venturing into new territory. "It would probably be a good idea if you would take a minute each morning to sort of brief the ghost in the hayloft about your plans for the day. Just to reassure him that we're restoring the barn and not destroying it. That might make the job go a little easier."

"Uh, sure Liz. No problem." Glenn has been dealing with neurotic customers all his life. Nothing fazed him. He called over to his helper Brian who was unloading the truck. "Brian, what we need to do is have our daily job meeting in the hayloft so that the ghost can listen in and won't be upset when we start tearing up siding or doing demolition."

Brian gave Glenn a blank look and just nodded.

"Oh, and Brian, don't say anything to Sanchez."

It's a good businessman who knows both his customer and his crew.

The restoration was completed without seeing hide nor hair of the ghost. Sanchez's tools disappeared a few times, but they always turned up sooner or later, generally in the hayloft.

The following spring, once the barn work was paid off, I decided to complete the kitchen remodeling by restoring the loft above the kitchen. This was more out of necessity than aesthetics. Birds had been getting in from somewhere under the eaves and I was tired of chasing them around the house and cleaning bird shit off the coffee table, which they were apparently using for target practice. The loft was the sleeping quarters for the original one-room stone cabin. It wasn't a large job, just some insulation and drywall, leaving the beams exposed, and refinishing the two-hundred-thirty-year-old floor.

Brian had the lead for this job. He liked to get to work early, so it was not unusual for him to be working in the loft by 6:00 a.m. Glenn was more of a night owl; his schedule had him starting work around mid-afternoon and finishing up in time for the 10:00 p.m. nightly news. They did good work at a reasonable price so I learned to live around them.

The stairs to the loft hadn't been installed yet so the only access was via a step ladder in the kitchen. I had greeted Brian on my way in from mucking out the barn and was now showered and dressed for work in my navy blue suit, navy-tinted stockings and matching leather pumps. I was calling up to say goodbye to him when he asked, "Do you have a minute?"

Thinking that he wanted to discuss some detail of the job, I climbed up the step ladder until my head appeared above the floor in the loft. Brian was sitting on the floor rubbing the floor boards with a tung oil rag. He had two fans running for ventilation.

"How's it going?" I chirped.

"Did anyone ever die up here?"

"What?"

"Is there any record of anyone ever getting very sick and dying up here? " Brian asked. He was a pretty straight up kind of guy, and was obviously really concerned about something.

"It was used as the family bedroom for a hundred years before the front house was built, so chances are pretty good that at least one person died up here. Why?"

"The other day I was working on sanding the floors and I smelled a strong, almost overpowering smell of meat cooking. It was like a lamb or strong stew. It got stronger and stronger until it made me nauseous. I ended up getting sick to my stomach."

"Maybe you don't have enough ventilation. I'll go get another fan."

"I've been painting for twenty years and never smelled anything like that. I figured it was one of the ghosts. I tried talking to it, you know, like we did with the barn. Just explaining that I was restoring the loft and was making it like new again. I just don't think I got through to it."

"Brian, this is unacceptable." I have to admit, I was agitated. Brian is a good person and a talented craftsman. He should not have to put up with this kind of treatment on the job. I found myself saying, "We can't let them do that to you! These are house ghosts; we have to take a strong position on house ghosts. I live in this house. My nieces and nephews will be playing up here and sleeping here. It is my time to be here, they had their time. You have to be very firm and make it clear that this type of thing is absolutely not allowed. Otherwise they'll be walking, or is it wafting, all over us."

"Ok, I'll try to be more firm with them."

"Terrific. What day did you say that was?"

"Last Tuesday. I remember because it was April first."

I got in the car, turned the key in the ignition and started off to a meeting on improving patient access to outpatient clinics. Suddenly, it occurred to me that I had just had a seemingly reasonable conversation with my contractor about how to keep disembodied spirits from impacting the construction schedule. Were we completely out of our minds?

These sorts of things never happened in the safety of the suburbs.

It's been pretty quiet since the last remodeling project. Every once in awhile a glass slides off a table and breaks when no one is in the room or the phone rings after the sound of a slamming door. Or sometimes, on a quiet evening when everything is settled down and I'm in the living room with the dogs, the old Labrador will look up at the staircase in recognition of something or someone, and I'll turn at the gentle thumping sound of his wagging tail.

Services

It's not so much fear of the dead but fear of the living—fear of life—that usually motivates us from point A to point B. Through years of evolution, we have rearranged our environment to go beyond the basic needs for oxygen, food, and shelter to the need for a continual droning of television, hair dryer, electric shaver, and blender. We've developed certain expectations which over time have become inalienable rights. Rights to cell phone signals, electrical power, air conditioning and heating, cable TV and roads that are plowed after a snowstorm. Certainly, these are things that should be expected, taken for granted even, especially for hardworking, taxpaying citizens of the good old US of A. We're not a third world nation after all. But I had been warned. My well-meaning friends all told me from the safety of their neutral décor condominiums with Berber carpeting and ironclad maintenance agreements that services in the country would not be what they were in the safety of the suburbs. I was going out there beyond the moat, out on my own where anything could happen and there was nothing, short of selling out, that I could do about it.

My first experience with a loss of inalienable rights was a power outage. A power outage has become the Great Force in today's society. Intellectually we've gone beyond our primitive superstitions and fear of ghosts. Our modern fears are more tangible; we are vulnerable. At any moment in time our service can be cut off, an event tantamount to sending us immediately back to Cro-Magnon status.

Power outages in civilized areas, even the most severe ones, usually last no more than three or four hours. This gives the family a chance to do things together like play Parcheesi by candle light. Anyone who works in a maternity ward can tell you what most people do during a blackout. If the electric goes out on May first, it can be predicted that the staff will be mighty busy right around Groundhog Day.

I believed the rhetoric, I was sure that out in the country, unlike in the civilized areas, power outages lasted for days. So that Friday night in May when the lights flickered, went out, came back on and then went out again, I sensed trouble. Luckily, a warm weather power outage is a cake walk. It's kind of like being Amish. You get up with the sun, go to bed with the sun, do everything by hand around don't take a bath every day.

In one of my past careers, I worked for a power company, so I knew that the blink-flicker-restore-blink-flicker-darkness sequence was the proverbial kiss of death for the residential consumer. It meant that the folks who "manage the grid" were switching the power from line to line and substation to substation trying to keep up the delicate flow of electrons without overloading any of the sensitive grid components while the entire infrastructure was going to hell in a hand basket. The people who managed the grid surely had sweat stains under their arm pits and were frantic as gerbils in a cat house by this point. No question about it, I was in for a long haul.

I hurried into the house to make The Call. I knew from past employment that power restoration is an example of the squeaky wheel getting the grease. It is actually a game of "biggest bitch wins." The electric company responds to a request for a power return in a particular area only when a certain threshold number of calls have been received. The more people that live in the area, the more calls that will be received, the more violent the exchange, and the faster the customers get their power restored. Which may explain why outages are shorter in the cities and the suburbs: the denser the population, the more calls go out to The Electric Company, so the faster the electricity gets restored. The Call to the Electric Company is not to be missed. First off, it's necessary to let them know that you are out of power because they have no way of figuring this out on their own. Of course they could just wait until billing time comes around and notice that you didn't use any of their product. But since the meter readers rarely make it out this far, chances are that they would do an "estimated" bill and charge you more than what you normally pay anyway.

The Electric Company is never embarrassed that someone has successfully called them using a telephone with lines that run along the exact same utility poles as their non-functioning wires. You are greeted by an unabashed female electronic voice who assures you that your outage is the most important outage ever and that the entire power company is working twelve-hour shifts to restore your particular power within two hours. You can call as many times as you want, it's always two hours. The voice is preprogrammed to say "two hours." It gives the power company an opportunity to thrill suburban residents by restoring their power within one hour and forty-seven minutes, thus "exceeding expectations." On the other hand, it doesn't matter that it's day two of the outage, power restoration is still two hours away. To add insult to injury, the electronic voice then offers to wake you up any hour of the day or night by calling you to tell you that your power has been turned on. As if you wouldn't notice your lights on, television blaring, hairdryer blowing, and the margaritas you put in the blender just as the power failed starting to mix!

I assumed, mostly because the farm was located on a dirt road in the middle of nowhere, that my place was not at the top of the power company's priority outage restoration list. So I expected the worst and began to shift into disaster mode. In retrospect, a power outage should have been anticipated, and plans should have been in place. I had been warned. I'd spent half my career as a project manager, dammit! How shameful to be caught with my proverbial pantyhose down during my *bona fide* power outage. Contingency plans should have been drawn up, lists should have been made, and provisioning should have taken place.

I established priorities based on the Flower Hill Farm Hierarchy of Needs. First, an inventory of the Chardonnay supply determined that I had enough to withstand at least a three day outage. Second, toilet flushing. Thanks to a bachelor's degree in mechanical engineering, I figured out that one of the wonderful things about septic systems is that toilets can be flushed by dumping a bucket of creek water into the bowl. I also learned that it's a bad idea to use a pickup truck to transport open buckets of water from the creek to the house. If there are a lot of gullies, you'll hit the front door with a wet truck and a dry bucket. Third, personal hygiene: Diet Pepsi can be used to wet a toothbrush when all bottled water has been consumed.

As I completed my preparations for the "long haul" I couldn't help noticing how my more seasoned neighbors had already been prepared. Most simply walked out to the side porch and started up the diesel-fueled generator that was permanently installed and hooked to the main breaker. A few farmers hastened home from the fields, backed the tractor up to the basement door and plugged 'ol Bessie into the electrical system. Problem solved. The neighborhood came alive with the sound of diesel engines keeping the home lights burning.

As the sun began setting I suddenly remembered the most important need: a light source. Flashlights are useless in a power outage. First of all, their batteries had been taken out long ago to power the boom box during the fence-painting party. Second, they are always stored in some deep recess of a kitchen drawer or back broom closet where they can't be found in broad daylight. No, flashlights were useless. Like Cro-Magnon man, I needed sustainable fire.

The problem was getting that initial spark, that small smoldering ember from which all other lights could be kindled.

In ancient times, someone was put in charge of making sure that the tribe had a continual fire burning. When the tribe had to move, this anointed individual was responsible for carefully gathering and packing the glowing embers to make sure that there would be fire at the new destination. Because of this, the Firestarter was a man of power, a Holy Man. I am not amongst the highly esteemed Firestarters. I now confess that I hid a "strike anywhere" match in my shoe during the test for the Girl Scout survivor badge and fired it up when the counselor wasn't looking, proudly holding my flint and steel above the roaring kindling. So there was neither flint, nor steel, nor match, nor lighter on the whole farm.

I remembered some scented candles in a carton in the garage, still unpacked since moving. As daylight failed I frantically pawed through the move boxes until I came upon this set of teaberry-scented votive candles. I soon found myself in the front seat of the pickup truck trying to light the things using an electric cigarette lighter. It took a few attempts (the trick is to fire up the lighter several times in succession so that it becomes very hot), but eventually I had access to FIRE. And a very festive front cab what with the teaberry scent and all. Using some tribal mandate stored deep in the heart of the collective subconscious to Never Let the Fire Go Out Once It's Started, I lit several candles while still sitting in the truck. Step by step I crept closer to the house, shielding the little votive candles, protecting the flame.

Just as I was about to reach the house, I heard the welcome and very familiar sound of margaritas in the blender. Crisis over.

At least for me. I could still hear the sound of diesel engines echoing across the little valley. Perhaps no one noticed that the power was on. Used to such inequities, people living in the country fire up their generator the minute the lights go out and don't even bother calling about the problem. Long after power has been restored to the region, the folks in the country are still blindly running their generators. When I noticed that they were still running on Sunday morning, I decided to take a walk and did some investigating.

As it turns out, Flower Hill Farm is not on the same grid as everyone else. It may be that the farm is uniquely situated on some auxiliary power line that provides backup power to a hospital, nuclear power plant, county emergency system and/or CIA operative. Best not to ask a lot of questions it being post-911 and all.

Since power outages did not seem to be the Armageddon event I expected, I took the next six months worrying about the next potential for disaster in this foreign land of limited services: The Winter Snowstorm. The real danger of a snowstorm in the country is boredom. Short days, long nights, and being trapped on the farm at the mercy of the township snow plow schedule leave little to do. As Bootleg Road is rarely traveled and only halfway paved, the north end being a rutted dirt and gravel pathway between two farms, I expected to be the last resident in Pennsylvania to be plowed out.

A few precious hours can be spent digging little human habitrails from the house to the barn or digging out the pony, donkey, pig or goat. Since wheelbarrows aren't any use at all in the snow, a Muck Bucket Luge Track can be built to allow the manure bucket to gently glide from the horse stalls to the manure pile. Once these tasks are done, however, the silence sets in. What would a single woman living alone in the country do while waiting three days for the plow to show up? The answer is quick and simple: wallpaper.

With the first ominous forecast, while others rushed to the market to clear the shelves of French toast ingredients, I was at the Home Depot buying discount wallpaper. I bought it cheap, since I am not overly particular as to pattern as long as it is self-adhesive, strippable, with not too much of a repeat pattern. I was headed to the checkout with my arms brimming with several selections from the Super Saver bins (among them : "Rocky Mountain Song Birds" with an attractive "Raptors and other Birds of Prey" border) when I ran into one of my neighbors. They were on the "other grid" electrical service and were in the midst of a fairly intense bidding war with another couple over the last remaining diesel generator.

"Guess we'll be stuck a long time till the plow comes through," I said, making conversation while at the same time trying to avoid the subject of power outages. Even though it isn't my fault, the neighbors get their noses just a little out of joint when they've been out of power for a week and then see my farm lit up like Christmas Village.

"Waiting for the plow? You never have to wait; your farm is one of the first on the township list. Our road is the one that doesn't get plowed," said the neighbor.

"Why is that?" I asked naively, feeling a little like Marie Antoinette asking why don't they just eat cake.

"Your land is right next to Skull Hill Dairy," the neighbor explained with a hint of impatience. "The township plows the dairy farms out first. The milk can't sit. To get out you have to go past Skull Hill Dairy, over to the Dan-Lyn Dairy, then to the Farmer in the Dell Goat Farm, then to Highland Dairy, past the township building, past the township supervisor's house, then past where Charlie who drives the plow truck lives, then just one more dairy farm on the left and that puts you on the highway. Just stay off any state-maintained roads and you'll be fine."

Within a year-and-a-half I had a pretty good sense of the reliability of traditional services. Due to what is probably either a great relationship with my guardian angel, or living proof of the maxim "God takes care of drunks and fools," electric and road services were a lock. The farm has its own water and septic, cable was never going to be a possibility, the phone service was fine (except when the ghosts messed with it), and cell phones just don't work anywhere in Bernville.

The mail arrives as often as one would expect given that the mail carriers have to use their own cars and are sometimes relied upon to deliver verbal messages from farm to farm, report fires, and return lost dogs or stray goats. They are, on occasion, also called upon to find the farmer and let him know that they just passed a cow calving in his field. When Kathy, who does the mail sorting, is on vacation, things fall apart a bit, but everyone knows who lives where, so it's not too much trouble for the homeowner to put the misplaced mail in the right box on the way to the feed store.

LESSON 6

What Every Woman Needs is a Good Metal Man

What I had yet to learn was that country life requires other essential services over and above the usual electric, phone, water, sewer, and high-speed bandwidth. These are provided by the unique professionals to be found in and around the various townships, the type of people you'd never meet in an area that sports sidewalks. They only thrive in a country setting.

The livelihood of some of these individuals is garnered from the collection and redistribution of some form of manure. For instance, the "Mushroom Man" will pick up horse manure at no charge. That is *only* if the farm has at least seven manure-producing horses with beds exclusively in straw.

Straw makes a wonderful bedding material. It's soft, absorbs urine like a sponge, and improves a horse's disposition in general. Unfortunately it requires three times the labor and eight times the volume of other bedding methods.

I quickly learned that at no time can anything but straw and manure be put into a quality Mushroom Man manure pile. Manure piles are regularly inspected to make sure that they contain no sawdust, rags, or dead pigeons. If that happens, the pile is summarily rejected and is doomed to remain where it is until the next millennium.

In addition, the Mushroom Man only makes his rounds when he is good and ready. By the time he arrives, if you are lucky enough to meet all the manure criteria, your stash is about the size of a three bedroom rancher. It's also been heating up as a result of the "ripening" process, and has matured to the point of combustion from its center. At that point it becomes a fire hazard.

The endearing thing about the nature of manure is that it must be relocated from one place to another if it is to be useful. And as any BMW owner who has followed too closely behind a manure truck on a rainy day can readily confirm, the stuff is quite a pungent and resilient product. It's also very democratic, and can be found anywhere in the country.

There is a hierarchy in the manure world. Bat guano easily claims first place in terms of balance of minerals and nutrients. It is, however, available in such small quantities as to be useful only in flower beds. Cow manure is second, and is prized by the Amish. They empty their barns every spring, much to the delight of the neighbors in nearby housing complexes who purchased their homes in a rural area to enjoy the clean country air.

Duck manure is another prized excrement. The Duck Manure Man will come, for a fee, and put a large pile of duck crap just about anywhere you specify. For some reason, not clearly understood or articulated, Duck Manure Men will only dump one pile per property.

Mitch, the farmer who leases my fields, purchased a pile of duck crap one year. But he threw his back out before he had time to spread it, and for weeks it remained a mountain of concentrated fertile, ripe, aromatic excrement. There is little in this world that smells worse than duck crap. And it doesn't get better with time, I can attest to that.

One thing does smell worse though. I have no idea what it is, but the neighboring farmer regularly spreads it on his fields. It is sprayed out of the back of unmarked tanker trucks that rumble down Bootleg Road in the wee, dark hours of the morning. The morning after one of these pre-dawn anointings, the air is so thick that it can almost be tasted. During the short walk from the house to the car the scent will settle on clothes and remain pungent for the rest of the day. People at my office sniff the air suspiciously and then check their shoes to see if they stepped in dog dirt. Or they'll look in their office trash cans to see if garbage was accidentally left overnight. When I sit down in the cafeteria people move to other tables. I am a Manure Pariah. To add to its charming appeal, the scent also attracts stray dogs. But I have to admit that the neighbor's fields grow faster and display a greener hue than anyone else's in the area.

Hard to believe, but woman cannot live by manure alone. There are other specialized services that are required. Fortunately the country has professionals with skills often handed down from generation to generation to meet a woman's every need.

Witness the following conversation:

"Have you found a Metal Man?" a friend asked one day. Debbie and her husband had just moved into their new home on a twelve acre piece of land in the small town of Leather Corner Post. The house was imposing and perfect in every detail, modeled after an Irish castle, right down to the turrets and drawbridge. We were sitting on a broad veranda overlooking a beautiful stream and pasture, enjoying the view with a glass of Chardonnay.

"I'm still looking," I sighed.

I knew that I should have found a Metal Man by now, but sometimes one thing leads to another. I needed to focus on the important things in my life.

"Well, not to worry, I'm sure one will come along when the time is right," Debbie said, while patting my hand with true sympathy. Although I tried to remain optimistic, it was clear that at this late date the prospects of finding the perfect Metal Man were waning.

I agreed with Debbie's quasi-spiritual comment on the lack of a good Metal Man in my life. Like the perfect husband, a Metal Man only appears "when the time is right." And you certainly don't want to push the process. Marriages and Metal Men encounters shouldn't be forced.

Metal Men don't advertise in the Yellow Pages or even the local trade paper *The Merchandiser* (which is thrown out of a speeding car into my rose bushes every week). Metal Men just happen along, and the really good ones are worth waiting for. For some reason, owners of fixer-uppers don't provide Metal Man references. Like a great recipe for taco salad or the name of a good divorce lawyer, you don't share this kind of information.

Life's greatest changes come along when you least expect them. My defining moment, Metal Man-wise, came early one morning at about 6 a.m. I had stopped at the local Redner's Gas and Grocery for a fill-up on my way to work. Just an ordinary stop at an ordinary gas station on an ordinary day. When I came out of the store with a donut and a Diet Pepsi for the long commute, I stopped dead in my tracks. There, at pump number five, with eight dollars of regular reading on the gauge, was a faded blue pickup truck.

This moment was burned indelibly into my psyche as Tammy Wynette blasted over the gas station speaker system begging me to "Stand by your man...." The sides of the truck bed were built up with four fence posts connected by gray wooden boards, and it was filled to overflowing with old lawn mowers, rusted box-wire fence crushed into two-foot squares, iron pipes, bicycle frames, and old chains. Clever woman that I am, I realized that these were telltale signs. I was in the presence of a real Metal Man.

I peered through the store entrance at the cash register to see if anyone in line looked like a Metal Man. A few patrons did, but none close enough to be counted as a true sighting. The Mission: To identify and isolate the Metal Man.

I stood by my car and tried to act nonchalant. No sense in appearing too anxious or excited. A few minutes later a man came out and approached the truck. He was about five-foot-three inches tall, probably approaching seventy (but then again may have been ninety), and his pate was covered by a John Deere hat. Really, there was nothing too distinguishing about him. Except for the contents of his truck.

I made my move. Slowly and from an oblique angle, not wanting to scare him off, I crept up to the side of his vehicle.

"Excuse me, sir. Are you a Metal Man?" I said almost in a whisper.

He started and looked around.

"*Darn*," I thought, "He's going to bolt and then I'll never find him again."

"Who wants to know?" the man asked suspiciously, his truck keys at the ready, with one hand on the door handle.

"I have an old farm and barn on thirty-six acres. I bought it a couple years ago and have been fixing it up. There is a lot of metal in the outbuildings that has to go."

I knew better than to use the work "junk" to describe the rolls of barbed wire, broken bicycles, rusted tractor parts, and crumpled galvanized pipe gates. The Junk Man will charge to take these treasures away. The Metal Man is a prospector, a real professional.

"I'm not sure what all is out there, I did see an old anvil and some aluminum storm windows," I said in an attempt to bait the trap.

Untapped outbuildings, one hundred pounds of solid iron, and the prospect of recyclable aluminum was a temptation too much to bear. He was hooked.

"I can probably stop out tomorrow night to take a look."

"I'm over toward Centerport. Here, I'll give you directions," I said, excitedly fishing in my purse for a pen and some scrap paper.

"I know where you are," he said with a smile, and in a twinkling he was gone.

For several moments, I stared at the space where the Metal Man had been but now only a small puddle of fresh oil remained. I shrugged it off as another Bernville social encounter and went on to work.

True to his word, he arrived the following evening. Like most Metal Men, he was a retired farmer who sold his land and was now living in a too small a house in town with too much time and too little to do. He missed the land and the daily struggle that farming entails. In other words, he was in his wife's hair all day.

"I go to work at 6 a.m.and don't usually get home until late," I said, setting up the ground rules. "You can come anytime and go through the barn loft, hoghouse, or the sheds. None of my stuff is in there yet and you are welcome to whatever you find. Take your time and come out whenever. The only deal is, if you take some metal, you have to take all of it."

The Metal Man couldn't help but smile. He was looking at a three-month task out in the country on a farm with absolutely no one to bother him.

"What if I find something valuable?"

Loaded question. If I said that he couldn't have it, he would have to think about whether he wanted to spend all this time sorting through the outbuilding treasures. If I said he could have anything he would assume I'd already gone through the buildings and knew that they contained nothing of value. Again he'd lose interest. It was a very tense moment.

"If it's made of gold or sterling silver or if you think I should see it, I would like you to put it aside for me to take a look at. Otherwise everything you find is yours." I replied. Given the history of bankruptcy and sheriff sales that plagued the property there was no way any gold or silver remained; anyway, he was after aluminum.

The Metal Man went to work. Although I rarely saw him in person, I found evidence of his progress as the weeks progressed, with more and more space being cleared out in the hayloft and the outbuildings. One day, I came home from work to find him waiting for me.

"I found some things that you need to take a look at," he said.

I walked across to where his blue truck was parked next to the back shed. Four items were neatly laid out for inspection. The first was a square contraption with a broken shaft and some sort of plate that was once secured by four bolts. Now it had only one, which gave it the appearance of a tooth about to fall out. My confusion was obvious.

"It's a motor for a hay elevator," he said softly. "It doesn't work right now, but it can be fixed."

"Oh," I said, wondering how badly I needed a motor for a hay elevator which I did not own.

I moved deliberately onto the second item—a rusted red-and-white gasoline push mower.

"It can be fixed," the Metal Man said encouragingly.

"Ah," I answered thoughtfully, picturing the added fun I could have using a push mower as opposed to my silly garden tractor.

The next item was a blue motorcycle frame. Both wheels were missing along with most of the parts. It was covered with dirt and roots as though it had been recently dug from an archeological excavation.

"This would take a bit of work, but it can be fixed."

I envisioned myself in the basement, a naked bulb hanging from a wire overhead, surrounded by motorcycle parts in various stages of repair. My hair would be tied up, I'd have on blue coveralls and a grease smear would be running across my face, like Betty Jo, the youngest daughter in "Petticoat Junction." The one who married Glenn the crop duster. Cute at age twenty-four, pitiful as one approaches middle age. No, the motorcycle skeleton had no place on Flower Hill Farm.

The final item was a large exhaust fan. You know the kind. They are used to suck the air through large chicken houses.

"I suppose that this can be fixed also?" I said, wondering what it would be like to be in the poultry business, encircled by squawking fowl all day long.

"No Ma'am," The Metal Man said with a hint of surprise in his voice. "That fan works just fine. It clanks some when you first start it up, but then it goes along good as new."

I walked slowly down the row of items to give them one last once over, letting the Metal Man see that I knew just how valuable they were and that I would be an idiot to part with them. I nodded thoughtfully while visions of hay and poultry farming interspersed with motorcycle gang activities passed through my mind. The metal man stood nervously with his hands in his pockets, trying not to look overly anxious.

"Thank you," I said finally. "I can see that these are valuable items, and that they should be repaired or otherwise put to some good use. I am afraid that at this time in my life, I'm not in a position do right by them. Would you take them and find someone who will?"

"You bet I will!" said the Metal Man, carefully lifting the treasures into the back of his truck. "You bet I will...."

The Metal Man had found the pot of gold at the end of the rainbow. In the process my excess metal problem had been solved.

In suburbia you do well to have connections in the corporate world of high-powered executives with its meetings aboard jets, tickets to Phillies games, and your own table at Judy's. But all this can't possibly compare to having connections in the edgy world of Metal Men.

Pet Karma and an Ass Named Irene

Some women are born man magnets. Others bring art or beautiful music into their lives. I have been blessed with Pet Karma. All I have to do is mention in passing that I might be interested in an animal of any type and within hours the phone rings. It's always someone who knows someone who just spoke to someone who is related to someone who happens to know where one can get whatever animal I mentioned. Nine times out of ten the animal must be rescued from a horrible fate.

One challenge for any new farm owner is to avoid taking on everyone else's unwanted animals. Take peacocks, for example. When I first mentioned that I was buying a farm, experienced farmers were quick to warn me not to accept any gift of peacocks or any unmarked packages that might contain peacocks. They can come from anywhere. Farms have been known to be overrun with peacocks before anyone realized what was happening. I was amazed at the number of people coming out of the woodwork with spare peacocks that they were more than willing to drop off.

Turns out peacocks are the hallmark and the bane of the first time amateur farmer. True, they possess an aura of elegance and aristocracy. They feed the fantasy of the genteel green lawn with a beautiful male peacock, feathers fanned out in full display, standing discreetly to the side of a pink and violet-hued rose garden. One imagines peacocks producing a cash crop of peacock feathers year after year, perhaps enough to help pay off the mortgage.

The truth about peacocks is that they scream. They let loose piercing, obnoxious sounds any hour of the day *or night*. Their tail feathers fall out easily, are immediately damaged or broken beyond repair, and grow back slowly. Male peacocks are extremely aggressive, challenging anything that moves in their vicinity. It is difficult to have more than one male on a farm at a time unless they are each given their own separate pens, preferably spaced far apart. Otherwise they will try to kill each other.

All of this obviously rules out low maintenance peacock-feather-growing. The hens are neither intelligent nor attractive and generally get lost or stuck under a shed or do something that requires a lot of human intervention to fix. It is, unfortunately, considered socially unacceptable to eat them.

I learned all this from a farmer friend who had not taken precautions and wound up with an incurable peacock infestation. Fortunately, I was able to dodge the bullet on peacock acquisition. The next challenges were the "petting zoo dissolution" and the "Ranger Rick Wildlife Sanctuary dispersal." Offers for three-legged raccoons, de-scented skunks, and bottle-fed groundhogs were politely refused. It wasn't as much out of experience or wisdom (that would come later), but just dumb luck that these animals required special permits from the Fish and Game Warden, and I didn't have a clue how to get one.

I caved in when it came to the home-raised Easter pets. Within the first few months of farm ownership I ended up with two ducks (Carson and Sophie) and my biggest mistake: Frank and Nancy, the American Heritage Turkeys.

Frank and Nancy were hatched from a group of mail order eggs and hand-raised in a friend's kitchen. The eggs had been guaranteed to be from different gene pools, but the sex could not be determined in advance and the hatching produced a surplus of male turkeys. As is the case with peacocks, the average farm can't be big enough for two Toms. Frank was the loser in the male turkey superiority contest.

"If you don't take this turkey, I know that Something Terrible will happen," my friend implored on the phone. "He gets chased and beaten up all day long. That big Tom of mine tries to take his hen away. It's so pitiful to watch him day after day. He's getting more and more despondent." Somehow this reminded me of the famous National Lampoon cover that announced "If You Don't Buy This Magazine We'll Kill This Dog."

Deep down I'm a softie. I was also new to farm life and couldn't bear the thought of a despondent turkey quaking in fear of losing the only hen he'd ever loved.

"I guess I'll take them. When do you want me to pick them up?"

"They just happen to be in my truck right now. I'm on my way to your place."

Despondency aside, Frank was an overweight and overbearing Tom turkey. He did have beautiful copper feathers that absolutely glowed in bright sunlight and his tail feathers were perfectly shaped. When he displayed them he looked like an Audubon rendering of an American Wild Turkey. His head was bald with a distinctive texture that looked like the surface of a brain. Its color was an indicator of his emotional state. If his head was light blue he was content, but tentative; pale grey meant that he was frightened. It was pink when he was eating. It was absolutely crimson when he was sexually aroused.

Most of the time, Frank's head was crimson. He was the horniest turkey that ever walked the farmyard. As fate would have it, he was too fat to breed effectively, but that didn't stop him from chasing poor Nancy around for most of the daylight hours. He was relentless in his pursuit.

Frank and Nancy were not a happy couple. Nancy was a pretty hen, but somewhat reserved and quiet. On the outside she seemed to accept her fate as one whose genetic makeup requires her to Mate for Life to someone she wasn't crazy about. Truth was, Nancy wasn't going to accept being hitched to Frank if there was any reasonable alternative in the immediate area.

One day I received a phone call from one of the neighbors who lived about a quarter of a mile away. Their son had borrowed his father's turkey call and was playing it on the rear deck of their house. Nancy must have heard the call and decided that, whoever he was, he sounded a lot better than the loser she was stuck with. Natural order of things aside, Nancy made the decision to leave Frank for whatever was on the other side of that turkey call.

She walked the quarter-mile up the road to the house, up four concrete steps, and began to peck insistently on the front door. When no one answered, she spotted some brightly-colored wind chimes set decoratively in a potted plant. She started pecking at them and raising quite a racket. The neighbors felt that Nancy was also an unsuitable mate for their eleven-year-old son and called me to come and remove my turkey from their front porch. I pulled up in the Honda, put Nancy in the trunk, and headed back home.

Nancy was never the same after that. She became very broody. Although she never laid any eggs she built a nest and started trying to hatch inanimate objects. She became fiercely protective of her collection of two burned out light bulbs, a couple of golf balls and a Mason jar. Frank, probably convinced that she was in the "family way," pretty much left her alone, and they lived peaceably for several months.

One morning, I went out early to feed the barn animals. Nancy was just fine, preening and rearranging herself on her nest as usual. A few hours later, Frank was scurrying all over the barnyard making a major commotion. Nancy was dead.

The folks down at the feed store assured me that this kind of sudden death syndrome sometimes happens with turkeys. They offered to try to find another hen, but I declined. Nancy was irreplaceable. Frank was destined to be the last turkey ever to reside on Flower Hill Farm.

As Nancy was the first pet demise on the farm it was time to select a location for the Pet Cemetery. Those of you who have ever lost a pet know how important it is to get this right the first time. A Pet Cemetery should be close enough to the house to allow for an occasional visit, but not so close as to be a continual reminder of one's loss. Shade trees are nice, but roots present an obstacle to digging. The cemetery should be located downstream from the well and in an area with minimal shale or bedrock. Even though one may be prostrate with grief, it's important to use good judgment when selecting the site. If you plan to have a lot of animals, it's also helpful to remember who went where so as to avoid confusion when interring future cemetery residents.

We are all a product of our past experiences. The Clark family template for a pet funeral was established with the death of Alexander the Hamster when I was about nine. When he (we always assumed Alexander was a he) died at a ripe old age of five he was placed in a small shoe box carefully lined with toilet paper. A hole of sufficient depth and breadth was dug under the canopy of a weeping beech tree in the corner of the yard and the coffin containing Alexander was carefully lowered into it.

The service continued as all six children gathered around as Dad read the Episcopal Service for the Burial of the Dead from the 1928 prayer book substituting the word "Hamster" for "Brother" at the appropriate times. As the body of our dear departed hamster, Alexander, was committed to the ground, each child put a shovel of dirt on his little coffin. The only exception was my older sister Vicky who was the only one in the family with any musical talent. She brought her cello outside and played "Amazing Grace" at the appropriate point in the service. We then marched back to the house singing "Onward Christian Soldiers," a hymn chosen not for any particular significance, but only because we all knew most of the words.

It was a proper burial and a good template. However, lacking five available siblings and a cello, I went about the sad and lonely duty of committing Nancy to the earth all by myself. Goodbye, Nancy, we'll see you at the Rainbow Bridge.

Frank adjusted to being a widower by becoming an indiscriminate lover. He was particularly fond of humping muck boots. His courting ritual consisted of approaching his intended from the rear, while the person occupying the muck boots was cleaning a stall or painting a fence or weeding the garden. Then he began a weird pacing, accompanied by a circling sort of dance, while at the same time making strange clicking noises. His head glowed bright red and his *snood* was fully extended. (It's not what you think it is. A snood is the flap of skin that extends down over a turkey's beak. Somehow the name seems appropriate.) He completed his mating ritual by snapping his wing feathers down, displaying his tail feathers and drumming with his feet like an overweight cast member of *Riverdance*. After five minutes he must have felt that he had made sufficient foreplay to make the muck boots swoon. He would then make a move to mount them. No amount of kicking, screaming or turning the water hose on Frank could discourage him when he had his heart set on wooing a fine pair of muck boots.

Frank's ardor knew no anatomical bounds. He made one pass at Alvin the pig who promptly bit off a couple of Frank's tail feathers. He tried to hump one of the horse's hocks. This resulted in Frank becoming airborne for the first and only time in his life. Finally, Frank discovered automobiles.

He loved to chase cars. He was especially happy to chase the mail lady's station wagon because it approached slowly and he must have felt that he actually had a chance of catching it. Bonnie, the mail lady, was really quite fond of Frank. She'd pull away slowly and then speed up, watching Frank through the rear view mirror, his wings spread, gobbling and running with all his might in a hysterical overweight wobbly gait looking much like Quasimodo being chased by a swarm of bees.

Frank was ever hopeful of catching and bringing down the U.S. Mail, which is probably, technically, a Federal Offense. If no mail lady was around, he would stand in wait in the middle of the road until an unsuspecting vehicle came along. When the driver stopped to avoid running him over, Frank, seeing a large male turkey reflected in chrome, would peck violently on the bumper. If the driver was game enough to get out of the car, Frank would immediately hump his or her shoes just to show the reflection who was top Tom around here.

This all makes one kind of wonder why Benjamin Franklin proposed the turkey as the national bird. The man had either an incredibly keen understanding of the human condition or a great sense of humor. Or both.

Frank had one other side to his character. Every year, about three weeks before Thanksgiving, he would fall desperately ill. The first year that this happened, I found him keeled over in the barnyard. Naturally, it was a Saturday night and the vet's office was on "emergency service." I didn't like the turkey all that much to begin with, and certainly didn't like him enough to incur the one hundred and thirty-five dollar fee for an emergency weekend vet call.

Unwilling to have the animal suffer, though, I brought him into the barn, made a nest of straw and placed him in it with a hot water bottle. Then, with no turkey healthcare knowledge to draw upon, I found some antibiotics left over from my last emergency room visit that I vaguely remembered someone telling me were turkey appropriate.

I mixed the antibiotics with water and filled a plastic syringe (for a second I considered putting the medicine into a turkey baster, but the irony was just too much). Sick as he was, it was still a challenge to get the antibiotics down Frank's throat.

I thought he might also need an efficient source of calories. A tour of the kitchen cabinets produced a set of "snack pack " cereal boxes that I'd bought on sale the last time the nieces and nephews had come to visit. I selected the Chocolate Cocoa Puffs, mixed them in a bowl of warm water and put the bowl within Frank's reach.

Miraculously, three days after Thanksgiving, the turkey fully recovered (probably more in spite of my ministrations than because of them) and was soon out terrorizing the neighborhood once again.

The second year, first week in November, Frank was once again lying prostrate in the barnyard. This time the mail lady was the first to discover him. She drove over the hill to the local Pennsylvania Dutch "Pow Wow" healer, Lillian, to ask for aid. Pow Wowers are an ancient and essential part of Pennsylvania Dutch culture, a type of shaman for the local farmers; they are skilled at healing both man and beast. Pow Wowers do not advertise or boast about their skills. The trick is to know where to find one.

Fortunately for Frank, Lillian lived nearby. I'd already started the antibiotic and Cocoa Puff treatment when the healer arrived. I didn't hear her come into the barn and she startled me. She seemed to appear out of nowhere. She had a large woolen shawl wrapped around her slight frame, her hair in a thick silver braid down the middle of her back.

"He is very sick," Lillian said, with sympathy in her voice.

"Yes, it just may be time for Frank to join Nancy at Rainbow Bridge," I replied, trying hard to sound disappointed at this possibility.

Frank was lying on his side, not moving. The Pow Wower closed her eyes and began to breathe deeply. She bent at the waist and passed her hands over Frank three times, standing upright and exhaling after each pass. Then she put her hands on Frank's head, passed them down his neck and over his body. When she took her hands away, Frank immediately stood up and started eating the Cocoa Puffs. Lillian came back over the next few days for follow up treatments. Soon Old Frank was good to go for another year. When the mail lady saw him up and about in the barnyard, she put notes in all the concerned neighbor's mailboxes letting them know that Frank was on his way to a successful recovery. Some things defy explanation.

With Pet Karma, it isn't necessary to go out looking for animals, nor does one have to stick to the run-of-the-mill dog, cat, pony, turtle or goldfish. If you are truly in the "zone" all you have to do is think of an animal and it will be manifested within a few short weeks, or perhaps hours for the truly blessed. This requires tremendous mind control and discipline so that one doesn't start daydreaming about pythons, peacocks or three-towed sloths and end up manifesting far more trouble than one bargained for.

That's how Irene showed up at Flower Hill Farm. It was a brief, fleeting thought brought about in a poignant moment while unpacking some of the things from my mother's house.

Dad had died suddenly a few months earlier and Mom decided to move out of their large house in New Jersey to her childhood home by the Jersey Shore. A lifetime of possessions had been carefully packed into boxes or moving vans and distributed to myself and my five brothers and sisters.

My boxes included numerous figurines that had been displayed for as long as I could remember in my parents' house on the bookshelf in the family room on the wall opposite the fireplace. I carefully unwrapped them and tried to find a special place in my home for them all.

There were two Hummel figurines, a bronze Labrador, two China playing kittens, and a small porcelain donkey. My father had always held a deep regard for donkeys, believing that they played a more important role than most of the disciples in the beginnings of Christianity.

A donkey carried Mary to Bethlehem in her time of need and with great stealth spirited her and the baby Jesus (additionally burdened by gold, frankincense and myrrh or, as my niece tells the story; gold, common sense and fur) out of Bethlehem to Egypt to escape the evil Herod. And it was a donkey, not a disciple, who was entrusted to carry Jesus into Jerusalem on Palm Sunday.

Donkey envy has been with us since the dawn of time. Even in the Old Testament, chiseled in stone on tablets brought down by Moses is the tenth commandment, "Thou shalt not covet thy neighbor's Ass."

Donkeys were definitely the star of the Biblical show in Dad's book. He claimed, after a trip to Israel, that he had visited the "Sacred Church and Sepulcher of the Holy Donkey," a claim that most took in stride since Dad was known for pulling people's legs.

I stroked the little donkey figurine and thought, "Maybe it would be nice to have a donkey someday...."

These thoughts were interrupted by the sound of the telephone ringing. It was Gayle, highly animated and out of breath.

"You have to help. Sue from Womelsdorf has a friend in Allentown who knows someone in Northampton who grooms dogs for a woman in Bath who lives next to a someone who raises show chickens who knows a man in Orefield who has a cousin in Mifflintown who heard of a man in Bird in Hand who has a petting zoo and is not taking care of his animals. He's stopped feeding them and is going to send them to the SALE!"

"What animals does he have?" I asked, trying to keep my guard up against taking on any aforementioned pythons, peacocks or three-toed sloths.

"The Horse Rescue people have found a home for the llama and the pony and there is a goat lady in Bucks County who will take the sheep and the goats. The only things left to save is one little chocolate donkey and some peacocks!"

"I'll think about taking the donkey," I heard a voice that sounded much like my own saying WHAT WAS I SAYING???!!!! I no more needed a donkey than I needed a Brazilian wax. Was it self defense against accidentally ending up with rescue peacocks? Or was it my late father gently nudging me from the Great Beyond to take in a hapless donkey?

One of the fundamental rules of animal rescue is: Once you say "yes" there is no going back on it. And "I'll think about it" is almost as good as a yes. But, because it isn't a solid yes, it means the rescuers have to do more persuading. Their goal is to get you to the "yes of no return."

The next morning an unmarked envelope appeared in the Flower Hill Farm mailbox. I knew what was inside without even opening it. The animal equivalent of the Save the Children photos: hastily taken Polaroids of a pathetically thin little chocolate donkey standing in a bare dirt pen with no visible feed or water. Also included was the obligatory "cute" photo of the donkey looking up to sniff the camera and the painful "distance" photo as the photographer is walking away, leaving the donkey to her fate in the small, grassless pen.

Works every time. Flower Hill Farm was destined to become the new (and final) home for a little chocolate rescue donkey. Completely defeated, I called Gayle as soon as I saw the photos.

"I'll take her, but I have to work every day this week and can't get over to pick her up."

"Not a problem. By coincidence, she happens to be on a trailer right now headed up Route 222. She'll be at your place in about twenty minutes."

"I'll go bed another stall."

So perhaps this pet magnetism isn't karma after all. Maybe it's just plain old-fashioned love of animals or positive proof of the maxim "There is a sucker born every minute." Whichever way you look at it, it doesn't matter, because at the end of the day, what it means is that I'm now blessed with a house, barn and farm full of needy, greedy, whiney, hungry, bossy, funny, entertaining, life-affirming beasts, each of them always tottering on the brink of disaster

What you Let in the House
Becomes Family

A road separates the house from the barn at Flower Hill Farm. It also (for the most part) separates the Barn Animals from the House Animals. House Animals are pets in the civilized household way as opposed to pets in the Frank and Nancy don't-get-too-close-to-the-clean-clothes kind of way that Barn Animals are.

Philosophically speaking, I require three things of house pets. First they must be reasonably housebroken. Second, everyone must get along (no biting), and third, when it comes to things like food, the good spot on the couch, and the first one in the bed, I would appreciate being known as the Alpha Bitch. These rules also extend to live-in boyfriends.

I came to Flower Hill Farm with only two house animals. One of them was an ancient black Labrador mix. He was a rescue of sorts. He had been thrown out of a car in front of a friend's place in the country. He was terrified, and it took two days to coax him out from under a trailer. At the time of the move to the farm, he was about fourteen and was beginning to slow down. He was not terribly useful as a watchdog because his fear of people sent him tearing upstairs to hide under the bed at the first sign of a stranger.

The other house animal was a Jack Russell terrier named Molly. She was fierce in any demanding situation, but being the runt of the litter and weighing only eight pounds, her usefulness as a guard dog was limited to sentry and alarm and occasional ankle biting.

I felt vulnerable. I had to face the fact that I was a woman living alone far out in the country where the nearest neighbor was a quarter-mile away and all were fast asleep by eight p.m. There was only one solution: a Doberman Pinscher.

I casually mentioned to a friend in Kentucky that I was thinking about getting a Doberman. The next day, someone from South Carolina called to tell me that someone in New York had a friend in Florida whose cousin in Minnesota had an ex-husband who knew someone in Virginia who had Dobermans and was expecting a litter. I called the number and, after a forty- five minute interview to determine if I was suitable enough to enter the candidate pool for Doberman ownership, I was duly judged to be marginally qualified to be on the waiting list for a male puppy.

The puppies were born on July thirteenth. As luck would have it, there were enough males in the litter to ensure that I could enter into the next phase of the dog matching process. In addition to genetic testing, the breeder also had the dogs psychologically tested by an independent testing group to ensure the right match between dog and prospective owner. The tests included observing the dog both with his litter mates and alone, making loud noises to test the puppies' reactions, and problem solving exercises with puppy psychological testing toys.

Agility, fear, and aggression responses, problem solving skills, ability to work and play with others, and leadership potential were all carefully assessed and scored. Each puppy came with a seven-page personality profile prepared by the puppy psychologists. The breeder then matched the puppies with the prospective owners based on an extensive set of interviews, completion of a two-hundred-question multiple choice psychological profile from each member of the applying household, an extensive criminal and background check and four personal and professional references (at least one from a veterinarian). Match. com had nothing on this process.

I received a call in September that I was a match for a puppy that was old enough to go. I got up at 4:00 a.m. and drove seven hours to a very small town at the southernmost part of Virginia. I followed the local highway as far as it went and turned onto a dirt road that meandered for a few more rugged miles to a little bungalow surrounded by a white picket fence. There in the yard were eight identical rust and black Doberman puppies, each with a different-colored ribbon tied around their neck.

Based on temperament and psychological testing, I was supposed to get the green-ribboned puppy. He was all the things that someone like myself could desire in a dog. Loyal, obedient, kind and gallant, it matched my psychological profile to a T. Here was my puppy equivalent of a soul mate.

The puppy was apparently unaware of our cosmic connection. He pretty much stayed over in a corner with the blue-ribboned puppy chewing on an old shoe. However, the red-ribboned puppy had other ideas. He ran out to greet me when I arrived and jumped into my arms, and he wouldn't let any of the other puppies near me.

The breeder was surprised. "This is very strange. According to his profile, he is not the right dog for you. He is very independent and headstrong. He's an intelligent dog, but he has his own mind about things. Funny, he's never gone up to anyone before. It's your choice, but this dog is going to be a challenge for you."

The red-ribboned puppy seated on my lap looked up at me with soulful brown eyes. I was hopelessly hooked. "I'd like the red-ribboned puppy," I said. Fools rush in where angels fear to tread.

His registered name was "Bootleg's Vincent Von Bern" but everyone calls him Vinnie. Except for some of the neighbors who call him the "Vinister of Defense." He thinks his name is "Vinnie No!"

Vinnie has spent his entire life in a state of total and complete self-actualization. There is not one apology in this dog. He has been the most destructive animal ever to grace Flower Hill Farm. Many puppies chew, but he takes it to new levels. He has gone through over three-dozen pairs of shoes. I no longer replace the boots at the first chewing. Since Vinnie works from top to bottom, I can usually get a few more wears out of the ones that he's not quite finished with as long as my pant legs are long enough to cover the damage.

Every knowledgeable breeder, veterinarian or talk show host will tell you that puppies should be crate-trained. Vinnie, the Houdini of dogs, has escaped from every crate ever designed. Some dogs may tear up a pillow or two. Vinnie has demolished three rooms of carpet and a complete set of dining room chair pads. And he is not content to merely destroy. To him, property destruction has artistic purpose.

Once, when he escaped his crate and had free run in the kitchen for a couple of hours, he got into the dish detergent and sprayed it all over the kitchen. Then he tore up the *Lancaster Farming* newspaper. He crafted a sticky collage of Pennsylvania Dairy Princess finalist pictures, Grand Champion Angus Bull photos and advertisements for manure storage facilities. I arrived home to find the artwork plastered all over the kitchen cabinets and appliances.

If painting is being done anywhere on the farm, Vinnie will be sporting the latex de jour. If construction crews are on the farm, Vinnie will borrow their tools for "projects" of his own. One day he stole a roll of duct tape. By the time the theft was discovered, he had taped the old Labrador fast to the front porch column.

When left to his own devices, Vinnie's games can turn macabre. For example, he sometimes plays "cub scout" by taking wood from the wood pile and stacking the logs into little "campfire" sites on the front lawn. Then he places his dog and horse toys in a circle around the "campfire." The cat and groundhog squeaky toys are placed on top of the logs. Beyond reading the fine print in his psychological evaluation, I haven't even tried to find an interpretation. Bill Murray in *Caddyshack* came to mind.

As much as Vinnie appears to be an animal out of control, the dog is, in fact, completely obedience trained. He will "sit," "stay," "heel," and "down" as long as he is attached to some sort of leash. Once loose, he is totally aware that there is nothing anyone can do about him so he's off in his own direction.

At the urging of my relatives, neighbors and the Bernville tourist board, I once hired a professional dog trainer to evaluate Vinnie and see if he could get him under control. The advertisement boasted that the trainer could train any dog in three weeks. But after fifteen minutes with Vinnie he announced that he wouldn't take the job.

"The dog knows what you want. He simply doesn't care, and views the whole obedience thing to be your problem. He's pretty happy with the way things are. I'm not going to take your money. This dog cannot be trained."

I receive a lot of pet advice. Every Christmas, birthday or major holiday brings a new collection of books, videos, DVDs or magazine subscriptions about dog training from friends, relatives and sometimes even neighbors I've never met. People call whenever a dog training special appears on television. The advice is all well-intended. My library now includes: *Training YOU to Train Your Dog, Dog training for Dummies, Is Your Dog Bad or Just Misunderstood, Dog Behavior and How It Can Work for You, The Problem Dog,* and *Dog Whisperer.* Vinnie usually eats them before I can get past chapter two.

It was from one of these books that I got the brilliant idea that dogs could actually be kept off of the furniture. In this particular case, I was seated on the living room floor, back against the leather couch where the three dogs were comfortably settled in, each on a separate cushion. I was well into a chapter on "Setting Boundaries with Your Pet" when the subject of pets staying off of the furniture was discussed. The author was of the firm belief that animals should either sit or lie upon the floor while humans occupy the chairs, couches and beds of the household. I had to admit from my spot on the floor that I was slipping down from the position of Alpha Bitch.

The author prescribed a method for reestablishing human rights to the furniture through the use of mousetraps. In the author's opinion, mousetraps set on the furniture would serve to discourage the animals from jumping up and napping on the furniture by startling them, but without actually causing them harm.

I thought this was a brilliant idea and dashed off to the Home Depot to buy a dozen of the things. When I returned home, I realized that mousetraps do not come with instructions. My only prior experience with them was in kindergarten. Children glued seashell macaroni to them, sprayed them with gold paint and presented them to their grandmothers as recipe holders. Even in the suburbs I had always relied on cats to manage the mouse population. I had never actually set a mousetrap in my entire life.

The setting of mousetraps is apparently obvious to the mousetrap manufacturers. In spite of a degree in mechanical engineering, an extensive search of the manufacturer's website, and two hours of dogged determination, I was unable to set the thing. Forget, "Build a better mousetrap and the world will beat a path to your door." How about writing down the damn instructions and maybe it will work just fine the way it is?

A phone call to a friend with cat allergies straightened everything out. The traps were set. I went into the parlor and waited. It wasn't long before the first trap SNAPPED. The Labrador, horrified by the experience, ran upstairs and sat at the top of the staircase with his back to the living room. A second SNAP sent the Jack Russell terrier upstairs to join the Labrador. Fifteen minutes of silence followed. Then the third "SNAP."

Suddenly, Vinnie burst into the parlor frantically barking and running in circles like Lassie trying to tell June Lockhart that Timmy had just fallen into a mine shaft (yet again).

I responded coolly. "I know about the mousetraps and I'm not going to do anything about them."

Vinnie stared incredulously. He sat down and cocked his head, one ear standing straight up and one flopped over. He clearly did not believe what he was hearing. He barked a few more times, but I refused to budge. He turned and left the room to return to the living room (Did I imagine it, or did he actually roll his eyes?)

Curiosity overtook me and I tiptoed to the living room door. Vinnie was rummaging through the basket in the corner that held his large collection of dog toys. He pulled out bones and squeaky toys and rawhide until he found what he was looking for; his big orange squeaky ball.

Carefully he walked over to the couch and bounced the ball on the cushions. SNAP went the trap. The ball bounced back to him. He repeated the process until all the mouse traps detonated. Satisfied, he jumped up on the couch, put his head on a designer pillow and fell fast asleep. I remembered reading something somewhere about the "use of tools" being strictly the domain of the human species.

Vinnie lives a purposeful life. His purpose is to guard, a calling that he fulfills completely and joyfully. No one had to teach Vinnie how to perform this task. It is his purpose, his Tao, his mitzvah, his jihad. Vinnie spends most days on patrol, sprinting full speed from one end of the yard to the other. His endless patrolling has worn dirt pathways across the lawn.

Occasionally, his enthusiasm for his work gets the best of him and he will run so fast as to career out of control and scrape a shoulder or hip on a porch column. No pain, no gain. When you gotta' guard, you gotta' guard. There is no getting around it.

One defining incident stands out in the relationship between Dog and Owner. It was five o'clock in the morning, and I had an important 6:30 a.m. meeting at my job, an hour's drive away. The Chair of Surgery, CEO, COO, CFO, CIO and all the EI EI O's were going to be in attendance. I'd worked for over a week to prepare for the meeting and had the agenda and a complete statistical analysis on Operating Room Performance for the past year. Being late was not an option.

I finished the barn work and was just getting out of the shower when I heard a man screaming hysterically in Spanish. Bernville is not high on the diversity scale. Although it is the primary language in downtown Reading, Spanish is not often heard in Bernville, a mere twelve miles and several galaxies away.

With trepidation I grabbed a small towel to cover whatever I could and peered out from behind the curtain of an upstairs window. Suddenly, I remembered the call from the Dumpster People. The dumpster on the front lawn, supporting the current remodeling project, was filled to the brim and the hauling company had promised to pick it up "first thing in the morning."

First thing in the morning for Dumpster People is apparently 5:00 a.m. The gentleman of Mexican origin who had been sent to pick up the refuse didn't realize that a one-hundred-pound Doberman was on duty. The scene that greeted me below was that of a very concerned, and apparently quite spry individual standing in the twelve-foot by twenty-foot dumpster on top of a pile of old kitchen cabinets, drywall, and other construction waste. He had been chased there by Vinnie who was delighted to find that, after three months of inactivity, the dumpster had suddenly sprouted someone for his entertainment.

I racked my brain for some appropriate Spanish phrase for this occasion. Unfortunately, I only had one semester of high school Spanish and my conversational skills were mostly limited to: "Good morning, Carlotta, would you like some hot chocolate?" and "The library book is on the table by the hat."

I had also acquired some lifeskills-type Spanish including: "The subway tracks are very dangerous," and "Wash your hands to avoid the spread of germs." Although each had their place, none of them seemed quite appropriate in this instance.

I screamed my one remaining phrase, "*Uno momento!*" and frantically found some sweats, put on barn boots without socks and ran outside to collar Vinnie. Nothin' doin.

This was Vinnie's Moment in the Sun. He finally had both an opportunity to guard and a potential perpetrator. He circled around the dumpster joyfully. He zigged, he zagged, and he evaded every attempt to catch or corner him, his little stubbed tail wagging the whole time. By this time, the man in the dumpster was laughing enough to bust a gut. Half-an-hour later, covered with mud from slipping a dozen times, I finally caught the dog and put him in the house while apologizing profusely to the now very amused man in the dumpster. Then I hurried to get cleaned up enough to go to work.

Dressed in my navy blue suit, navy-tinted stockings, and matching pumps I sped the fifty-five miles to work, arriving at the meeting fifteen minutes late. I girded up my loins and stood tall, then opened the door to the meeting room.

The Chair of Surgery and all the assembled Ei Ei O's glared at me. I paused, and decided to go with an abbreviated version of the story. I smiled at each of them in turn and said, "I apologize for being late for this important meeting. I was naked, and because of my limited grasp of Spanish it took half-an-hour to get the screaming man out of the dumpster. I have the agenda and the background material. Shall we begin?" No one said a word. The meeting continued without a hitch.

Some animals are house pets, some animals are barn animals. We are introduced to this concept at a young age when we learn that dogs go "bow-wow" and cows go "moooo" and each lives in its proper environs. Things were so clear then. That was before Alvin the Pig. A tweener, he started out as a house pet and wound up being a barn animal.

Alvin came into the world at the end of the "potbellied pig craze." Marketed as smarter than a dog (they are) and smaller than a cocker spaniel (they aren't), the Vietnamese potbellied pigs were touted as the ultimate "must have" designer pet. They initially sold for over one thousand dollars and because they breed like rabbits caught the interest of many a would-be "potbellied pig breeder."

The craze was brief, and fizzled out quickly. Pigs, after all, are pigs, and there is a lot of baggage that goes with that. They are initially adorable and will walk on leashes and sit up for grapes. They are easy to house train and get along well with dogs and children. As they get older, they often get more and more like, well, farm animals.

Pigs, like humans, are one of the few mammals with an infinite capacity to gain weight. They only stay small for the first six months. Adorable at twenty pounds, they were less so at three-hundred-and-fifty pounds. Piglets are inquisitive, friendly and cute. Older pigs are boarish, pushy, and opinionated. Hadn't we all learned our lesson from Dorothy in the *Wizard of Oz* not to play around the pig pen?

As local planning boards rapidly passed ordinances against keeping farm animals within town and city limits and pig owners became less enchanted with having a hog in the house, shelters and animal rescues filled up with potbellied pigs. Alvin came disguised as a Christmas present from a soon to be ex-potbellied pig breeder.

"He's the last of the litter and we just couldn't imagine him going to just ANYBODY, so we wanted you to have him!" They tied a red ribbon around his neck, shot him in through the kitchen door and ran like hell.

He was not beautiful. If you can imagine a one-hundred-fifty-pound slate-colored football with four short legs, a large snout, tusks and a Mohawk of black bristles on an otherwise hairless body, you have pretty much described Alvin as an adolescent pig. He had a straight tail with some bristles on the end that he would wag while eating or when he was otherwise pleased. His ears were small and looked like leathery leaves glued tightly to the sides of his oversized head.

Alvin had a few issues with early social development. He was easy to get along with as long as things went his way, but when perturbed in the least he would scream bloody murder. His screams were so ear-piercing that when Alvin had an "episode," the dogs would run upstairs and dive under the beds and the cats would disappear for two days. After a tussle with Alvin, my ears rang as though I had just come from front row seats at a Jethro Tull concert. "Perturbations" included any attempt to restrain, pick up, relocate, or redirect Alvin. He had no "bottom" to his screaming and would keep it up as long as anyone was messing with him. It took four days to get the ribbon off his neck.

Alvin did, however, respond very positively to food of any kind. When it was time for Alvin to go out, I learned to throw a grape out the door. Alvin would scamper out after it before "doing his business." Instead of teaching him to come when called, it was simply a matter of opening a box of Whole Wheat Triscuits and Alvin would come running.

For the first few months, he was the perfect house pet. He was easily house broken, got along well with the dogs, and slept quietly on the dog bed. Then came spring and the first smell of fresh soil. It is indelibly inscribed in the genetics of pigs to root. Think truffles. Alvin started pushing the kitchen chairs around with his nose, and then graduated to the kitchen table and the living room furniture.

It was more of an inconvenience than a problem. At the end of a long day at the office, it was not unusual to come home to find all the furniture rearranged in whatever pattern suited Alvin that particular day. The day I came home to find the refrigerator pushed three quarters of the way across the kitchen, unplugged and defrosting, was the same day Alvin moved to the barn.

The move went surprisingly well. Alvin had a small stall, sleeping bag, night light and access to a small, grassy, walled-in barnyard. After he settled in, Alvin developed a daily routine. He woke up in time to greet the neighborhood children waiting for the school bus and coerced them into giving him at least a part of their lunches. Then it was back to bed for a few hours, getting up in time to get a dog biscuit from Bonnie the mail lady. After a couple hours of sunning in the yard, Alvin retired for another nap, waking quickly to get carrots if anyone stopped to see the horses. If time permitted, Alvin lay down for another short rest and then got up at four o'clock to greet the school bus and eat any lunches left over from the neighborhood kids. Then it was back to bed until five thirty when dinner was served.

One day I was off from work and had just finished my early morning mucking when I was surprised by a small, thin woman standing by the barnyard gate. She was dressed in a pink jogging suit and appeared to be a very spry seventy-year old.

"You are Liz," she proclaimed. "I've been waiting to meet you and to tell you that your pig saved my life!"

At the sound of her voice, Alvin came trotting out from under his sleeping bag grunting happily and wagging his tail. Clearly they were already acquainted with each other.

"Please go on," I said.

"Well, this past spring I had a heart attack and had to have bypass surgery. When I came home, my doctor said that I had to start walking. I was so depressed I couldn't get out of the house.

One day my husband came home and said, 'That lady down the street has a little pig living in her barnyard and if you want to see it you are going to have to walk there.'

Well, I just love pigs and wanted to see him so badly, but my husband wouldn't take me. Every time we went out in the car he went down the road the opposite way so that I couldn't get a peek at the pig. One morning I got myself up and decided I was going to see the pig and that was that. It was the longest walk of my life, but I finally got to your barnyard and sat on the wall to rest. Well didn't this little pig come out and start talking to me. I've walked here every day since to have a little conversation. I hope you don't mind, I give him a few crackers. He seems to be particularly fond of Whole Wheat Triscuits."

One life, one action always touches another. Alvin's banishment to the barnyard corresponded exactly to this woman's time of need for healing.

Alvin enjoyed the company of the other barnyard animals. His presence discouraged hawks from attacking the chickens. He became quite protective of his little flock and hung out with then like an attentive shepherd.

He would also, from time to time, come back to visit his indoor roots. If he smelled something particularly tasty cooking in the kitchen or if company was around who might not know the "no feeding the pig in the house or on the front porch" rule he could be found hanging out behind the porch swing ready to charge through the door at his first opportunity.

One Saturday morning in early fall, I rose with the sun and picked a basket of apples from the trees by the barn. Alvin had been making regular trips to the apple tree to eat the fruit off of the ground. This, combined with the bus stop lunches, mail lady biscuits, and the heart attack lady crackers made Alvin one fluffy pig.

In spite of his size and his huge stomach that dragged on the ground between his short stumpy legs, Alvin was agile. This particular morning, he hid behind the porch rocker by the kitchen door. Seeing his opportunity when I opened the door to let the dogs out, Alvin rushed in. Once inside the kitchen, he got a good whiff of baking apple pie and decided that he wasn't leaving without a taste. Trying hard to hold true to the "no pigs in the house" rule, I chased him around the kitchen table in an effort to herd him back out the door. We did two laps around the kitchen before Alvin peeled off and ran up the staircase to the second floor.

There are a few pure truths in life. One of the cruelest by far is that it is easier for pigs to go up stairs than it is for them to come back down. Alvin and I realized this at the same moment. Having my "country life fantasy morning" shattered, once again, by the livestock, I screamed at the pig at the top of the stairs, "Serves you right and you are just going to have to figure this one out because I can't carry you back down."

Alvin, equally pissed off at his predicament, screamed back at the top of his lungs.

I shouted, "I AM NOT LISTENING. I AM NOT LISTENING TO YOU. YOU CAN JUST STAY UP THERE FOR ALL I CARE."

Incredibly, Alvin found new energy and cranked his screaming up a notch. The window panes rattled.

Not to be outdone, I turned up the volume and shrieked, " I AM DONE WITH YOUR SCREAMING AND BEING PUSHY AND JUST DOING ANYTHING YOU WANT AROUND HERE AND THINKING THAT EVERYONE ELSE JUST HAS TO DO WHATEVER THE PIG WANTS."

It was then that I turned around to see my darling little neighbor, ten-year-old Adrianne, with her mother standing at the kitchen door. Adrianne was all dressed up in her Girl Scout outfit, complete with hat, badge sash, stripes, pins and bars, and Girl Scout knee socks. She stood frozen in horror, with her Girl Scout Cookie sign-up sheet held in her trembling hands. As the little girl's mother doubled over with laughter, I tried to compose myself. I walked over to the door and did the only thing I could do under the circumstances, I bought eight boxes.

A Four Year Old Will Kill You

In spite of a lifetime of achievements as a mechanical engineer and health care executive, membership in numerous societies and prominent positions on several boards, what really counts in my book are horses. In fact, the total purpose of having a career at all is to provide funding for horseshoes, horse feed, and riding lessons.

Before I "bought the farm" my one and only horse lived in the comfortable world of the boarding stable. Here, in this idyllic, near Disney environment, horses are simply fun and games. Boarders show up when they want to ride, return to their lives afterward, and have no idea of the reality of real horse ownership.

The stall mucking, hay growing, feed buying, water bucket filling, herd refereeing, teaching the horses manners and all other such horse-related tasks were the responsibility of the stable owners, most of whom preferred that boarders just stay out of the way.

Showing up after all the chores are done for a pleasant ride or a pre-paid lesson is a win-win for the horse, the owner and the stable manager.

I lived peaceably in my role as boarder of an aged show horse whose former owner had ridden him to blue ribbons in every horse show up and down the East Coast. I bought him in his early twenties and spent a few wonderful years learning from this experienced School Master and even winning a few ribbons myself at local shows.

New Shot was now in his late twenties and retired due to chronic lameness. His infirmities did not come upon him suddenly. They represented many years of faithful service, a price paid for thousands of fences jumped in perfect form and thousands of acts of forgiveness for a rider's bad spots, bad hands and poor balance. The toll taken for a lifetime spent at the top of the game.

Such gallantry deserved a comfortable retirement of carefree turnout in grassy pastures, a chance to live out his days at Flower Hill Farm. This came at a time when Naomi, my horse trainer, and her husband were also retiring and selling their lesson/boarding business to move to Kentucky.

For a few months, New Shot lived alone at Flower Hill Farm with Alvin the pig as a pasture mate. Horses have a natural herd instinct and in the absence of other horses will form a "herd" of sorts with other animals. As the only horse on the farm, New Shot quickly adopted Alvin as his best pal and honorary herd member.

This instinct is so strong in horses that they will become panicked if they lose sight of other herd members. Alvin, equipped with a wry sense of humor, took full advantage of this. Many times New Shot's screams of terror would get me running from the house to the barnyard only to find Alvin hiding behind one of the stall doors, no doubt snickering to himself.

Alvin's behavior bordered on mental abuse of this gentle herd animal. Soon I was in the market for a free pony to keep New Shot company, a need I casually mentioned to a friend.

The next day someone from California called a dog groomer from Atlanta with a friend in Amsterdam who had just sold a horse to a woman in West Chester, who knew someone in Oyster Bay with a cousin who went to aerobics with the veterinarian who was recently married to the brother of a woman who owned the stable where a free pony was looking for a home.

For forty years Duncan had been the "walk-trot" beginner lesson pony for most of the children under the age of ten in eastern Long Island. He had outlived his usefulness and the owners no longer wanted to support a pony that had been "sadly outgrown." They stopped paying his board and left it up to the stable owner to find him a new home.

After a brief conversation, shipping arrangements were made and within the week the "free" Duncan arrived at the farm in a big, shiny silver tractor trailer with the shippers logo and "comfort assured air ride" painted prominently on its side. He was the last pickup in a van of horses shipping to the Harrisburg National Horse Show for the Grand Prix jumping competition. The van was carrying eight horses, each worth well into six figures, and Duncan, the free pony.

He stepped down the steep van ramp like Napoleon himself, flipped his nose back at his high-priced traveling companions and surveyed his new surroundings. He was a shaggy gray/white pony with what appeared to be large coffee-colored manure stains on his belly, back and rump. His mane and tail were matted and his forelock completely covered his eyes. His tiny legs were crooked and bent with arthritis and his feet had the telltale "ski slope" shape caused by at least one past episode of founder. He didn't come with any papers, background information or even feeding instructions. There was only a small paper tag attached to his faded blue nylon halter in a child's handwriting that simply said "Duncan." The shipping bill was at least three times what any normal person would have paid for a much younger pony in the local market, but Duncan clearly felt that he was worth it. He embraced retirement like a fifty-five-year-old steelworker.

Whatever love Duncan ever had for children had apparently vanished in his waning years. He was more than willing to stand at the fence and be fed carrots by adults and was pleasant and sweet to children in strollers or under the age of four. But if any child of "riding" age set foot on the farm, Duncan scurried off to the back pasture. He would not let a child near him if he could avoid it.

If he let his guard down enough to be caught and bridled, he would politely let a child ride him for about fifteen minutes. When their time was up, he would either scrape them off on a nearby fence or drop his head suddenly and let the little darlings tumble off over his neck. He would then do a spin that would be the envy of any cutting horse and high tail it out to the back pasture, kicking and bucking the whole time. Sometimes it took a day or two to coerce him back to the barn.

It is no wonder that Long Island has produced some of this country's most savvy and talented equestrians. If they could survive Duncan, they could handle anything.

Forty-something year old Duncan got along famously with twenty-something New Shot and an amicable and well-managed herd was soon established.

Life is pretty much about hot pants. Horsemen throughout the ages have learned that the secret to getting a horse focused is to take hot pants out of the equation. For mares, choices are to leave her alone completely for the days when she is "in season" or to put her on the equine equivalent of "the Pill." For males, it's more straightforward. You simply cut off their nuts.

When interest in dating and mating is over with, the only thing left to do is eat as much as possible and maybe get a job. Most geldings make fine horses for the amateur horse owner. They live simple, hormone-free lives. My well-behaved, if somewhat feeble geldings led me to believe that I knew what I was doing as far as horses were concerned.

An important part of horse ownership is for the human to attain and retain the role of Herd Leader. Herds have a hierarchy which helps them decide who eats where, who comes in first, and who gets to roll in the best mud. It is important for every herd to be aware of who the herd leader is, the one who can simply look at another horse and back them off ten feet. I had been doing a fair job in this role. I didn't ask much from the herd and, having an opposable thumb, I was able to operate the lock on the feed bin and the latch on the pasture gate better than the others. The horses allowed me the job of herd leader without much debate.

Truth be told, I got a little cocky. I began to believe that I knew all there was to know about horses and was just the cat's meow when it came to equine ownership. And, as with most people who know everything, the knowledge just got all backed up in there and it had to come out somewhere to relieve the pressure. I felt obligated, if not compelled, to give advice to all my horse boarding friends.

As all knowing and awe inspiring as I had become in the horsey world, it was now time to take on a new project: a green horse I would personally train to levels of greatness. Without much money to spare, I looked around for something cheap, maybe even free. But nothing is more expensive than a free horse.

Gracie was just such an animal. Her mother, Mary, was a Thoroughbred racehorse, a stakes-placed mare with some good bloodlines. The purpose of a retired race mare is to produce foals. One every year if she's any good. Gracie had been Mary's seventh and last foal. She was a beautiful filly, blood bay with perfect conformation and wide, soft brown doe-like eyes. But foaling is a treacherous business and things often go wrong.

In this case it was a ruptured uterus in Mary. Loss of blood and infection were the most immediate problems, and in the end her future as a broodmare was over. The challenge switched to keeping her alive long enough to nurse the foal.

She had several severe convulsions, causing the breeder to have to take the little filly away from her mother for periods of time for her own safety. It may have been genetics or it may have been environment but Gracie was a fighter. She didn't care how sick her Mom was; day-old Gracie kicked, bit and jumped on the poor mare several times a day to make her struggle to her feet so Gracie could nurse. This tough little filly ran the show from day one.

It may have been too much human handling or lack of discipline from her mother or the fact that they had been kept separate from the other horses because of the mare's illness. Whatever the case, Gracie did not develop normally. She became completely and totally socially retarded.

Following the training regime of most race horses, Gracie was started under saddle at eighteen months of age. After sixty days of basic breaking, the breeder sent her off to the racetrack for race training. Gracie lasted only two months; she never raced, and never finished her training.

She was fine in the shed row and working on the track all by herself. But when she got to the part where she was supposed to work with other horses her lack of equine social skills proved to be debilitating.

If a horse came up behind her she tried to kick it. If a horse came up beside her Gracie stopped and let it pass, clearly not a good trait in a race horse. If too many horses were on the track Gracie would simply stop dead in her tracks, plant her feet and refuse to move, and no force on heaven or earth would compel her to move forward. She didn't like these horses, she wasn't going to play with these horses and she sure as hell wasn't going to RUN with these horses. They tried everything up to and including beating her until she had welts on her back and sides, but this only made her more determined. It made Gracie hard. A race horse that isn't going to race isn't much good in a racing barn, so Gracie's status changed to "free to good home."

My animal karma came into play again. As luck would have it, I just happened to be visiting the breeder's barn when Gracie came off the trailer, returning somewhat in disgrace from her failure at the track (having run up enough in training, board, and vet bills for a down payment on a three bedroom ranch house).

I muttered those fateful words, "She's so pretty, I wish I could have her."

SHAZAM! With little to no warning I was suddenly holding one end of a lead shank with a rearing, striking twelve-hundred-pound filly dancing on the other end. She was probably just a little riled from being at the track, I said to myself. All there was to do was get her home and she would settle right down, blend in with the group and start a new career.

Gracie's second career was going to be as a show horse. I looked forward to my new project: retraining a young Thoroughbred fresh from the track into a quiet hunter prospect using my newfound expertise. But as an amateur, more accurately and honestly a "rank amateur," I soon learned that I had neither the experience, agility, nor just plain guts to get the filly to do what she was supposed to do.

Each day's training session would start off just fine. The filly went smoothly along with the saddling, mounting and warm-up routines. Then, after about ten minutes, it was like the quarter ran out in the carousel horse in front of the supermarket. Gracie would suddenly stop, plant her feet and stand motionless, and no punishment or reward could budge her.

"What that horse needs is discipline," said Stefanie. Stefanie was the classic "Dressage Queen." Tall, athletic, nauseatingly thin and perfectly turned out in black riding breeches, custom-made calf leather boots, and a long black dressage whip that she always seemed to have at her side. She was dating a male friend of mine and they had stopped out at the farm just as I was in the middle of one of the hopelessly frustrating training sessions with Gracie.

"Would you like to try?" I asked.

So far the session had been a pitiful blend of urging, cajoling, and begging in an attempt to get the horse to take a single forward step. Gracie was planted in the middle of the riding ring like a bronze statue.

The woman got on and immediately cracked Gracie with the dressage whip. The filly stood motionless except for a barely perceptible grinding motion in her jaw. Stefanie cracked her again, harder this time. Gracie kicked out with one hind leg and pinned her ears. Then a third crack.

Up went Gracie into the air. She came down, stuck her head between her knees and with one big buck landed the source of her abuse in a heap in the middle of the ring. Gracie then walked calmly over to the mounting block and stood by it. She looked back at Stefanie as if to say, "Care for another round, Sweetheart?"

Gracie's third career was that of broodmare. At this point, she was three, coming four years old and represented an investment of close to forty thousand dollars. So far she hadn't run a race, jumped a fence, or done anything of any use. After careful consideration of the thousands of stallion prospects a suitable (aka affordable) husband for Gracie was found at a farm near Harrisburg.

Thoroughbred breeding is a risky business. Most mares will only allow a stallion anywhere near them during the few days that they are "in season." At other times they are much more likely to kick the amorous stallion and send him on his way. More than one stallion has even been killed by misunderstanding the mare's lack of willingness to participate.

Where over twelve hundred pounds of testosterone meets twelve hundred pounds of (hopefully) willing mare, the breeding shed is no place for amateurs. Gracie was sent away to meet her intended, get the deed done and come back when she was at least two months settled in foal.

Gracie returned from the stud farm a "mother-to-be" and a changed woman. She hadn't gained much respect for me during her brief career as a show horse. In fact, she had developed a bit of a vendetta after the experience with the Dressage Queen.

With hormones raging, the newly-pregnant mare let me know she had very specific requirements for being handled. Gracie's rule number one: no one was allowed to look her in the eye. If anyone did, she pinned her ears back and rushed at the bars in her stall with teeth bared. Secondly, any grooming was limited to the neck and shoulder area only. Attempts to go further back were met with a raised hind leg, and a swift and well-aimed kick if this warning was ignored. Third, no tying or restraining. When she tired of standing while being groomed, Gracie would simply pull back and back and back until something broke. It was either the halter, cross tie chains, eye hooks or the beams they were screwed into.

Morning turnout in the paddock was the ultimate power struggle. If she was the first to be taken out, Gracie would pull back on the lead rope and rear and strike. Alternately, she might decide to walk placidly out though the paddock gate, but once the lead shank was unsnapped, she would spin, run and kick, splattering me with mud. She would then stand by the gate and kick and bite the other horses as I led them through. If she was not the first horse to be turned out she reared in her stall and was completely unmanageable. Daily turnout thus became a dreaded chore.

Gracie became the undisputed herd leader. Unfortunately her lack of social skills made her a *very* stressed executive. The job of the herd leader is to keep a look out for wolves and mountain lions and to find water and food for the other horses. Since there was an ample supply of food and water and a scarcity of wolves and mountain lions in the immediate neighborhood, the Lead Brood Mare technically had very little to do.

Anyone who has worked for a bad boss knows that they are at their worst when underemployed. Gracie spent her underemployed day relocating the herd.

The geldings were content to graze just about anywhere, but this was not acceptable to their new supervisor. With ears pinned and teeth bared, Gracie moved them from the lower left to the top right corner of the paddock. Ten minutes later, with equal ferocity, she chased them into the lower right corner. Not content with that she made them do laps around the paddock in the midday sun. She worked those geldings like a lesbian drill sergeant. New Shot became thin and run down, and the pony took to hiding along the fence line in a large multiflora rose bush.

The twice daily trips to the barn were becoming a nightmare. An outside opinion was called for. I didn't need a Dressage Queen. I needed a genuine, dyed-in-the-wool, rootin' tootin' cowboy.

"A four year old will kill you," the cowboy said, leaning on the white four-board fence that surrounded the horses in the paddock. He was wearing faded-blue denim jeans, well-worn cowboy boots of brown leather with pointed toes, a denim cotton shirt, black hat, and belt with a silver buckle the size of a dinner plate. Requisite cowboy uniform. His suntanned skin was as leathered as his boots and his hands were gnarled and twisted from years of dealing with horses, broken fingers, sprained thumbs, and crushed nails. All part of the business.

Bobby knew horses. He had worked around them since he was six years old. He did a stint as a bronco rider and even performed as a rodeo clown. My farrier had recommended him, saying that Bobby has forgotten more about horses than most people ever knew.

"Start breaking a horse at two and it's pretty easy," Bobby said. "If you take your time, keep them listening to you, get them balanced, and stay quiet enough when you first saddle them and get on, they will usually just go along with you. Mostly because they're so surprised by it all that they can't think of anything better to do. At two they're off balance and don't want to fall over. The focal point of a horse's eye is farther out than ours. That gets them to thinking that you are bigger than they are. It's best to keep it that way. At three, they'll try a few bucks or maybe something a little more tricky. If you stay on, they won't try again. If you come off, well, then they've learned something they consider useful. At four, what you're dealing with is the equivalent of a seventeen-year-old kid. If you don't have their respect by now, you're not going to earn it during the fourth year. They've got balance, agility and speed. If they figure out that they've got weight and size on you, you're pretty much done for."

Bobby took another swig of Pepsi and kicked a stone. "Your horse here has figured all this out and more. A horse doesn't necessarily have to like you, but she damn well better respect you. My advice is to find this horse a stall in somebody else's barn. Nothing's more expensive than a free horse."

Not the advice I wanted to hear.

"What about if I love her?" I asked.

He smiled to himself and looked down at the drink in his hand. He answered softly, "There is no bottom to that horse. Discipline will only make her hard. If you're too soft on her she won't respect you. She has her own sense of justice. She interviews humans to see if they're qualified to take care of her. Most of them aren't. Don't ever assume she's agreed that you are in charge. If you win her heart, she'll give you everything. If you don't you're not going anywhere and you might get hurt. You can tell a gelding to do anything. But you damn well better ask a mare. You don't need permission with that mare so much as constant negotiation. She may just be worth it. But I'm glad she's yours and not mine!"

"What do I do?"

"If she doesn't do what you ask, don't quit until you make her do something." He added, "It's probably best to ask from a distance."

Depressed about the situation, I let it go for a couple of days. I cleaned the house, took mineral baths, vowed to do yoga for an hour at dawn and at sunset, drank nothing but wheat grass and carrot juice cocktails, cleaned out the trunk of the car and balanced my checkbook daily. At one point during this detoxifying soul-searching I went through the box of old books I'd never unpacked since moving in, the box marked "equine." It was filled with pictures, instructions, recipes, autobiographies of…you get the picture. It was an impressive collection. *John Lyons on Horses, The Horse Whisperer, Horses for Dummies, Shut Up and Ride!* You name it.

The books all stressed a common theme: horses are horses. They are not dogs, or cats or humans or dragons. Horses have no choice but to view the world through horse eyes. Horses are herbivores. They are prey and they know it. That one fact is present during every moment of their lives. All day long horses worry about lions jumping on their backs. They only lie down if they feel safe and secure. Otherwise they sleep standing up since it is easier to start running when you are already on your feet.

Their herd instinct drives behavior. A horse separated from the herd is easy prey for lions or wolves. "Fight or flight" is not modern guru organizational development theory. It has directed every horse's behavior since the dawn of time. Should I run, kick or bite? It's all about keeping the lion off your back. It's all about staying with the herd. Nature has rules and horses abide by them. When you are a prey animal, it's not like being in a Fortune 500 company. It really matters who is in charge of the herd.

It suddenly became clear. I needed to get the job of CEO of Flower Hill Farm back from the broodmare. I needed to become herd leader. The opportunity came one evening when I went to bring the horses in for their dinner.

Gracie decided that it was too nice to come in for the night. If she wasn't coming in NO ONE was coming in. The geldings trotted happily toward the gate looking forward to a nice meal in the peaceful solitude of their individual stalls. Gracie pinned her ears back and chased them from the gate like a quarter horse cutting cattle. In the same movement she kicked up her heals in my direction in an expression of pure distain.

This time I didn't flinch or back away. It was the Show Down at the OK Corral. I had a lead shank in one hand and a longe whip[1] in another. Recognizing that this was a dangerous mission, I was already wearing a riding helmet and steel-toed boots. That only served to piss Gracie off. She shook her head and trotted off, nose held high in the air. That gave the rest of the herd a chance to slip unnoticed through the gate into the safety of the barnyard. I closed the gate behind them. Now free of danger, the geldings munched hay and watched

---

[1] A longe whip is used for longing which is a method of training whereby the trainer holds a line attached to the horse's halter, forcing the horse to walk or trot or canter in a circle around the trainer. Longing can be used to train either a horse or a silly human intent on riding a horse.

with interest at the power struggle between the former and current Lead Brood Mares.

Gracie turned slowly and glared. We stood about sixty feet apart. I glared back, violating rule number one about looking her in the eye. Gracie flipped her head and stamped her foot on the ground. I did the same. The mare stood perfectly still, wheels turning in her brain. She faced her back side toward me and kicked out. CRACK went the longe whip as it harmlessly struck the ground. Gracie looked over her shoulder with a "Just who do *you* think *you* are?" look on her face. She turned slowly, no doubt contemplating a plan to come over and stomp me to death. CRACK went the longe whip again.

I redirected my gaze and focused on Gracie's hindquarter, just where a dominant horse would bite a less dominant one. Gracie started to walk in a circle around me. Every time she shook her head or stamped her foot, I did the same. When she stopped, I gently shook the longe whip to keep her moving. I moved the horse from the lower right hand corner of the paddock to the upper left hand corner. Then from the upper left hand to the lower right hand corner. I made her trot around the paddock in a counter-clockwise direction. Then switching the longe whip from right hand to left, I made the horse move clockwise.

The power struggle went on for almost an hour. At no time did the longe whip actually touch Gracie (an act that her sense of justice would consider the ultimate in Bad Form) nor did Gracie get close enough to threaten harm. Over the hour I went from glaring to gazing and from demanding to asking, as the mare made the same softening transitions. In the end both mare and human were soaked with sweat and physically and emotionally exhausted. Then, Gracie lowered her head, and while licking her lips in submissive horse language, walked over, put her head against my chest and let out a long sigh. I rubbed her ears gently. It was never going to be easy, but from now on it just wasn't going to be quite so hard.

The ultimate purpose for the domestic horse is to be ridden. Gracie was out, New Shot was lame and well past riding age, the pony was too small and Irene was, well, an ass.

The horse for sale ad in *Lancaster Farming* proclaimed the horse, "Ships, clips, broke to ride. Dirt Cheap." I called the number and set up an appointment to meet the owner. When I arrived, a young woman was riding the colt in a small ring. I watched for awhile and, as things seemed in order, I got on. The horse was inexperienced, "green," but went along nicely enough. He was nice looking, but a little undernourished. "What's the horse's name?" I asked.

"It's a Secret."

"You can tell me, I'll have to call him something."

"That's his name."

"What's the secret?" I asked. The girl didn't answer.

Instead she burst out, "I really need to sell this horse because I'm going into the Army next week. If you don't buy him I'm going to have to send him to the SALE."

I'm always a sucker for a good rescue. Secret's owner was talking about the New Holland Horse sale, where many of the horses not rescued by kind-hearted souls were instead sold for meat.

"How old did you say he was?"

"He's three coming four."

"What was it that the cowboy said about four year olds?" I thought to myself. A momentary red flag waved in my brain, and then I stroked his soft muzzle and gave him a peppermint. "Couldn't possibly apply to this little guy. He's a real sweetie," I mused

I paid three hundred dollars. Close to the meat price for a horse of this size and weight. Prices for riding horses can run into the thousands, ten thousands and even hundreds of thousands, mostly depending on the level of training the horse has received. But when you're paying forty cents a pound, you probably should be thinking that there might be a problem.

Secret loaded onto the trailer like a gentleman and was trucked off to Flower Hill Farm. Cautious with a young horse and only slightly humbled from my experience with Gracie, I left him alone with the rest of the herd for a few days to get acclimated. I worked with him on the ground in the barnyard for a few weeks after that. He was willing and obedient and soon it was time to try him out. Just to be safe, I asked Gayle to come over for the inaugural ride. Secret was an angel, going around the ring quietly and willingly. This horse was a real steal!

Feeling every inch the Horsewoman of the Year after my successful fifteen minute ride, Gayle and I arranged a time to work Secret again. The following day, we set about the same routine. After a little ground work we carefully but confidently walked over to the mounting block. As Gayle held the bridle, I gently stepped into the stirrup, swung one leg over the horse's back, and settled a bit uncomfortably into the saddle.

Without warning, the horse lunged forward. Gayle, seeking self-preservation, let go of the bridle. The horse madly bucked, twisted, and reared. Falling off wasn't a matter of *if*, it was a matter of *when*. I didn't last the full eight seconds designated by the American Rodeo Association's definition of an accomplished bronco ride. I landed in a heap with an acute pain in the side that was later diagnosed as three cracked ribs.

So THAT was the secret. This horse was a head case. It happens. A horse can be quiet as Ol' Shep one minute and then something, maybe some small insignificant little thing, something that the rider may not even notice, a mouse fart in the next field for example, sets them off. Then they become a half ton of total panic. For Secret, it was landing on his back just a little too hard. Cold backed. Good bucker, though. Eventually, after six months, three thousand dollars in professional training fees for him, and two thousand dollars in medical bills for me, he found a home with a cowboy. The little horse made quite a name for himself on the rodeo circuit under the handle, "Secret Weapon." He only has to work for eight seconds and only then on weekends. Don't bet against him. Not many cowboys make it to the whistle.

With Secret "down the road" and Gracie in an unridable, yet blissful state as mother-to-be, the problem of what to ride was still staring me in the face. My next attempt at getting a riding horse was a huge seventeen hand Thoroughbred mare aptly named, U R Not Funny. The horse had a series of lameness issues that kept her off the track (growing pains, her owner confidently assured me).

The owner was trying to find a loving home for her, and had rightly pegged me as a sucker. "She's broke to death and would never hurt you!"

"How old is she?"

"Three, coming four."

Normally, I'm a bright woman with good judgment and a sense of self preservation. But when it comes to horses, my common sense flies right out the window. In hindsight, the four-year-old rule really should have sunk in by this point.

"I'll take her," I said.

Funny had issues. She needed special shoes, special feed, special medication and a long time to warm up. She was clumsy and would occasionally trip and fall over. But she was kind and she could be ridden on the days when she was sound.

One beautiful Saturday afternoon Glenn and Brian were working on the roof finishing up the barn restoration. I took Funny out for a ride. It was delightful to finally be on a quiet, gentle animal. I walked her around the fields, then brought her into the small barnyard for a little bit of structured work. A white sports car passed the barnyard, going faster than cars usually did on Bootleg Road. As the driver gunned the motor, the young mare spooked and started to stumble. As she caught herself, I was thrown off balance and landed on the mare's back just behind the saddle, where the horse's kidneys are. This scared Funny even more. She put her head down and started to buck.

A seventeen-hand mare is five-feet-eight-inches at the back. I fell over her head at the full height of her third buck.

Conservatively, I probably fell about eight to ten feet. I hit the ground hard enough to see stars, even with a helmet on. At first I couldn't see. Not that I was actually blind but it was more like my brain could not make sense of the images. I lay on the ground, stunned.

Glenn scrambled down from the roof. "Are you all right?" he asked with worry in his voice.

"Where is the horse?" I gasped.

Funny, terrified by the afternoon's events, had run into her stall in the barn and, in spite of wearing a saddle and a bridle, was trying very hard to pretend that she had been there all along.

"I have to get back on her," I said, stumbling across the barnyard to get a longe line from the tack room. "Just for a minute. Otherwise she'll learn that she can get away with bucking people off and I'll have another Secret on my hands."

I clipped the line on the horse and led her over to the mounting block. As Glenn held the mare I started to get on. It was then that I noticed a peculiar bowing between wrist and elbow in my left arm.

"I can't do this, my arm's broken," I said, with the clear logic that comes from experiencing acute head trauma. "You'll have to do it."

Not wanting to further traumatize me, Glenn said, "I'm from New Jersey. I can't ride a horse. Heck, they don't even let us pump our own gas. Brian, you grew up on a farm. You get on."

Brian had been watching the proceedings in disbelief from the other side of the barnyard fence. "I'm not getting on a horse that just broke someone's arm," he said.

Brian makes a lot of sense that way. Cooler heads prevailed and Glenn and Brian talked me into skipping the ride.

"We still have to feed the animals," I insisted.

"Liz, your arm is broken and you're seeing double. We have to get to the hospital."

"I have enough adrenaline in my system to last about another thirty minutes. After that I'm going to be miserable. I'm not going to want to feed animals when we get home, so we have to feed them now. It's not like we have a choice."

Once the animals were fed, Glenn poured me into the front seat of his car and set off on the one-hour ride to the medical center. As soon as we were out of Bernville and within cell phone range, I called Patty to tell her why Glenn would be late coming home.

The laughter lasted for a full thirty seconds. "Can't believe you fell off another horse. Which arm did you break?"

"Left."

"That's good, at least you can still muck stalls."

Broken arms barely count as injuries in the farming community. Sprains, strains and bruises don't make the sympathy list either. (Unless they are caused by a tractor roll accident, which engenders a great deal of sympathy since this type of accident often results in damage to the tractor). If you want sympathy in Bernville, it has to be a broken leg, rotator cuff surgery or significant chest or abdominal pain resulting in hospitalization.

We went to the hospital where I worked. It was a Saturday, and I didn't know any of the staff that was on for the weekend. "A chance to be a Secret Shopper," I thought vaguely. The ER wasn't busy and a head trauma generally trumps everything but chest pain, so I was quickly admitted and assigned a room. As part of the triage the nurse asked, "Are you afraid of anything?"

"No, but I probably should be."

Before leaving the nurse asked, "Is anyone hurting you?"

"Must be a concussion test," I thought. Best to answer each question carefully and slowly as not to be forced to remain overnight or worse yet, give the wrong answer and be committed under a 302. I looked around the empty room and slowly replied "No."

Glenn stayed while I got X-rays and a CT scan of my head. My arm was broken, head was not, just a concussion. Glenn was pretty hungry by this time so he stepped out to get something to eat. As soon as he was gone, a very concerned nurse stepped into the room.

"Who hurt you?" she asked.

"U R Not Funny," I replied a little sleepily. Short answers, stick to the truth.

"I'm not trying to be funny. According to your electronic medical record you have a long history of trauma injuries. How did you break your ribs?"

"It's a Secret," I answered, the pain medication clearly taking effect now.

Suddenly it dawned on me. These were the mandatory questions health care workers ask if they suspect domestic violence. "Oh, no, no one's beating up on me. It's a lifestyle choice. I own horses!"

"That explains it," said the experienced ER nurse. "We have a lot of jockeys come in here from the racetrack up the road. They are crushed and broken with very serious injuries and all they can say to us is, 'Don't CUT MY BOOTS!' You horse people are a little strange."

"Not really," I said. "A good set of custom riding boots can easily run a couple thousand dollars."

Glenn and the orthopedic resident returned at the same time. "We're going to set your arm, but it will probably have to be pinned later. This will get you through until your appointment with the surgeon," said the resident. He pulled out an eight-inch-long needle, "This will take care of the pain."

"I just bet it will." I said, turning away from the needle and holding onto Glenn's hand for dear life. Glenn, having a naturally inquisitive mind and an easy way with people, chatted with the resident, asking questions about everything that was going on and getting a good education on bone setting. At some point in time, the resident caught on to the fact the Glenn was probably not my significant other. Aware of patient confidentiality requirements, the doctor asked, "What is Glenn's relationship to you?"

"He's my renovation contractor," I replied.

Glenn nodded enthusiastically. "I'm always looking to learn new skills!"

A titanium plate and eight screws later, my arm was good as new. In addition, I became a whiz at one-armed stall mucking. Something good eventually comes out of every experience.

After that incident, I decided to give up riding for awhile. But nothing could diminish my dream of raising horses. It was all up to Gracie the reluctant broodmare.

That first year, Gracie gave birth to a chestnut filly. Naming the foal was a bit of a challenge for me. Thoroughbreds all have unique names. The Jockey Club has an online database where you can try out potential names to see if they've been used already. Since this was my first time as an official "Breeder," I felt an awesome responsibility to get the name just right. I tried at least a hundred names but each was already in use. I bought the 2,000 baby names book from the grocery checkout, I consulted all the "beget" chapters in the Bible, but nothing seemed suitable. The little red filly's barn name was "Emily." She was a sort of a high lace collar kind of girly-girl filly with a very high opinion of herself. As the registration deadline neared, I finally said, in a fit of frustration, "She can just be Emily!" And so her name is Just Be Emily.

The second year, Gracie gave birth to a dark bay colt. Naming him was easier. He was all male from the start. Foaled in five minutes, he was up and running in ten. He was named Bootleg Jack because of his address on Bootleg Road. He was a bit of a pistol, though, and probably should have been named "Hell on Hooves."

The Flower Hill Farm herd had grown to six horses and a donkey. In the course of developing the herd I had suffered two concussions, three broken ribs, a broken arm, a sprained ankle and minor knee surgery. I was wiser, humbler, quieter and poorer. In spite of it all, I still had nothing to ride.

From Things That Go Wump in the Night Good Lord Deliver Us

As much as I love animals and respect nature and living things, if any of said living things compete with the livestock for food, carry diseases, create hazards, or are just plain scary or annoying, they have to go. Or at least some attempt has to be made to persuade them to do so.

Take bats. I hate bats. I have an insurmountable fear of them and will do anything to make sure I am never within a thousand miles of a single one of their species. If I visit a zoo, I skip the small mammal house because it might contain bats in cages. I never watch nature shows because they often feature flying oddities. Batman comics give me the creeps. It's a bottomless fear. A bat phobia.

This fear and loathing goes back to a significant episode that occurred when I was six years old. Every Saturday afternoon from fall until spring, without fail, Dad would pile my siblings and myself, *sans* seatbelts (this was in the dark ages before child safety seats had been required) into the back of the Chevy station wagon and drop us off in front of the Brookline Movie Theater. There we joined all the other children dropped off by their dads for an afternoon of cinematic wonder. The movies were fifty cents and the double feature ran for just about three hours. Joy for us, a nice break for our parents.

One day, the projector broke ten minutes into the first film. The theatre was forced to close and, as it was pouring rain outside, all the children called their dads to come get them. This was something none of us would ever, ever do again. The daddies showed up tight-lipped, barely masking their annoyance. Nobody said it, but it was clear that the dads of the Brookline Theatre clientele were not the least bit bothered about having to spend the entire afternoon home all alone with the moms. It wasn't until I was in college that it dawned on me why the daddies were so unhappy about a broken Brookline Theatre projector. The lesson learned was: No matter how bad, or scary, or child inappropriate the films were, children knew not to call their parents until the closing credits ran out on the second feature. As we grew older, we realized that we could pocket the fifty cents and hang out all around town until the theatre let out as long as all of us were standing out front when the blue Chevy station wagon pulled up. Unfortunately this didn't occur to us at the time. With age comes wisdom.

The first feature film on this particular Saturday afternoon, when the projector was working just fine, was a typical Disney light-hearted animal tale where semi-domesticated raccoons or otters or skunks or something mammalian had delightful adventures with humans. It included the obligatory "animal trashes the house" scene where the starring animal accidentally gets into the house while the family is out, gets tangled up in yarn, steps into paint, runs through peanut butter, floods the bathroom, knocks over honey jars and flour canisters, and then is pursued out the back door by a Great Dane who gets blamed for the whole thing.

The second feature was titled "The Bat Man." You can see where this is going. In all innocence, everyone thought that the film would feature the comic book hero and his naïve sidekick Robin. Didn't matter, though, we had been trained to never, ever go home before the second feature was over. The plot details were somewhat over the head of this first grader. My recollection was that it was about a man who was paid to kill people by putting bats in their rooms at night. The movie was in black and white, and featured scene after scene of a man in a trench coat with his hat pulled down to cover his face walking down narrow apartment hallways with high doorways and transom windows. As the music grew progressively spookier, he slowed down and stopped at a certain apartment number. Then, with black-leather-gloved hands, he opened the transom window and released a single large black bat. This was followed by terrified screams from within while the camera remained fixed on the apartment doorway. The scene next morning showed the doctor and the coroner exiting the room slowly while shaking their heads. What has occurred inside was left up to the imagination of a precocious six-year-old.

My nightmares went on for years. This is all told so that you will understand that I do not have a run-of-the-mill fear of bats. This fear goes well beyond the boundaries of paranoia.

The attic in the Bootleg Road farmhouse came complete with a major bat infestation, one of those fun little extras I didn't even have to pay extra for. The first bat escaped the attic rafters and appeared in the upstairs hallway during the hottest part of July. I'd just returned from a particularly robust Bastille

Day celebration and had slipped out of my *Vive la France* blue, white and red cocktail dress and gone to bed humming the Marseilles to myself. Suddenly I heard the unmistakable "flip-flop-flip-flip" of a grounded bat just outside the bedroom door. I screamed and jumped up and was now standing on the bed in a T-shirt staring at the crack under the door and shaking uncontrollably.

At least there was no transom. Still, I needed a plan. A plan and an Outfit. It was a warm evening, about eighty degrees. I donned a sweatshirt, sweatpants, cotton tube socks pulled up over the sweatpants so the bat couldn't climb up my leg, and finished the ensemble with Isotoner gloves and a ski mask to protect my face. I shivered while slowly turning the door handle to open it, knowing full well that a half-ounce bat with huge fangs lurked on the other side. When I saw the bat helplessly stuck on the floor in the hall, I screamed to wake the dead and immediately slammed the door shut. The combination of flooding the hallway with light, opening and slamming the door, and screaming hysterically disoriented the bat so badly that it scuttled under the door and into my bedroom. I was now trapped in my room with a bat blocking the only exit. I considered climbing out the window, walking across the porch roof, cutting the screen and climbing in through the guestroom window. Instead, I took the more logical action. I screamed. I grabbed the queen size bed spread and threw it over the bat. I screamed again. Then I picked up the bedspread with the squeaking, growling, and fiercely defiant bat in it and threw the whole thing out the second story window while screaming the whole while.

Then I sealed all of the doors to the attic and to the upstairs rooms with bath towels and duct tape and spent a sleepless night in my complete bat outfit with a sheet pulled over my head.

The next morning, after retrieving the now batless bedspread from the front lawn in the relative safety of daylight, I called Gayle for advice. "You handled the problem fine," she began, "Just be thankful you're single. A married woman would have had to endure the sight of a middle aged, balding, beer-bellied man with a hairy back leaping around the bedroom in a pair of baby-blue boxer shorts flailing wildly at the poor creature with a tennis racket. You should not be afraid of them. Take a good look at one. They have cute little faces like miniature Welsh Corgis."

Point well taken. It adds a whole new dimension to pictures of Queen Elizabeth on vacation at Balmoral Castle with her Corgis staring adoringly up at her. Gayle also suggested calling the Cooperative Extension Agent to see if they had any additional information.

The Cooperative Extension Service is an essential resource for all farmers. They are generally affiliated with large universities and have the latest information on soil testing, crop rotation, organic farming, and artificial insemination of dairy cows. In addition they have excellent tips and brochures on turning your tool shed into a chicken house or maintaining high density orchards. The inexperienced farmer has the Cooperative Extension County Agent on speed dial. Extension agent jobs turn over infrequently. They may in truth be inherited, sort of like a "divine right of kings" succession system. The agent has a status similar to town mayor. They are experienced and highly knowledgeable educators, used to solving any problem a rural settler may encounter. Unfortunately, hysterical women wanting to exterminate every bat in the county are referred to the summer coop student. The conversation went something like this:

Liz: "I have a bat infestation and need the name of a very good exterminator."

Suzy Sunshine Summer Student: "Bats are actually Wonderful Animals. They eat millions of insects every evening, live in highly complex social groups, are very intelligent, and bat guano—excrement—is one of the best fertilizers available."

Liz: "Last night I had a bat in my bedroom. They have to go NOW!"

SSSS: "Have you considered a bat house? We have some excellent literature on building your own bat house."

Liz: "I am living in a bat house. In fact I am apparently living in the most perfectly suitable bat house that bats could ever imagine. I need to know how to make my house *less* suitable for bats. I have a lovely, large barn. Is there any thing that I can do to encourage them to migrate over there instead?"

SSSS: "You are very lucky to have bats. They are a vital part of our ecosystem. We are fighting to have bats declared a protected species. I only have literature on attracting bats. You need to learn to appreciate bats. Did you know that their faces actually look like little miniature Welsh Corgis?"

It was clear I was on my own. I tried sealing up all the openings in the attic. I pumped eighteen cans of "Great Stuff" spray foam sealant wherever light could be seen coming into the room. I filled the abandoned chimney with insulation, old clothes, outdated *Lancaster Farming* newspapers and fiberglass fabric and sealed the whole thing with stucco. I left lights burning and the stereo blaring with old Lawrence Welk tunes in the attic for a month in the spring to discourage the bats from settling in.

Still they came. They came by the hundreds, by the thousands. Every July, during the hottest nights of the month, the older bats would push the younger "pups" out of the colony. In spite of doors sealed with duct tape and shut windows, the adolescent bats would find their way into the lower parts of the house and wreak havoc.

Eventually I became de-sensitized to the sight of bats swooping across the living room and accepted their presence to a degree. I still scream but more for ritualistic effect than from actual fear and not as loud as I used to. What I did do was perfect a humane technique for getting stray bats out of the house. It involves two yellow dust mops. One to swat the bat out of the air and the other to place underneath the bat, sandwiching it so that the animal and the two mops can be thrown out an open window simultaneously. Not wanting to leave anything to chance, I first practiced with Reese's Peanut Butter Cup wrappers until I had the technique down pat.

On the morning after a very hot summer night, there may be up to eight yellow dust mops strewn around the front yard. I can now humanely dispatch a bat while carrying on a phone conversation and never miss a beat. They're not so bad, after all. Did you know that they look just like miniature Welsh Corgis?

The other flying varmint in my chosen world is the pigeon. Pigeons, aka "rats with wings," are the plague of both town and country. In the city they are content to hang out in the square and crap on statues of Civil War heroes or ex-Presidents. This may be distressing, but they are not inherently dangerous. In the country, they can be found in and around silos and hay lofts defecating on the hay and the feed, thus spreading disease to the livestock. They will also roost in the run-in shed and fly wildly out whenever a human approaches. This spooks the horses and creates a great opportunity for being Stomped To Death. Most annoying of all, pigeons have a very distinctive and rather lengthy mating process during which they sigh, grunt, coo and moan continually. They have an uncanny sense for doing this whenever intelligent and inquisitive nine-year-old boys are visiting.

Not all of the pigeons were born in the wild. A few of them around the farm have little bands or miniature timers on their legs which indicate that these are lost racing pigeons. Berks County is on the fringe of the racing pigeon industry of Eastern Pennsylvania. All I know about pigeon racing I learned from a pair of bachelor farmers living over toward New Tripoli. Pigeon racing was their passion. Two or three times each year Leon and Clyde, fifty-something and never been married (never been kissed) bachelor farmers pile into their conversion van with a couple cases of Yuenglings and a few cages of pigeons and head south until they get to a designated spot in the Middle of Nowhere, South Carolina. There they pull off to the side of the road at some exact mile marker, attach a miniature stopwatch to the pigeons, click the start button and release them into the air. They then turn around and head back home to watch and wait.

Apparently other pigeon racers are given similar instructions to drive to Other Towns in the Middle of Nowhere, South Carolina and release their pigeons equal distances away from their respective farms. When the pigeon arrives home, the farmer clicks the watch off, takes the timer off the pigeon's leg and mails it to the official pigeon racer time keeper and referee. The pigeon with the fastest time over the prescribed distance wins Cash and Fabulous Prizes. Well, actually, it's the pigeon's owner that wins. The pigeon gets nothing for his or her efforts.

I've been led to believe that the prizes can run into the ten thousand dollar range. Last year was a bittersweet one for the bachelor farmers. One of their pigeons returned to the farm in what was surely the winning time, but it decided to rest on the roof of the barn instead of going directly into the roost to have his little miniature timer removed. "That must have been very frustrating for you!" I exclaimed. "Heck no," Clyde replied, " I just called back to the house for my brother Leon to get the shotgun. Leon's a good shot; he got the pigeon down but didn't hurt the timer. We celebrated with some pigeon pie." I could not make this up.

On Flower Hill Farm, the pigeons were a problem. They were everywhere and so were their "leavings." There was pigeon poop on the farm equipment, horse trailer, hay, and even the horses themselves if they spent too much time in the walk-in. "You need to shoot them," friends advised.

This advice, though well-founded, was a problem. In addition to having no tractor, Flower Hill Farm has no firearms. In my mind, a gun is just another accident waiting to happen. Every year hundreds of hunters are accidentally shot by their dogs. It was pure madness to take a chance on Vinnie getting his paws on a firearm. Most of the neighbors can relate at least one account of shooting their houses by accident while aiming for a skunk or groundhog.

The closest thing that I have to a firearm is a homemade potato cannon made of a four-inch diameter PVC pipe "chamber" glued to a two-inch diameter four-foot-long PVC pipe "barrel." You load it by shoving a potato down the barrel with a broomstick, and filling the chamber with an extra-hold aerosol hairspray that has ether and/or alcohol as the first ingredient on the label. It's then sealed off with a screw cap which has a grill starter drilled through it. When the button on the grill starter is pushed, the spark ignites the hairspray and propels the potato a good six hundred feet. The potato cannon provides great entertainment at parties and is lots of fun when you're sitting on the front porch with nothing better to do, but it is not good for precision shooting. I have considered stuffing it with newspaper and Brussels sprouts for a shotgun effect, but in reality, it should probably be considered a Weapon of Last Resort for most purposes. This clearly was not a solution to the pigeon crisis.

One winter night around ten, I had just started a fire in the fireplace and was sitting down for one of those rare evenings with time to enjoy a good book and a glass of Chardonnay. I heard the distinctive chug of a rattle trap pickup truck pull up to the house, followed by voices in the front yard and footsteps on the front porch. I looked out the side window and saw a large red and white extended cab pickup parked across the bottom of the driveway, effectively blocking any chance for escape. I then heard a knock at the door that started my heart racing.

The only downside to living this far from civilization is that, well, it's far from civilization, and nobody is close by if you are in imminent danger. I thought about the potato cannon resting against the refrigerator in the kitchen. Too far away, and only good for one shot. There were at least three strangers outside. I reached down, held Vinnie tightly by his collar, and opened the door.

The man under the front porch light was about six-foot-two-inches tall. He wore olive green mechanic's overalls, bright yellow leather gloves, and lace up work boots. He had on an "aviator" type hat with two black flashlights duct taped to either side of his head facing forward. Thankfully, the flashlights were turned off. His two companions, similarly clad, were walking around the yard, apparently trying to get accustomed to their head-mounted flashlights. Beams of light were bouncing everywhere creating a laser light show in the snowy winter landscape.

"Knock it off," said their leader, glancing over his shoulder. Obediently the two turned off their headgear and joined him on the porch. One was holding a very large green fishing net on an aluminum frame. The other had a burlap bag in one hand and a huge black metal flashlight in the other. I was as close to passing out from fear as I had ever been in my life. My legs were numb and my mouth was dry. Even Vinnie was too stunned to do anything but press himself close to my leg and stand silently.

"Ma'am, we were wondering if you had any pigeons, Mitch said that you might."

I remembered complaining to Mitch, a nearby farmer, about the pigeon problem last summer. He said he knew of a few fellows—"Pigeon Catchers"—who might be interested in taking them on. According to Mitch, they generally came around in the winter. This dark, cold, winter night Flower Hill Farm was receiving a visitation by the Pigeon Catchers. Could anyone be more fully blessed?

"Yes, uh, yes…um…pigeons, pigeons indeed. Yes, there are many pigeons over in the barn." I sputtered, as a wave of relief washed over me. "They are in the hayloft, the silo and in the walk-in shed around the back. Sure, uh, catch all you want. They're everywhere."

One of the companions spoke up, "Are there a hundred of them?"

"Well, no. There aren't quite a hundred of them. I could safely say that there are at least fifty."

"Is that all?"

"Shut up, Troy. Pigeons is pigeons," said the leader. And there is a lot of truth to that.

"Just how do you catch pigeons?" I asked, still recovering from my initial shock while trying to make some pigeon-related conversation. Wrong question. I had clearly sunk much lower in the group's estimation.

The leader was polite and patient, "When I shine a flashlight on them they freeze. Then Troy here throws the net on them and Billy slips them in the burlap sack. Simple enough, but we don't want you to get frightened if you hear a lot of crashing around in the top of the barn."

"Not a problem," I said with a stupid smile plastered on my face.

I didn't have the nerve to ask what the crashing would be about and what they were ultimately going to do with the pigeons. I blithely assumed, of course, that they would be retrained as racing pigeons. Since every last one of them is now gone thanks to the Pigeon Catchers, without a doubt they are happily flapping their wings between South Carolina and Bernville, Pennsylvania with little stop watches tied onto their legs.

Pigeons and bats can be distressing and worrisome, but not outright dangerous. The most feared of all varmints on a horse farm is the groundhog, aka *grundsau* [in Pennsylvania], aka *marmot* [west of the Mississippi], aka *woodchuck* in other parts of the country. Although they can be aggressive and vicious when provoked, they are generally slow to anger. They are content to sleep in a bit, rise at around ten in the morning and amble about eating grass for a few hours, occasionally standing up on their hind legs to check out the surroundings. The real danger lies in their burrows.

Generally a groundhog burrow has at least two openings: one wide one that serves as a front doorway and another that is usually smaller and harder to find that provides both ventilation and a quick escape from predators. These openings can spell death for a horse unlucky enough to accidentally step in one and break a leg.

Flower Hill Farm has a great many groundhog holes. One of the "can't miss" farm chores is a weekly pasture patrol with a shovel and a wheel barrow filled with rocks to find and fill them in. Unfortunately the little buggers are determined and will reopen the holes time and time again. They dig through dirt like a fish swims through water. Groundhog holes are no joke on a horse farm.

The Groundhog Hunters started out as normal people: a group of friends that get together to watch Eagles football games, meet for happy hour here and there, and have the occasional summer barbeque. Normal folks with normal jobs, normal families, and reasonable social skills. A few own small farms and can relate to the problems associated with buying a fixer-upper homestead.

During one typical summer barbecue, I happened to casually mention that the farm was overrun with groundhogs. It was more of a conversation starter than anything. But the excitement in the air became palpable. A small crowd began to gather. They picked up their lawn chairs and formed a tight circle around a cooler of Yuenglings. The Groundhog Hunters were coming into their own.

"Liz, if you don't mind, we'll be happy to come out some evening to check out the situation. We'll bring a couple of rifles and have the problem taken care of in no time," said Scott, a soft drink salesman by day, who was soon to become the Lead Groundhog Hunter in Bernville, Pennsylvania.

"Be my guest, you can come out anytime. Just don't scare the horses."

Two weeks later, I was driving home on my one-hour commute from work. Admittedly I was preoccupied and driving on mental autopilot. Suddenly, before I could hit the brakes, a large, seemingly despondent and possibly suicidal groundhog leapt into the side of my moving car. Unable to maneuver, I heard the sickening thud as the car hit the animal, or perhaps as the animal hit the car. Either way, he was a goner. I was briefly angry at myself for my human arrogance and how I had allowed preoccupation and thoughtlessness to wreak such destruction. I admit that I channeled my thoughts toward humanity's responsibility for global warming and the disappearing rainforests. I felt bad, but in total truthfulness, it was an accident and I wasn't overly sorry that one less groundhog was reproducing in the world.

I pulled into the driveway with thoughts of a quiet evening alone at home. The back porch looked like a scene from the movie "Deliverance." Two Groundhog Hunters were seated casually in chairs tipped back on two legs. They wore jeans and baseball caps with the brims turned backwards. Cigarette packs were rolled up in their t-shirt sleeves revealing a "farmer tan" and their rifles were leaning against the stone wall of the house. They had been there for some time judging by the two empty Yuengling bottles under each chair and the half-empty bottle in each of their hands. The day before, I'd bought a case of beer and put it in the fridge. I suspected it was a six pack short by now. A small pile of cigarette butts lay on the floor beside one of the Groundhog Hunters and a freshly lit one was dangling out of his mouth. My three farm dogs were lying lazily at their feet completing the "backwoods cabin" look.

"How many did you get?" I asked.

"We walked the entire property and didn't see a one. No luck at all. We saw lots of burrows, but not one groundhog out in the open. We looked and looked and couldn't find a one of them."

"Well, I got one more than you did," I replied.

Impressed, and slightly cowed, they helped themselves to a couple more Yeunglings. As it was now getting toward evening and was too late for groundhog hunting, they decided we should head for the Blue Marsh Canteen for dinner.

I had to feed the barn animals, change my clothes and pick up the mail so I said I would meet them there. As I crossed over to the barn in the deepening twilight, I accidentally stepped on an equally preoccupied groundhog. I screamed, he screamed. We ran in opposite directions. As I caught my breath, I turned to see the tail lights of the Groundhog Hunter's pickup truck fading in the distance.

The Groundhog Hunters are self-proclaimed experts in the animal's habits, psychology, and physiology, and are well-versed in methods for their extermination. They pass this valuable knowledge on only reluctantly and only after they are plied with a Yeungling or two.

"One important fact about groundhogs is that they lack the ability to belch," began one evening's conversation. This was a surprise to me, and I was curious to learn how someone had discovered this little tidbit of information.

"What government-funded pork belly research project came to that insightful conclusion?" I asked. I was ignored.

"Their inability to belch can be exploited by putting Alka Seltzer tablets and Double Bubble bubble gum into one of their holes. When the useless varmint eats the Alka Seltzer and bubble gum, the gases will start to expand, thus bloating the groundhog."

"What about farting? Is the groundhog able to get rid of the gasses by farting?" I asked. I was serious.

"He may fart once," the Groundhog Hunter continued, taking another swig of beer, "That will only serve to propel him out of his hole. After that, the bubble gum blows up and effectively makes a seal between his stomach and intestines, trapping the hot gasses."

The image of farting, distended groundhogs being propelled at high speed out of their holes only to end up filled with hot gasses wafting on the summer breeze was more than I could bear. Besides, what was to guarantee that the groundhogs would eat the Alka Seltzer and bubble gum at all, much less in the proper sequence? I had to politely reject the Alka-Seltzer/Double Bubble solution.

The "pour a bunch of gasoline into the hole and light a match method" wasn't even considered as one of the Groundhog Hunters had spent several weeks in a burn clinic due to an unfortunate farming-related experience many years before.

Believe it or not, the local hardware store carries "groundhog gas bombs." They look like small red sticks of dynamite, but instead of nitroglycerin they contain poisonous gas. For the sake of safety, the only way to light the bomb is to use a special fuse. The fuses are about eight inches long and are made of a mixture of gunpowder, paper and wax. They are designed to burn underground and to do so slowly enough to allow the bomber to get a safe distance away from the hole. Fuses come "free" with the gas bombs. Government regulations require the retailers of these devices to store the fuses separately and to provide them only to legitimate purchasers of groundhog gas bombs. Furthermore, the fuses cannot be kept in the same bag as the bombs since they may accidentally migrate over to them, insert themselves by puncturing the top of the groundhog gas bomb, and spontaneously ignite and cause a calamity. It is the nature of these fuses to become lost (or be forgotten at purchase), or to be accidentally thrown away, among any number of other things. Once lost, fuses cannot be purchased separately under any circumstances.

I learned this the hard way when I misplaced eight fuses which corresponded to eight bombs that I had purchased. I returned to the hardware store later the same day to replace the missing fuses.

"Excuse me, I need to buy eight fuses for my groundhog gas bombs."

"The gas bombs are over by the garden hoses," said the store clerk, barely looking up from her copy of *Lancaster Farming* as she pointed in the general direction of the agricultural fertilizer and poisons aisle.

"Yes, I know. I bought some this morning. Only I misplaced the fuses and I need eight of them."

"The fuses come with the gas bombs."

"Correct, only I misplaced mine this morning. Could I buy the fuses separately?"

"We keep the fuses separately from the groundhog gas bombs because of Government Regulation."

"Would I be able to buy just the fuses by themselves?"

"Fuses don't come by themselves."

"But if they did, how much would they cost?"

"They don't cost anything; they come with the groundhog gas bombs."

In America it's easier to buy semi-automatic weapons and Teflon-coated armor-piercing bullets than it is to buy fuses for groundhog gas bombs.

The Groundhog Hunters were both undaunted and clever. They put together makeshift fuses made out of "sparklers" and prepared to gas a particularly large groundhog burrow. If one gas bomb would do the trick, imagine how much more effective all eight bombs would be. They covered the vent hole of the burrow with a large rock, lit the sparkler/fuses and threw the bombs in while screaming, "Fire in the Hole!" They rolled a larger rock over the mouth of the groundhog burrow and ran and crouched behind the pickup truck which was parked about twenty feet away. Then they waited...and waited...and waited.

After awhile, the sparklers stopped fizzing and there was neither sound, nor spark, nor smoke coming out of the hole. Dismayed, the Groundhog Hunters started walking toward it. When they got to within three feet they were suddenly enveloped in yellow, putrid, poisonous gas. The groundhog burrow they were gassing was actually the entrance to a sort of mini-underground groundhog "co-op" complex, and the gas was billowing out of about half-a-dozen secondary holes. They all ran for the pickup truck and got the hell out of there. As they pulled away they spied four groundhogs who had been watching the entire proceedings from a safe distance underneath a multiflora rose bush.

The Groundhog Hunters had been at this for several weeks without a single confirmed kill. So it was not surprising when they showed up late one Sunday afternoon with a couple of guns and assorted boxes of ammunition. One of the rifles was a bit scary. It was a World War II British army something-or-other, designed, from the looks of it, to take out a tank. The brass bullets for the gun were easily three inches long.

"What are you going to do with that?" I asked.

"Desperate times require desperate measures," was the response.

The group sat on the front porch. One of the many joys of country living is the front porch. The farmhouse has a wrap-around porch with cream-colored pillars set on brick pedestals. Hanging baskets of purple and magenta "million bells" adorn every column and attract hummingbirds, especially in the evening. The two concrete steps to the front lawn have large urns on each filled with purple and white wave petunias, with smaller pots of begonias and geraniums. The flower beds are filled with irises, roses, giant zinnias, and marigolds, giving a full display of colors from spring until fall. The front porch furniture is a comfortable mix of wicker and wooden rocking chairs. A two-person porch swing hangs from two sturdy chains.

We began discussing plans for this year's modification to the Tree House which is used for watching sporting events. The Groundhog Hunters are avid Eagles football fans. They smoke both cigarettes and cigars, though not at the same time, and like to eat delicacies like bratwurst with sauerkraut while cheering on their team. In addition, they view the football game with the television picture on, the sound off and the commentary coming from a local radio station. The radio is augmented by a steady stream of somewhat cutting and often raunchy commentary by the Groundhog Hunters and their guests. In addition, they have one friend (a friend of a friend, actually) who can clear an entire room in seconds by passing gas after eating bratwurst and sauerkraut.

All animals need their lairs and burrows, including *Homo sapiens.*

When the wives and significant others of the Groundhog Hunters suggested that they find some place other than the living rooms of the wives and significant others to watch the games, the Tree House was born. It was built in the woods on one of the Groundhog Hunter's farms about four hundred feet from the house. The core of the Tree House is a twelve-foot by twelve-foot room built fifteen feet up in the air and anchored between three trees. It is paneled and carpeted, with a drop ceiling, one window, one door, and several electrical outlets. There is a counter for crockpots, a TV mounted on the ceiling in the corner (complete with cable), a small refrigerator and electric baseboard heat. Lighted beer signs and Eagles posters adorn the the place. The "carpeting" is green artificial turf painted to look like a gridiron. The main room is surrounded by a front porch and side deck large enough to accommodate a grill, picnic table (with patio umbrella) and a couple of benches. It also has a shingled roof and is covered with at least three different shades of putty-colored vinyl siding rescued from the dumpsters at a nearby construction site. It is affectionately dubbed the "Eagles Nest." This year's planned modification was a modest one that captured the new "green" spirit: the design and installation of a PVC piping "beer bottle disposal chute" to send the empty bottles of Yuengling down the full fifteen feet to the ground level recycling bin.

Suddenly, all Tree House conversation stopped. Scott, the Lead Groundhog Hunter, stiffened. He reached slowly and cautiously for the British Army Tank-Stopping gun. No one dared breathe as he brought the gun to his shoulder, sighted in on something across the road on the hillside which was easily two hundred yards away, and carefully squeezed the trigger. BOOM! went the cannon/rifle. The sound reverberated around the valley and shook window panes in both the house and the barn. It took the Groundhog Hunter a couple of seconds to regain his balance after being stunned by the repercussion. In retrospect, it probably was inadvisable to shoot off a gun that large while seated in a rocking chair. Once upright, he set the gun down, leaned forward in the chair and lit a cigarette, all the while staring steely-eyed at the target across the road.

"Did you get one?" Rick, the other Ground Hog Hunter, asked excitedly.

"Yep," Scott answered simply, taking a long drag off his cigarette, "I did." It was a Clint Eastwood moment for sure.

"Are you sure you should be shooting a gun across a roadway?" I asked.

"It's Sunday," came the reply.

Not sure whether it being the Christian Sabbath actually gave dispensation for shooting across public roads, I shifted the conversation.

"Let's go over and see," I said. I'd been paying pretty close attention and didn't actually see a groundhog, only some dust being kicked up by the bullet hitting the ground.

"We can't now. There may be more of them."

"It will be sunset in an hour, can we go then?"

"No, it would be too dangerous. There are a lot of groundhog holes up there. Someone may step in one and break a leg."

"I'll go out tomorrow morning."

"He probably won't be there by tomorrow."

"Why not?" I asked.

The Groundhog Hunter paused for an extended period of silence.

"Coyotes?" asked one of the other men.

"Coyotes," he replied while twisting open another bottle of Yeungling.

The only confirmed Flower Hill Farm groundhog mortality was probably more from natural causes than the result of an actual "kill."

Before the arrival of Vinnie the Doberman puppy, the groundhogs had free run of the farm. The old Labrador had pretty much given up groundhog chasing and the Jack Russell terrier was discouraged from taking on creatures five times her size (although she was ready and willing). The elderly groundhog that lived in the hole by the decaying smokehouse was definitely dog savvy and managed to stay clear of the rapidly maturing Doberman. It wasn't all that difficult. Vinnie has the stalking skills of an African bull elephant on the rampage. His MO was to charge out of the house while barking furiously and then run a couple of laps around the perimeter of the property chasing cars, joggers, children on bicycles, Canadian geese in flight, or airplanes flying overhead before getting down to actual groundhog chasing. That left more than enough time for the critter to retreat to his burrow.

One Saturday morning, for whatever reason, Vinnie caught the senior groundhog away from the safety of his home. The young dog's prior hunting experience had been limited to playing with an extensive collection of squeaky toys and attacking flowers and vegetables in the garden. Without a clear plan, Vinnie resorted to leaping wildly around the aged groundhog, barking furiously. Exasperated, but not frightened, the animal prepared to teach this young inexperienced whipper-snapper a lesson or two. But as he reared up on his hind legs, he suddenly clutched his chest with his little groundhog paws and fell over backwards, stone cold dead. Technically, the groundhog was probably annoyed to death.

That didn't stop Vinnie from taking full credit for the "kill." He picked up the groundhog and shook it furiously. Then he carried it to the front porch, set it down proudly on the top step, and sat like a bronze statue with the dead groundhog at his feet for a good seven hours.

Occasionally, the need to patrol the property became overwhelming. Not willing to leave his trophy, he picked up the carcass every half-hour to run a few laps around the perimeter, or chase a jogger or bicyclist or family with a baby carriage. Just another way to endear oneself to the neighborhood.

I tried several times to distract Vinnie from the groundhog corpse long enough to get it onto a shovel and off the front porch. Nothing doing. This was Vinnie's first kill and he wasn't sharing. Finally, around dusk, I coaxed him into the house with the promise of table scraps with dinner. Once inside, I slammed the door and was able to bury the critter appropriately in his empty burrow.

For a couple of days, Vinnie fancied himself quite the critter killer. That was until he discovered the groundhog hole by the outhouse behind the garage. It was Monday morning around six thirty and I was running late and trying to get off to work. I heard Vinnie's barking followed by fierce growling and snarling. Suddenly the barking turned to loud yelping, and Vinnie came tearing around the back of the garage. He ran around me and hid behind the skirt of my business suit. His nose was bleeding profusely from a scratch delivered by the groundhog as Vinnie had stuck his nose where it didn't belong. Thus ended Vinnie's career as a groundhog killer. He carries the scar on his nose to this day and proudly displays it when in the course of a cold snowy evening folks get together to compare war stories.

Thou Shalt Not Covet thy Neighbor's Tractor

One of the supposed joys of gentlewoman farming is tractor ownership. I can bear witness to a multitude of friends, acquaintances and unnamed members of Tractor's Anonymous who, upon acquiring a few acres in the country, have run themselves into near bankruptcy in the pursuit of the perfect used tractor. This was not a trap that I was willing to fall into.

Tractors, in short, are both dangerous when they are being used and expensive to fix when they break down. They roll over easily, lurch forward at unexpected times, and run into things on a whim. A hot tractor engine parked too close to baled hay has burned down more than one Berks County barn. I had taken an Introduction to Farm Safety course at the Cooperative Extension Service and had seem some nasty photos of what happens when man meets machine in the farming community. The lecture was given by "Lefty" Miller. Enough said.

Flower Hill Farm is a great proponent of the "Accidental Farming" agricultural philosophy. Most first-time farmers make liberal use of their tractors with associated attachments to perform even the most minor tasks, like getting the mail and stirring the paint. Some even use them to cultivate their fields. A more than rational fear of power equipment and tractors has led Flower Hill Farm to be not so much cultivated as "allowed to evolve."

For example, if the kitchen remodeling happens to take six months and the twenty-cubic-yard dumpster is left on the lawn until all the grass dies under it, leaving an unsightly brown patch, *that* is the perfect location for the expansion of the herb garden.

If I'm driving around on a Saturday morning and see an auction sign, and the auction happens to be a nursery closeout, and I get a little carried away because daylilies, river birch, pin oak, variegated *Artemisia*, and wormwood are going "dirt cheap," *that* defines the landscaping motif.

Since I have no tractor and I basically fear all power equipment, most landscaping is done by hand. At Flower Hill Farm, trees are carefully placed wherever the Doberman has started to dig a hole in the front lawn. Or, if the trees are especially lucky, they are set deeper in vacated groundhog burrows where their roots have more of a sporting chance. There is also the Darwinian "Survival of the Fittest" program. Shrubs and perennials are placed in shallow indentations where the grass has been scraped off, and their roots are then anointed with a mixture of horse manure, pine shavings, and a double dose of "Miracle Grow." This is followed by a liberal watering, and from then on the plants are left to fend for themselves.

The farm is not totally tractor-free. The farmer who leases the "upper twenty" has a large collection of tractors, hitches, attachments and farm equipment of all kinds, all of which can be found in various stages of repair.

At any given time there can be two or three vintage tractors stalled in the field, a couple of broken hay balers, a manure spreader with a broken chain, and a seed drill, all in various stages of rust. The "better" equipment is stored in the barn to await repair. From what I have seen, most of the local farmers seem to do more buying of farm equipment than actual using of farm equipment.

The market for farm equipment is quite exclusive: it is either *used* or *very used*. It's not entirely clear who buys the equipment when it is new. Private sales of farm apparatus are rare, but they do occasionally occur. More often equipment will be bartered for other equipment, tractor parts, livestock or drywall services.

The grand festivals of all farm equipment sales are the consignment tractor and farm equipment auctions. These "can't miss" events are at their best when held in the spring when the wafting odors of soil, daffodils and lilac blossoms fill the eager farmer's mind with thoughts of effortless planting with a new (used) tractor and disc harrow. This is followed by images of clear, low-humidity summer afternoons riding through sun-drenched hayfields on a shiny green John Deere with the hay being chopped, baled, and thrown into a wagon with little or no human intervention.

Surely, equipment being sold under the anonymous guise of a consignment auction has been barn kept, lovingly cared for and meticulously maintained. It will be far better than the stuff lying out in the field. Gets them every year.

In my third year of farm ownership, the Groundhog Hunters, Scott and Rick, decided that it was high and past time that I broke down and bought a tractor. This was prompted by the appearance of a full page ad in *Lancaster*

Farming for one of the largest farm equipment auctions ever staged in the Susquehanna, Lehigh or Schuylkill Valleys.

Not your ordinary consignment auction, mind you, the advertisement exclaimed that this sale of sales was prompted by the fact that Dorothy and Clyde Ziegenfuss were retiring after a lifetime of farming. They were selling their entire inventory of tractors, farm equipment, garden tools, milking equipment and a few select pieces of pink Fostoria Depression glass. The tractors alone, when parked side by side, covered over three acres. No one could actually say that they personally knew Dorothy and Clyde, but whomever they were they definitely had an impressive collection of equipment.

The sale was set to begin at 8 a.m., with tractors scheduled to be sold at noon. This is an old auctioneer's trick. The intent is to get people in early to look at the tractors while at the same time maximizing their blood sugar level. This is accomplished by stuffing them with high carb/high fat breakfast offerings involving lard, powdered sugar, bacon, sausage and other permutations of pork products lovingly prepared by the ladies auxiliary of the North Penn Rod and Gun Club.

The attendees are then further whipped into a buying frenzy by having the auctioneer's out-of-town cousins walk around the equipment saying, "That's a beauty, you'd have to be a fool not to put a bid in on that one" and "I bought that same tractor ten years ago, and it's been running non-stop ever since. I do all my planting and harvesting with it and then hook it up to the house and use it as a generator all winter long."

The prime target is the urban pioneer, but pretty soon even more experienced and hardened farmers get caught up by the sight of all those hydraulics and three-point hitch attachments. Before long the tractor that sat on someone's front lawn for six months with a "For Sale" sign on it until the grass grew higher than the rear tires has now become more coveted than the Maltese Falcon.

As the day of the auction approached, the Ground Hog Hunters' anticipation hit a fevered pitch. Their respective spouses and significant others had forbidden them to look at any more farm equipment for themselves. In other words, they were on "tractor probation." No more tractors or pieces thereof were to be brought home under any circumstances. Their only ticket to the sale was under the premise of providing technical consultation in support of a tractor purchase by someone else. Someone like me.

Sitting on the back porch while enjoying a couple of Yuenglings, the Groundhog Hunters mulled over the desirable tractor characteristics for my farm. The upshot, arrived at half-way into beer number three, was that mine would have to be four-wheel drive with new tires, less than fifteen hundred hours on the engine and a hydrostatic transmission.

I firmly stated, as I had on all previous occasions that found the Groundhog Hunters in auction discussion mode, that I was not going to buy a tractor, period, no matter how good the hydraulics were and how few hours were on the engine. That was final. The end. No more discussion.

On Thursday, two days before the auction, I had an appointment with the dermatologist for some minor Moh's surgery to remove a small spot on my face. The intent of Moh's surgery is to gently remove a layer of cells at a time until all the offending tissue is gone. Easy enough, right? The offending blemish had been biopsied and had come back negative for cancer, but probably needed to be taken off anyway. Being a fair-skinned woman "of a certain age,"and having lived a lifetime outside in the sun, this was not unexpected. What was unexpected was the outcome.

The surgery session started at eight in the morning.

"Don't worry," the physician's assistant with perfect skin and the cute "upturned nose" purred, "It would be very unusual in a case like yours to have to go more than two or three layers deep."

After having the first layer removed, the patient goes to the waiting room with a large bandage (in this case on my nose) and sits with ten or so equally nervous patients waiting to see if another layer has to come off. On this particular day, with this particular patient, cancer cells turned up in the first layer, and the second, and the third, and the ninth and the tenth and the twelfth. By the time 4 p.m. rolled around, all the other patients were gone, the office staff was packing up for the day and I was missing half my nose while suppressing a panic attack.

"This is very unusual," mused the surgeon, "We found a tumor below the skin and had to keep going until the cancer was gone. We got all of it. Now, I'd like you to meet the plastic surgeon who is going to put your face back together. He will have to take some cartilage from your ear, skin from your forehead and a few other places. It will take at least six weeks of total seclusion before you can go out into society without frightening small children and causing cattle to stampede. Unfortunately for you, due to a shortage of operating room block time, we can't start putting your face back together until Monday. It will be the first of three operations. This one will take about four hours, so be prepared for a couple days of complete bed rest. Keep the bandage on your face. You won't be able to wear contacts or glasses (even though you need them to drive). Your face should stop swelling in about twenty-four hours. We'll see you on Monday.

Yep, this was unusual, we didn't expect this. Before you go, do you mind if we let a dozen or so residents have a look at it? Have a nice day."

Even though every fiber in my body screamed "NO, NO, I DON'T WANT A BUNCH OF RESIDENTS TO LOOK AT ME," I smiled and nodded agreeably. I was well aware that I was now at the mercy of the Medical Community and its Operating Room Block Time and I didn't want to take even the smallest chance at pissing someone off. Sure, bring on the whole platoon!

They filed into the tiny exam room, a sea of white coats with stethoscopes and little laminated cards tucked into their pockets with key medical terms and I'm sure "What to do in case of emergency" all spelled out for them. They peered and made assorted comments using a lot of medical terms. A few in the back (newer ones, probably) stood with their hands over their faces like bystanders at a car accident. A few took pictures with digital cameras. Then they thanked me and wished me luck. I did the same for them. Have a nice day.

Boom. Home alone with half a nose.

After the initial shock (and the first dose of painkiller) wore off, I began the requisite Wallowing in Self Pity. Perhaps I would not go through the surgery, instead choosing to wear a black veil, hiding by day, occasionally pulling back a lace curtain from an upstairs bedroom window with my delicate porcelain-fine hand to take a peek at the world that had once been a vibrant part of my life. I would only go out at night to glide silently through beautiful flower gardens. If a passerby would happen to catch a glimpse of me in the moonlight, they would see a willowy figure clad in black with sad blue eyes looking mournfully through a black veil. Vampires would be my only friends.

Reality check: My figure moves more toward "butternut squash" than "willow" the mortgage had to be paid, and animals had to be fed. The show must go on.

One bright spot gleamed in my otherwise dismal scenario. I would have to call off my attendance at the tractor auction. Couldn't be helped. I made a call to the Groundhog Hunters and left a message on their answering machine.

"I don't have a nose; I won't make it to the auction or anywhere else for the next fortnight." Using the word "fortnight" made me feel all the more heroic and Victorian, even though I was going to be out of commission for six weeks, a total of three fortnights to be exact.

Fifteen minutes later the phone rang with an obviously agitated Groundhog Hunter facing the very serious possibility of missing the spring tractor consignment sale.

"What does your nose have to do with buying a tractor? What you need to do is to get out of the house; it will do you good to take your mind off of this. It will be fine, I'm sure no one will even notice."

He had a point. Fact of business is, one could surround any sale tractor with half-a-dozen naked Dallas Cowboy cheerleaders and the entire cast of the Victoria's Secret Valentines day lingerie show, and if the hydraulics are good enough and it had a PTO, no one would take note of them except to wonder why these babes were standing in the way of a pre-purchase look-see.

Weakened by loss of blood, sore from bodily trauma, and feeling the mind-numbing effects of a steady dose of Percocet, I caved in and agreed to go. It would be, after all, my last public outing before Monday's surgery and a six week confinement period.

Sale day arrived. The Groundhog Hunters all arrived, no doubt exhilarated at their prospects. With a budget of seventy-five-hundred dollars firmly established in both my mind and checking account, I slid into the pickup, face swathed in white bandages, looking somewhat reminiscent of The Mummy. After a few miles we turned into a dirt lane clearly marked "Spring Consignment Sale." There, just beyond a grove of walnut trees, was the largest collection of late model tractors ever assembled in one place on Earth.

It included not only the coveted Ziegenfuss Collection, but other consignments as well. Row upon row of John Deeres, Fords, Allis Chalmers, and orange Kubotas gleamed in the morning sun. There were custom-painted tractors, black with flames on the sides (go figure), tractors with names painted on them (like boats) or endearments like "Troy and Diane 4 ever" (no doubt a divorce consignment). These tractors obviously came from good homes. Caught up in the moment, I mentally ratcheted up the budget to eight-thousand-two-hundred dollars (And hoped that the auctioneer accepted Visa cards).

After a breakfast of a scrapple, an egg and cheese muffin, followed by a cup of coffee that would wake the dead, we began the serious business of scouting out a potential tractor. One of the auctioneer's cousins wandered up and asked the Groundhog Hunters what they were looking for.

The Groundhog Hunters were eager to comply. They sang a chorus of responses that basically boiled down to: "We need a twenty HP or more tractor with four-wheel drive, a PTO, good set of hydraulics, new tires, less than fifteen-hundred hours on the engine, front end loader, and set up for a back hoe attachment."

"A roll bar, good set of brakes, no more than two gears and a top speed of less than five miles per hour," I quickly chimed in. But I was ignored. Tractor auctions remain bastions of male domination.

"What's your budget?"

"Fifteen thousand dollars," the Groundhog Hunters said in unison.

I wondered how things had gotten this far out of control this quickly.

"Ten thousand!" I shouted.

I was ignored.

The cousin led them to an aisle of small- to moderate-sized tractors. "You might find something here that will sell for that. This one here is a real SLEEPER!"

Not quite sure what that term meant and assuming it had something to do with provoking unconsciousness, I turned to ask him about it. But realizing that the Groundhog Hunters had already fallen in love, like Good Saint Nick, he had disappeared in a twinkling, to play Yenta to another set of farming fools.

It was a deep royal-blue Ford with silver trim. It had great hydraulics and tires that whispered "Buy me." It came complete with both a front end loader and a back hoe attachment, and was set up for an under- belly mower. It was, in short, the kind of tractor that farmer's dreams are made of. One Groundhog Hunter gently stroked the front end loader, while the other sat in the driver's seat fondling the gear shifts while making quiet "put-put-put" noises.

"Twelve thousand, but no higher," I stated, recalling that my home equity credit line could be tapped in an emergency such as this.

The auctioneer was getting closer and closer, surrounded by an entourage of excited bidders. Caught up in the moment, I could feel my heartbeats quickening. The Groundhog Hunters circled their tractor protectively, glaring at the prospective buyers in a well-intentioned attempt to warn them off.

The auctioneer began his pitch, extolling the virtues of the tractor parked before them. Then, when it seemed that I was destined to own a tractor, he added, "This one has a twelve-thousand-one-hundred dollar reserve."

The sun suddenly broke through the clouds, a choir of angels began singing and a sudden flood of relief came over me. I wouldn't have to figure out how to get the damn thing home, it wouldn't run into things, fail to start, leak hydraulic fluid, roll over or set the barn on fire. Flower Hill Farm would remain tractor-free for yet another season to come.

As I walked back to the truck with the now dejected Groundhog Hunters, I tried to contain my joy (which was not difficult as you will recall that my face was swathed in white gauze bandages).

"Liz," Scott said. "You should have bought that one. You missed your chance. I think you're just cutting off your nose to spite your face."

Rick slugged him hard in the arm.

All this is not to say that Flower Hill Farm exists entirely in the nineteenth century. It is, after all a thirty-six acre farm, and some equipment is essential. This is mostly due to a local ordinance that requires all weeds be mowed to a height of less than eighteen inches at least annually and no later than the fourth of July, wetland vegetation and planted crops not withstanding. Gentlewomen farmers live in fear that they will be found in violation of these obscure ordinances, and end up losing everything.

This is not so far-fetched when one considers the plight of the Amish farmers over in Bird-in- Hand. According to *Lancaster Farming*, they failed to comply with an ordinance that required them to pump out their "onsite septic systems" once every three years. These particular systems were *outhouses*, and nobody figured that you needed to pump out them out. Nobody except for the local township Board of Supervisors, who levied over two-hundred-and-fifty-thousand dollars in fines. Now, everybody is up to their eyeballs in legal fees and the shit has, indeed, hit the windmill.

I am, in fact, in possession of a ten-horsepower riding lawn mower, three broken push mowers (one of which is self-propelled), and a weed whacker.

The push mowers may not actually be broken. It's just that the average female lacks the upper body strength to put sufficient torque on the motor by pulling the starter cord. There are probably thousands of similar "broken" mowers owned by both females and male weaklings in homes throughout America.

One of the push mowers is in a perpetual state of "partial assembly." This is because I was naïve enough to buy the mower in its original crate and then attempt to put it together following the instructions written by newly graduated engineers on their first work assignment.

After four hours of trying to assemble the thing, I felt I had a pretty good mental image of who these people were: young pimply-faced whippersnappers, living in neutral décor condominiums with Berber carpeting and all inclusive maintenance agreements.

There they sit, oblivious to my plight, enjoying outdoor café happy hours on a Friday afternoon while sipping Mexican beers with limes stuffed in the bottle necks. Their talk involves stress management, the latest in electronic gadgets, Facebook and Twitter postings, and how their five-figure jobs just suck so much.

Meanwhile the consumers are sitting on top of anthills, baking in the hot midday sun, with a "flat head" screwdriver and a hammer attempting to assemble and/or repair a lawn mower using aforementioned whippersnapper's instructions, handily translated from English into French, and Spanish and Mandarin Chinese.

It probably should be a state or federal law that the assembly instruction writers for any lawn care equipment should be required to watch a videotape of the average consumer attempting to assemble their product.. The tape should begin with the customer/victim easing the merchandise out of its box by bracing it against one's feet. This would be followed by an attempt to unscramble the form-fitting cardboard that encases the thing while clenching the ubiquitous protective plastic bags that came filled with parts in ones teeth. Then comes the "part identification," where the parts list never quite matches the bill of materials. Undaunted, and with a leap of faith, the consumer would then attempt to fit tab A into slot B and so on, dutifully following the instructions until the product is functional (or not). Any such law would probably be challenged as forcing young engineering graduates, no matter how whiney and pimply-faced, to witness a level of consumer suffering that would undoubtedly scar them for life. Their sensitivities are delicate, after all.

The weed whacker is a necessary evil for any farm. There are places where one dare not take a mower, because in the space of a few feet the terrain can shift mercilessly from swampy to rocky. The typical weed whacker in Berks County has an operational life span of approximately fifteen minutes. After this one has to deal with a flooded engine, a tangled or broken line, debris caught in the rotating device, an incorrect fuel mixture, the cat needing the vet, or emergency eye surgery. As the ultimate in irony, the repair cost of the weed whacker is invariably equal to at least three-quarters of the initial purchase price, sitting right on the border of "Just buy a new one" and "May as well fix this one, it's cheaper."

If one is fortunate enough to get the tool buzzing along at full speed, say, along a fence line, the chances that the weeds being whacked are poison ivy increases exponentially. Since its purpose is to cover the operator with weed fragments propelled at high speed, this miracle of modern machinery can give you a poison ivy rash in places you never dreamed possible.

When all else fails, the newly-stalled weed whacker can be effectively used as a club to beat down the more prominent weeds, giving the impression, at least from a distance, that the fence line has actually been trimmed.

The Flower Hill equivalent of a tractor, the fifteen-year-old John Deere ten-horsepower riding mower, was acquired for a very reasonable price because the previous owners were getting divorced. There is no direct evidence that the lawn tractor actually caused the divorce, but the Mean, Green Lawn Machine probably had a checkered past, and a poor or non-existent maintenance schedule at the least.

It does have a few shortcomings: only two of the five speeds actually propel the rider in a forward motion, the blade height adjuster is perpetually stuck on four inches, the steering wheel has about ninety degrees of play in it, and most of the safety features are disabled. The twenty-four-inch mowing deck is also a wee bit undersized for a thirty-six acre farm.

In addition, and I will admit this outright, I'm known to be a little tough on farm equipment. Fortunately, I have an excellent relationship with the guys at the Bernville Trustworthy Hardware Store, where help is just a phone call away.

"The tractor is broken," began one of my many phone calls to Wade, who now recognizes my voice.

"Hi, Liz, what happened this time?"

"Somehow the mower blade went through the mower deck. It came right through the metal housing and is sticking up a couple of inches like a compound fracture."

"I don't think that's physically possible. Did you run it into the fence again?"

"No, this time I hit a rock. Well, first I hit a bees' nest and the bees started swarming. I put the mower in the fast gear and began evasive maneuvers. But then I had to swerve to miss the horse trailer. The right front wheel went into a groundhog hole which caused the tractor to spin one-hundred-eighty degrees until the wheel bounced out of the hole. I was headed straight for the swamp, but at the last second, I managed to make a sharp left. When I swerved to avoid an apple tree stump, the mower kind of bounced down a small embankment and somehow landed on a large rock. That's when the mower blade accidentally went through the deck."

"We're on our way."

Motivational Leadership: Transforming Guests into Free Labor

Initially, buying a fixer-upper farm on thirty-something acres gave me a brief celebrity status among my suburban compatriots.

I had ventured beyond the safety of sidewalks, curbing and Cable TV to "Green Acres," complete with a pig (mine was named Alvin instead of Arnold, but the thought was there). I had done what many of my friends had dreamed of doing. I had bought the farm, along with the skeleton keys to the simple life.

For a season, I was their Edmund Hillary, Amelia Earhart, Neil Armstrong, Captain Kirk, and Eva Gabor all rolled into one, daring to go where no one had gone before. And then they all followed me.

Some came out of curiosity, others out of concern. But most came to grab a taste of that place in the country, to return to their agrarian roots where the going was tough and the tough got going. Flower Hill Farm became a mixture of Camp Kiwanis and an Outward Bound experience.

I didn't really care why they came as long as they brought old clothes, closed-toed shoes and a pair of work gloves with them. Since the recent increase in the minimum wage and the high cost of benefits for paid labor, I had discovered that the Visitor was an asset to be both welcomed and exploited.

One of my early careers as a project manager in nuclear plant construction had prepared me nicely for turning unsuspecting visitors into high-functioning work teams. The trick to converting the Visitor from Innocent Bystander or, heaven forbid, Houseguest, into a useful resource is to set up the expectation of manual labor early on. With practice, this can be done both cleverly and subtly. Thus the correct response to "Hey, how about if we come out and see you sometime?" quickly evolved to "Great, be sure to wear old clothes!"

Even if someone is stopping out for an hour on their way to somewhere else it's important to know exactly what task can be assigned to this potential source of free labor. It's important to be well-versed in time management.

When Cousin Carl dropped in on his way home one evening to return a book he had borrowed, I was waiting with a new belt for the lawn tractor. He only spent twenty minutes putting the belt in place, a task which would have taken me half a day.

Work parties are also a useful ploy for getting free labor. As with any large gathering, successful work parties require some pre-planning. First of all it's important to have a lot of trash bags, a twenty-cubic-yard dumpster, and a wide variety of tasks to offer the company. Providing a choice, or at least the appearance of a choice, gives the labor a sense (albeit a false one) that they are in control. It's also helpful if the tasks have a clear end point, so nobody is tempted to slack off early.

Food and beverage should be made available only after a significant amount of work has actually been completed. Beer is a double-edged sword. If it is offered too early, the work party can become just a plain party and that ends up costing time and money. But if supplied at just the right time and in the perfect quantity, beer can motivate work crews to awesome levels of productivity. The whole process is really an art form.

For example, one can say, "Three more truck loads and I think Jeff's team could be ready for a beer!" This not only propels Jeff's team into high gear, but has a "halo" effect on Marcy's team who has been slacking off a bit on the fence painting.

It is important too that assignments fit the competency of the group. Jobs that require power tools should only go to those qualified, and only if they bring their own equipment and sign the appropriate waivers. In the end, the most successful work parties require a lot more brawn than brain.

The first Flower Hill Farm Cleanup Day attracted about ten people and four pickup trucks. The invited guests arrived at mid-morning and were immediately organized into individual teams.

Scott, the Groundhog Hunter, showed up equipped with a Sawzall so he was given a wide choice of tasks. He opted for cutting boards in the barn in order to transform four very small stalls into two large ones. As owner of the Power Tool, he was given a couple of minions to help carry out scrap boards to the Burn Pile.

Jeff had an open bed pickup truck and some military training in explosives, a rare combination. He was put in charge of the Burn Pile, and was tasked with transporting anything burnable from the barn, outbuildings, and fields to same. He also got a helper.

Vicky was in charge of finding and gathering all retired appliances that had been discarded into the back field and getting them into the dumpster in the driveway. She was assigned a truck and the remaining volunteers.

Debbie showed up in old clothes, but was handicapped since she had just gotten an eighty-dollar manicure. Not a problem. She was assigned to the newly-repaired riding mower.

You have to be flexible and play to people's strengths.

It was a day that would go down in Flower Hill Farm history. The crews tore through their assignments with gusto. One pickup truck load after another was transported to the Burn Pile. The appliance team found four clothes washers, three dryers, a dishwasher and a trash compactor abandoned in the back field. Their rusty bodies were quickly transferred by truck to the waiting dumpster.

As the day wore on, the Burn Pile got larger and larger, but Jeff carefully engineered the pile for safety and stability. By early afternoon, it was about the size of a three bedroom ranch house. All agreed that it was now time to start the fire.

Lighter fluid was doused on in generous amounts around the perimeter, and a couple of old tires were added get the fire going. Trucks were all moved a safe distance away. Buckets of water were lined up and an extra length of hose was added to the one from the barn so it could reach the Burn Pile in case of emergency. All was in readiness, locked, loaded, and ready to roll. The entire work party gathered around the soon-to-be bonfire to admire their work.

"Anyone have a match?"

Five out of the ten workers were ex-smokers. All present simultaneously patted the pockets in their clothes. No matches. The vehicles were searched. No matches. Nervous glances were exchanged.

All of this labor to build a Burn Pile and not a match to be found. One of the minions volunteered to make the six-mile trek to the nearest store to buy a box. I considered the tea berry candle/ truck cigarette lighter method I employed during the power outage, but the downside of that maneuver was that it had fried the lighter.

Dejected, the team started to dwindle away, since it was obviously time for a beer. Suddenly, from the direction of the Burn Pile, came a strange noise. "Pop, fssssssssssssssistttttt, KABOOM!" The burn pile was fully engulfed in flames! And near it stood Jeff , the conflagration now reflecting in his eyes, with a look of total satisfaction pasted on his face.

"What happened?" I asked.

Jeff replied, "I took up scuba diving and joined a marine rescue team. I just remembered that I had a flare gun in the truck. I shot a flare into the Burn Pile, and off it went."

The pile burned for three days. You can't buy that kind of labor at any price.

Old college roommates are another great well for free labor. Lou (Carol Louise) is one of those special friends that come along only rarely in a lifetime. She and I shared the same house while in college, and learned a lot about life during those years. We've been helping each other through thick and thin ever since.

Lou has a beautiful home in Naples, Florida, so I try to get down there every year to visit with her and her family. We go shopping, enjoy happy hours at wonderful dockside bars, and eat fabulous food at great restaurants. Entertainment includes going to the beach bar and watching the sunset over the gulf accompanied by the William Tell Overture, relaxing in the hot tub in the backyard or enjoying a weekend getaway to West Palm Beach or the Keys.

When Lou called to say she was coming to visit, I wanted to repay the gallons of free booze and all those lazy afternoons under a perfect sun that Lou had provided with something in kind. The nine-hundred linear feet of unpainted four-board oak fence surrounding the pastures seemed to be just the ticket. I ordered another twenty cubic yard dumpster, rented a compressor and a paint sprayer and borrowed an electric generator from one of the neighbors. I also filled the truck with five-gallon buckets of pinto-white opaque fence stain.

There is strength in numbers, so I invited a bunch of girlfriends to meet my college chum and paint the fence at the same time.

The painting was pure poetry. Lou turned out to have a knack for both speed and accuracy with the paint sprayer. Kathy and Vicky dubbed themselves the Holy Rollers. They finished off the boards in Lou's wake while Nancy and I painted the posts. It's all about creating atmosphere and experience to convert mere guests into manual laborers.

The Groundhog Hunters were also a great resource for free labor. Generous and helpful by nature, they are especially so after a couple of Yuenglings. They are also inclined to agree to almost any task after dinner over a Baileys Irish Cream.

After finishing a nice dinner at the Blue Marsh Canteen with a Baileys on the rocks they asked, "What's the next project at the house?"

"It's a big one. I have to get the kitchen done."

The kitchen was another example of the need for poor eyesight and great vision. I had long ago ceased looking at the cabinets with their sagging doors, the frontless drawers and the stove that served primarily as an upscale mouse condo..

Instead I saw stone walls re-pointed in Colonial style, a chestnut-beamed ceiling exposing the plank flooring from the sleeping quarters above, and granite countertops glistening over oak cabinets. The look would be complete with black-lacquered appliances and a rustic wood floor stretching out under a cast iron spiral staircase leading to cozy sleeping quarters above the kitchen. The loft bedroom would host a feather bed comfortably nestled below carefully-stained rafters.

"It needs to be gutted down to the walls." I added. "The plan is to clean it out, sandblast the plaster off the stone walls, and create a natural finish kitchen with stone, brick, and the original beams in the ceiling. That means taking out the paneling and at least three layers of ceiling."

"We'll help."

"It's a lot of work."

"We love demolition. It's one of the Things We Do Best. We'll be there tomorrow at nine o'clock sharp."

Judging from the number of Baileys the Ground Hog Hunters had sipped that night, I did not expect to see them until closer to noon.

The following morning, I finished the barn chores and began dismantling the kitchen myself. In preparation for this, I had already emptied all the cabinets, rolled the refrigerator into the living room and set up a toaster oven and microwave to serve as my temporary "mess."

To prepare for the long haul, I moved the washer and dryer onto the front porch and hooked the washer up to the garden hose that, due to the plumbing abnormality, ran only hot water. Then, using the duct tape and plastic sheeting bought to comply with the Homeland Security recommendations in the now famous "Citizens' Guidelines for Preparing for Terrorist Attack," I sealed the kitchen off from the rest of the house.

It was now ready to be destroyed. With the prep work completed, I now started the dismantling proper.

The first step was to rip down the drop ceiling. The paper ceiling tiles were removed easily enough, and except for having to dodge a number of dead bats and pounds of mouse droppings that rained down from above, the job was no sweat. This was going to be easy, a piece of cake. The metal grid that framed the ceiling tiles was attached by some overzealous installer who had soldered every joint of the frame and tacked the frame to the joists every ten inches with twisted steel wire. I pulled and pried and yanked and hammered and hack sawed and did everything except gnaw to try to get the metal frame down. In desperation, I attached a rope to it and tried swinging on it. Nothin' doin. When the first Groundhog Hunter arrived I was hunched up on the porch in tears.

"Step aside," he said heroically. "I was born for work like this."

True to his word, some loud banging, a few crashes and two or three curse words later, he had the ceiling grid down and out in the dumpster. Working on adrenaline, he ripped apart the second ceiling which was made of cheap paneling. By the time the second Groundhog Hunter arrived, the third bead board ceiling was dangling half-way down. With their combined demolition skills it only took two hours to completely strip the kitchen down to brick and stone walls and the original chestnut beam ceiling. At one point the dust was so thick that the intrepid crew got lost in the haze. It didn't slow them down a bit, although they coughed up black dust until the middle of the following week. Real demo men apparently don't use respirators.

Our kitchen demolition revealed iron horse shoes and corncobs placed strategically over all the doors and windows by previous owners. Scott, a grandson of a Pow Wower and therefore knowledgeable, claimed they were put in place to keep spirits and witches from crossing into the house.

"You didn't find three copper nails hammered into any doors or window sills, did you?" he asked.

"No, I don't think so."

"Well, if you do, it's best that you just leave them there."

"Why?"

"Some things you don't want to know."

Living in a house that has a Certificate of Paranormal Activity hanging proudly on the dining room wall, I left it at that.

Woman Cannot Live by Reconstruction Alone

The demolition and reconstruction cycle continued for four straight years. I put my social life on hold and focused on learning the finer points of spackling, plumbing and minor electrical rewiring. I arrived at the office with white dust "epaulettes" on my suit jacket shoulder until I learned how to hermetically seal my clothes closet from drywall dust with duct tape and plastic.

There was, of course, some social satisfaction gained from interacting with the Metal Man, the Duck Manure Man or any one of the farmers who were always up for taking a break by watching me paint an outbuilding or muck out a stall. But eventually, I needed more.

I longed for the elaborate "theme" parties I was famous for in my past life: my annual tree trimming parties, a highlight of the holiday season (and a fine source of new ornaments and good bottles of wine); the hat party where everyone had to bring a hat for someone else to wear; the "come as a criminal" party or the super soaker/water pistol parties held during the hottest days of July.

But best of all was the "Stranger Party." A fine tradition to commemorate the end of a romantic relationship, I would call friends from all walks of life (college, neighbors, old job, new job, church, horse boarding stable, garden club, etc.) and tell them to bring a dip and one person that I did not know (making it clear in the invitation that these were two SEPARATE items). Since I mixed the groups up pretty well, nobody could tell a friend from a stranger, and the parties were a blast. Everyone had a built-in conversation starter and some great new relationships were formed.

Behind my back, these events were referred to as the "Find a new date for Liz parties." But this didn't stop anyone from coming.

Finally, even though the house was not completely finished, I declared an end to my entertainment celibacy. A dozen friends from the wine tasting club provided the perfect answer. I invited them here for a brunch before touring the five wineries in the Bernville area.

Pennsylvania is a lot of things, but Napa Valley it ain't. Nevertheless, a thriving wine industry produces an eclectic combination of fruit wines, spice wines and varietals from local grapes grown in small hillside vineyards. Most of the local wine masters are still clinging to day jobs so they only open their cellars Friday through Sunday to share their bounty with the local tourists.

The pride and work that goes into every bottle is so evident that, with the slightest encouragement, the wine masters become generous to a fault with both libations and conversation. A five-winery tour, therefore, was an ambitious agenda.

I could keep the brunch short and the conversation lively so that no one would notice the mess I lived in, and hopefully by the time the afternoon was over, no one but the designated drivers would remember the details. In addition, the drivers would be so traumatized by the challenges of navigating the back roads of Berks County that my living situation would soon be long forgotten. A perfect plan.

I cleaned up as well as one can using an electric leaf blower, shut the doors to the more offensive rooms, covered up most of the holes in the walls with strategically placed furniture, and as an afterthought lit a case of teaberry-scented votive candles. With a few linen tablecloths thrown over the tool benches and sawhorses, the place looked downright sanitary.

A buffet of fruits and cheeses, smoked salmon, bagels, hot crab dip and asparagus wrapped with prosciutto completed the setup. I hoped the guests would focus on the Bavarian china plates and the highly polished sterling silver coffee/tea set and flatware rather than the missing woodwork, water-stained ceilings and outlets with bare wires dangling out of them.

After mixing up some mimosas and a pitcher of Bloody Marys and doing a quick sweep of the rooms to make sure there were no mice, bats or snakes lurking anywhere, I nervously sat down to await the guests. Martha Stewart I wasn't, but at least I had done my best.

They arrived exactly ten minutes late, as all good guests do, and were happily eating and drinking when the Groundhog Hunters materialized at the back door dressed in plaid flannel shirts and their usual baseball caps on backwards. Each had a rifle over his shoulder and a handgun shoved down the back of his pants.

"We thought we'd come out and try our luck with the groundhogs," they chimed in unison, while stealing sly glances past the door to the smorgasbord of brunch goodies that lay within.

"Have you had any breakfast?" I asked in my "Please, please say, 'Yes, we just had a huge breakfast at the fire hall'" tone of voice.

Something happens to Scott when he switches to Groundhog Hunter mode. He loses his sales manager demeanor and becomes something like a cross between a redneck hick and Zeke, the farm hand in *The Wizard of Oz*.

"Not a bite," Scott said, hanging his head and shaking it side to side slowly. "We were in such a hurry to git out and hep you out with those varmit groundhogs that we jest plum forgot. Sure are hungry something fierce, though."

I turned back to see my wine tasting friends peering at us over their flutes of mimosas. Some appeared quizzical, no doubt wondering what was delaying my reappearance.

"Won't you come in?" I said, resigned to a loss of whatever social standing I had with the group. "Just lay the firearms on the table outside." I felt like I was about to witness what happens when one introduces the "twice removed" out-of-town cousins to ones prospective mother-in-law.

The Groundhog Hunters set down their rifles and reached down the back of their pants and pulled out their revolvers, adding all to the arms cache now displayed on my antique table.

After entering, they then plopped down in the middle of my friends, filled the good china plates to overflowing with bagels and smoked salmon, and proceeded to regale the wine tasting club with the idiosyncrasies of groundhog behavior and execution.

"Got any Yeunglings?" they called over their shoulders. "Never mind, we know where they are."

I envisioned my name being erased from the Bernville Blue Book.

"I'll take one," said one of the senior members of the wine tasting club.

"Me two," said another.

As the Groundhog Hunters passed out bottles of Yeungling, I was distracted by another knock at the door. There stood two of the local farm hands stained with axle grease, with sweat dripping from the 'dew-rags' wrapped around their heads.

"Liz, we were just getting started haying when the baler got jammed. Do you have a pipe wrench, a pitch fork, flathead screwdriver, some duct tape and about twelve feet of garden hose?"

The hay baler jammed with the regularity of "Old Faithful." Long ago I had ceased to ask how it was repaired. It was either the strangest piece of equipment ever built, or my farming friends were using it as an excuse to restock their tool shed. Then again, maybe they were just on a scavenger hunt.

Without thinking, I reached under one of the linen table cloths and retrieved a roll of duct tape, pulled the pipe wrench and screwdriver out of the silverware drawer and grabbed the twelve feet of garden hose coiled in the roasting pan in my non-functioning oven.

"Pitch fork is in the barn," I said, handing the other items over. The farm hands hesitated, throwing furtive glances at the table of fruits, spreads, breads and bagels.

"Would you like to join us?" I asked, now resigned to the possibility that the day was going to be a total bust.

The men then reached behind them, removed the Colt 45s stuffed down their backsides, lay them on the table next to the Groundhog Hunter's cache of weapons and made their way inside.

Soon they were backslapping and yucking it up with the Wine Tasting Club/Groundhog Hunter crowd, all of whom, although they were at least two generations removed from their agrarian roots, seemed to have fond memories of summer weekends spent at grandma or aunt so-and-so's in the country.

The conversation turned from talk of sporty yet sophisticated Cabernets with a hint of blackberry, good legs and a crisp yet lingering finish to the merits of variable threshing speeds on combine harvesters, the pros and cons of duck manure and whether or not groundhogs make good eating. Although a fine time was had by all we never did go to the wineries.

Afterwards, I couldn't help but notice that I wasn't getting return invitations.

Having failed miserably with the high-browed cultural set, I turned my time and attention to a much more laid back, forgiving, and easily amused audience: children.

As part of my brother's annual visit from the mountains of Colorado to Grandma's beach house in New Jersey, portions of the family made a side trip to Flower Hill Farm. The particular group consisted of my "more sister than sister-in-law" Nita, who brought her two kids and their two cousins. She came partly to experience the joys of Flower Hill Farm, but mostly to escape a beach house crammed with seventeen alpha in-laws and one-and-a-half bathrooms.

For her inaugural visit I took the day off from work, cleaned the house to my own high standards, bought popsicles, black olives and other child-appropriate food and anxiously awaited their arrival. And waited...and waited. Long after their expected arrival time, I finally got a phone call from Nita.

"I'm lost." I've been driving around for two hours and have no idea where I am."

"Why didn't you call sooner?" I asked.

"Couldn't get a signal. Now I know why you call it radio-free Bernville. There wasn't a payphone when I stopped for gas."

"Could you have asked directions there?"

"I've been at the beach house for eight days. It was so nice to just have a few hours without anyone telling me what to do."

Recognizing a clear case of post-beach-house stress syndrome, I proceeded as gently as I could.

"Look around you and tell me what you see."

"Wire fences, cows, cornfields, an old red barn and some hay wagons."

"Anything else, anything unusual?" I asked.

"The kids are plugging their noses, I smell skunk."

"Well there you go," I exclaimed. "Is there a farmhouse with blue siding on your right?"

"Why yes." Nita said slowly.

"You're not far, just make a left at the bottom of the hill and keep going until you smell the pig farm, make the next right and go about a quarter mile. When you smell the chicken houses, it's the next left. My farm is on the right. You can't miss it, just follow your nose!"

Nita is great at all the things that challenge me. Like cleaning. Her definition of clean and mine are light years apart. She has high standards, but she's willing to act on them.

"You distract the kids and I'll clean the house" offered Nita as she set down her suitcase while simultaneously reaching for the vacuum cleaner. Nita and Mary Poppins must be related. Houses just straighten themselves out in her presence. Dirt runs in fear, and clutter just lines itself up like soldiers awaiting inspection.

It didn't take much persuading for me to take the kids and a pound of carrots out to the barn to introduce them to the animals rather than dust and polish. And Nita could have the peace and quiet she needed to get the house sufficiently sanitized so that the children wouldn't contract the bubonic plague, smallpox or hoof and mouth disease.

"Do you think the pig will like me?" asked five-year-old Jack.

"Of course he will," I replied, while filling Jack's pockets with sliced carrots and Whole Wheat Triscuts. "He'll like you just fine."

The farm is a miraculous place for children. These annual visits provide an opportunity to teach my nieces, nephews and godchildren highly transferable skills that will no doubt be useful in their chosen professions: how to fill water buckets, clean stalls, safely throw hay bales down from the hayloft ("Don't fall through the hole!"), groom horses and other such college-preparatory skills.

A visit to Aunt Liz's starts with rising at 5:00 a.m. to feed the animals, muck stalls, and ride whatever horses are deemed least likely to kill them. Then we head to the feed store, followed by the local creamery for ice cream. By then it's about ten in the morning.

If they get bored, I load the kids on the back of the truck tailgate along with a shovel and some heavy rocks. We drive around the fields and play "Groundhog Safari." Every time someone spots a groundhog hole we stop the truck and the kids jump out and fill it using the shovel and rocks. The work prepares, if not induces, the children for the perennial backache adults enjoy throughout their lives. Where else can kids today get that sort of experience in accelerated aging?

The fun continues with activities like bathing the turkey or trimming Alvin the pig's hooves with the tree branch lopper. Rarely do these activities result in injury. Statistically, only one in two children ever leaves the farm with a torn ligament or gouged eye.

A few more hours spent making forts in hay bales, playing hide and seek in the cornfield, or looking for crawfish in the stream and then it's time for supper and whatever marginally child-appropriate activity I've lined up for the evening.

As someone who has left childbearing to others, I struggle with the customary trips to Chuck E. Cheese, McDonalds or Sesame Place, especially when there is more appropriate entertainment available, such as the local rodeo. Here they offer mutton busting, where small children are thrown onto the backs of sheep and have to hang on for dear life while the sheep tears around the arena in a state of blind panic eventually flinging the child into the dirt. On off nights at the rodeo arena there is always the demolition derby. Berks County's answer to recycling, the amateur owner class is where you can get one last "hurrah" out of ol' Bessie before relegating her to the scrap heap.

I'm never one to turn down an evening at the Thoroughbred racetrack since it provides the children with an excellent opportunity to learn about probability and statistics. Any niece or nephew of reading age needs to know their way around a racing form, and I provide the venue. Although the state gambling commission has deemed them too young to bet at the windows, it doesn't hurt them to know how much a ticket pays if you go for a dollar box exacta and the first and second place horses go off at five-to-three and twenty-to-one respectively. It's not uncommon for the kids to get into heated debates over whether the jockey's earnings or the trainer's record is a better basis for handicapping while in their car seats on the way home from the track. This is music to my ears. Transferrable skills, that's what children need. I don't get the kids often, but they always return to their homes with an education.

Occasionally I am the one who gets the education. Children don't trouble themselves thinking about which questions are appropriate or sensitive or likely to stir something up. They just come out and ask, not because they are nosey, or "not minding their own business" or have an agenda or want to make a point. They just have an innate curiosity and a desire to know the answers to life's uncertainties. In short, they ask because their parents put them up to it.

It was an elegant day in mid-July, with low humidity and a slight breeze to keep the bugs away. The corn was high enough to hide in as I made my way though the neat rows with my eleven-year-old niece Caroline in tow to the edge of the cornfield. She was carrying an old copper pail, the Official Berry Bucket for Flower Hill Farm.

It is a well-known fact among the children visitors that when the bucket is exactly two-thirds full of wild blackberries there are exactly enough berries to make a batch of jam. Less than two-thirds, then all you get are blackberry pancakes. We walked along the edge of the field gently touching the delicate ripe berries so that they fell "plink, plink, plink" into the copper bucket. Caroline, finally having Aunt Liz all to herself, asked the question that had evidently been on the minds of the family for a long time. "Do you ever get lonely out here?"

I paused, concentrating on a particularly plump and hard-to-reach cluster of blackberries in the middle of a nest of prickly branches. "I have to think about that," I replied.

Lonely. When was the last time that I felt lonely? Where was that empty, echoey feeling from Saturday nights without a date, or the IT parties with the fabulous hors d'oeuvres and skim-the-surface conversations that left me with the overwhelming urge to run away?

Or the weddings, seated at the "remnants" table of mother-of-the-groom's high school friends, old maids and the inevitable out-of-town cousin, the one whose not-too-plugged-in-aunt is sure that he'll meet a nice girl someday and is hoping it will be me, not realizing all along that he is gay. As we chat I inevitably learn that he's in a committed relationship with some guy named Louis and prefers the same brand of pantyhose that I do. In the meantime, his aunt stops by every few minutes to see how we're getting along. She has that same look that my neighbor has the first time she puts the ram in with the sheep. When I once again fail to snag this gem of a catch, the same woman is at the ready to gently pat me on the hand. She assures me that I will someday find that someone special because "there is never a pot so crooked that there isn't a lid to fit it."

Where indeed was that hollow sound of isolation and inadequacy that rattled the walls of my perfectly appointed suburban existence like a wolf howling, "I'm soooooooooooooooo loooonnnneeeellllyyyy"? It was gone, departed, vanished. I don't remember when it happened, but it was definitely not present. Had it been replaced by sheer exhaustion, or had it been superseded by something else?

"I'm not lonely," I said thoughtfully. "There are plenty of visitors: farmers, Groundhog Hunters, Manure Men, Metal Men, and Pigeon Hunters. Even when I'm alone, I'm not lonely. There is always something to do, someone to think about, a part of the dream to put into place. Loneliness might be more about living without purpose than it is living without people." I felt surprisingly poetic and philosophical while imparting these words of wisdom to my little niece.

Apparently satisfied with my answer, Caroline continued, "Have you ever been in love?"

"Look! The berry pail is EXACTLY two thirds full!" I exclaimed.

Part of the family's annual visit always involves having the Pennsylvania relatives over for a picnic. Everyone was anxious to get some good family photos of this rare get together, so a makeshift studio was set up in the living room. Someone climbed up on a chair and adjusted the ceiling spotlights from illuminating the fireplace to instead lighting up the couch. When all the photos of all possible combinations of family members had been taken, my sister went to readjust the lights to their original position. As she reached for the chair, the lights moved themselves. First the right one moved and then the left one, each one defying gravity to return exactly to its previous position without any human intervention.

"That's it, I'm leaving," said my sister Vicky.

"I'm sure that they must be spring-loaded," said Nita, quickly reaching for a cause-and-effect explanation.

"Let's just not say anything about this to the children," said Cousin Hope, nodding to her husband David. Their three bright children can read the Bible in four languages. Hope has been a missionary all her life, witnessing famine and poverty of unimaginable magnitude. Part of her ministry includes counseling victims of abuse in South Africa. She has been there and done and seen it all. More important, she had just granted her kids permission to spend the night on the farm with Aunt Liz and was not about to let a couple of ghosts interfere with the first night in a dozen years that she and her husband would be spending alone. Best to just let it be. The Lord will protect and provide.

As the evening wore on, the adults were sitting on the front porch enjoying the peace of the summer twilight with a glass of Chardonnay as the sun was slowly disappearing over Skull Hill. The children had burned off the last of their energy playing tag on the lawn. Suddenly, Sandy, the youngest at age three, stopped in her tracks, obviously transfixed by something that caught her eye. With her eyes wide open, she began trembling, while slowly tiptoeing over to her mother on the porch. In a whisper she said, "Mom, look! Aunt Liz even has fairies!"

For a moment I froze in horror. What unimaginable thing were the ghosts up to this time? The little girl pointed across the road under the shagbark hickory tree by the barn where the blinking lights of the evening's first fireflies shown brightly. Since Sandy lives in the mountains of Colorado she had never seen fireflies before.

Children see magic everywhere. Especially at Flower Hill Farm. Magic! I'd never thought of it before: Flower Hill Farm wasn't haunted by the dead; it was haunted by magic. Now that explains everything. And these little visitors will always be welcome here to share it with me.

LESSON 14

Take Stock at the End of the Day

E ven the strongest of us eventually reaches a breaking point. Mine occurred after my first weekend off the farm in six months. I returned from a somewhat bohemian weekend at the beach to find the bathroom plumbing leaking down through the dining room chandelier. Again. (This would be the fifth time I would have to replace the ceiling). The roof was also leaking and the well pump was making a noise like a calf separated from its mother.

A call to the well company brought yet more bad news. In spite of the fact that the well water had passed every possible inspection and had been tested regularly, an analysis of the "nutrient management" plans filed by farmers within a seven-mile radius revealed some problems when reviewed by the county agent issuing the well repair permit. They showed that under the right topographical and meteorological conditions, a remote potential for higher than recommended parts per billion of something or other could slip into the well water. In short, the well had to be relocated.

The well pump people said that they couldn't come out to fix it because their Douser was down with the Amish in Lancaster being fitted for a new divining rod. I guessed that it was like some Harry Potter thing; you have to fit the rod to the man or something like that. I called my horse trainer and friend, Naomi. She grew up in this area of Pennsylvania and had recently retired and moved to a fifty-acre farm in Kentucky.

"Well, you need the Douser," Naomi said in a matter-of-fact tone. She clearly had not shaken off her cultural roots since the move. "The first thing we did when we bought the land in Kentucky was to find a reliable Douser. Saved us a lot of time and trouble locating the well for the house."

"What the hell is a Douser going to do?" I groused, "I'm not paying good money for Berks County hocus pocus!"

"Oh sure, then why don't you just find some well company in the Yellow Pages? They'll send some guy out with a backhoe at two hundred bucks an hour to wreak havoc on your lawn until he finds a well. In the meantime he will have dug about fifteen holes, crushed your septic drain field and ripped up any underground wiring that you may have. A Douser will spend ten minutes walking up and down the lawn and will pinpoint your well within inches, guaranteed. Then they'll only have to dig one hole."

"I can't do this anymore. This land is too foreign, the culture is too weird," I sobbed.

"Of course you can't." Naomi said gently. "You're not alone, nobody can do this. It's just too hard. No farmer ever gets everything finished. It will all be there waiting for you tomorrow. As long as the animals are fed and safe at the day's end, you've done enough. Take fifteen minutes at that point and sit quietly. Enjoy the place where you live, accept it for what it is and where it is right now. Drink in your surroundings. Listen to the birds in the spring, the locusts in the fall or the snow falling in the winter.

"Pat yourself on your back for whatever you accomplished this day, no matter how trivial, and forgive yourself for whatever didn't go right or didn't get finished. Just don't ever think you are supposed to get it all done."

Although I felt like I had temporarily tapped into an Indian mystic, I quickly realized that this was a sterling piece of advice, and I kept to it. Fifteen minutes of quiet communion every day from now on.

I learned to ignore Vinnie careening around the yard at high speed, occasionally knocking over the potted plants. I paid little attention to his vigilance and constant barking to make sure that NO ONE disturbed my quiet time.

I learned to shut out the endless list of things that needed to be done and to quiet my inner voices of doubt and despair and replace them with gentle hymns of thanksgiving. Taking stock meant seeing the little valley as it had been seen by farmers for two hundred years, green and lush with a golden sunset between rolling hills with fields of freshly-planted corn and hay. In silent stillness, I watched the hummingbirds come up to the potted petunias hanging on the porch, flitting their little wings for a moment before buzzing away. Cardinals, gold finches and barn swallows put on an elaborate air show before settling down for the night. All was well in the country world.

But the spell was soon broken. The trouble with staring into space is that the space becomes clouded with all the things that still need to be done. The corn crib, for instance, was an eyesore. It was listing dangerously to one side down and far past any usefulness. It also blocked my view of the horse pasture from the front porch. "Maybe I can chain it to the truck and drag it to the burn pile." I mused. Back to the toils and troubles of farming.

As I was far too tired to hitch the corn crib to the pickup truck, I enjoyed some end of the day reading. It was a tattered and torn book that I'd found in the loft during the kitchen remodeling: John George Hohman's *Long Lost Friend*, originally published in 1820. The authoritative work for Pennsylvania Dutch Pow Wow healers, the book contains recipes for a myriad of cures and protections. In it are instructions on how to make cattle return home and protect them from witchcraft, and recipes to cure colic in horses or children.

There were incantations for charming enemies, identifying robbers, and avoiding murderers, hints for removing worms from beehives, and spells to guarantee a win at card games or a successful outcome to a lawsuit. The book also identified words to be spoken while making divinatory wands (which made me consider finding the damn well myself with the right piece of ash or hickory or whatever).

I read *A Safe Remedy for Various Ulcers, Boils, and other Defects*: "Take the root of an ironweed, and tie it around the neck, it cures running ulcers; it also serves against obstructions in the bladder (stranguary), and cures the piles. If the roots are boiled in water and drank, it cleans and heals the lungs and affects a good breath. If this root is planted among grape vines and trees, it promotes the growth very much. Children who carry it are educated without difficulty, and are fond of learning all useful arts and sciences, and grow up joyfully and cheerfully." We could probably do away with federal, state and local government if everyone was just issued a generous supply of ironweed.

On this evening in mid-May I looked up to see Lillian, Frank the turkey's savior, crossing the yard to the front porch. She seemed to have a sixth sense about when my "session" was over and always appeared at exactly the right time. Instead of barking and running, Vinnie became quiet, as if grateful for her visit. As Lillian sat down, Vinnie rested his head in her lap while she patted him. It was stinking hot mid-July type weather, hazy, hot and humid (the dreaded three H's). Lillian had a frayed rope in her hand.

"Have you seen Thomas?" she asked.

"Did that goat escape again?"

"Yes, I've been working on clearing the woods of poison ivy and I had staked Thomas out in a new section this morning. I had quite a few patients today, mostly farmers hurting themselves trying to get the crops in while the fields are dry. When I came out to check on Thomas, he apparently finished off all the poison ivy and decided to finish his meal by chewing through the rope itself."

Lillian fanned herself with her hand. "I heard an eagle call and found three feathers on the dirt road."

I never quite understood what Lillian was talking about, but I was always certain that it was meaningful, if somewhat obtuse.

"Is that bad?" I asked.

"It means Destruction." Lillian replied ominously. Her grey-green eyes looked skyward as if Destruction was about to fall on us at any moment.

"If anything is going to get destroyed, I vote for the corn crib." I quipped.

"You need to be more thoughtful," Lillian warned, while taking a furtive glance at the book on my lap. "Always be careful when you finish you're prayers with a request. It just might be given to you."

"In that case, I'll just request that the corn crib be moved directly to the burn pile."

Lillian rose to leave. I felt bad, since she was clearly annoyed with me, and in truth I should have been more respectful. After all, Lillian was kind to both man and animal and was a skillful healer.

"I'll keep an eye out for Thomas," I said.

"No matter."

The next morning I was off for yet another day at the office. As happens with busy people, my conversation with Lillian was quickly forgotten in the rush of meetings, telephone calls, deadlines and the daily crises that is Corporate America. When I finished my last meeting at three o'clock and checked the local weather on the computer it looked like the Mother of all Thunderstorms was headed directly toward Bernville.

Having horses at home was still a novelty for me and I treated them like hothouse plants. I brought them into large, well-bedded stalls if it rained and slipped rubber boots on them if it was muddy. I also dressed them in blankets appropriately weighted to the forecasted temperatures after the first frost. These outfits all matched the gender and personality of their wearer in color and style.

One of my friends from my past horse boarding facility actually hired a "Palette Consultant" from a company aptly named "The Clothed Horse." For an outrageous fee, the consultant reviewed a series of photographs and hair samples taken from mane and tail and determined her horse's "season" based on a proprietary formula. She then prescribed color, print and fabric combinations for sheets, blankets, leg wraps and coolers. It was my friend's bad luck that the horse, being chestnut, ended up as an "Autumn" and the mare was stuck with paisley prints in rust, burnt sienna, and olive green as her ideal fabric and color combination. Being bound by a budget, my horses' sartorial choices were less plentiful. They had to endure a more "off the rack" wardrobe, and were forced to wear what was on sale.

I have since gotten over that kind of fuss, and they now live happily out in a field naked as the day they were born, except under blizzard conditions when I find, having lived in Bernville awhile now, that the best outfit is rip-resistant Kevlar in hunter-safety orange. But this is now and that was then. As the thunderstorm approached, I realized that the horses were out in the pasture without their rain sheets on.

As I sped east on I-78 I could view the dark clouds ahead, so I drove a little faster and turned on the local radio station. Nothing was mentioned about the weather at all. All I heard were the usual afternoon call ins by citizens claiming to have been abducted by aliens. I soon relaxed and even started to feel a little bit silly for all the fuss, thinking that I shouldn't keep running home every time the skies darken.

As I turned off the exit toward Bernville, I drove through a brief but intense rainstorm. Then the skies turned blue and the cooler air took on that fresh spring rain scent which fabric softener manufacturers brag about. I rolled down the car windows and drove casually home.

When I reached the back end of Bootleg Road I had to turn around since the road was blocked by a fallen tree, a not unusual occurrence. I drove around the Skull Hill Dairy to the other end of Bootleg road and turned toward home. There I was stopped short by a horizontal forest. Six trees had fallen across the road. As I got out to survey the damage, I was met by three of the neighborhood mothers and half-a-dozen children.

"It was a tornado!" gasped Carly, an attractive blond who lived at the corner. "I was just getting ready to meet the kids at the bus stop. I went outside and the skies were black as pitch. I heard a roar like a freight train and ran down to the basement terrified. It was ten minutes to four exactly. Just the same time as when the bus was supposed to come."

"Are all the kids OK?", I asked. My mouth went dry and I became weak in the knees as the seriousness of the situation sunk in.

"The bus was delayed because a car went into a ditch on Irish Creek Road and the fire police shut down all the roads from Centerport to Bernville. If the bus had been on time I can't imagine what would have happened. But it was over and the sun was out by the time the kids got home"

"Are your animals OK?"

"The horses were in the barn and the cows seem none the worse for it."

"Has everyone been accounted for, any homes damaged?" I continued.

"The Petersons were living in a camper while they build their new house. The camper was destroyed, but Sherry took the baby and went to the store at three thirty so she wasn't home. Lou was outside when he saw the funnel and started running for the camper. The wind picked him up and tossed him into a straw pile inside their cinder block barn. Boy was he lucky. The camper looks like a crushed aluminum can."

I could see through the fallen trees that the tornado cut a path right through my farm, but in leather pumps and a silk suit I was not equipped to climb through them to try to get home.

"Has anyone seen my animals?" I asked, trying to push away images of my beloved horses being hurt or worse.

"We'll go see," said a couple of the neighborhood kids, as they started climbing over the trunks of the fallen trees to head toward the barn.

It was then that I noticed Lillian standing in the woods next to the road on a dirt ramp that the kids used as a jump for their mountain bikes. She stood motionless, her long grey hair in a single braid down her back, her eyes staring straight ahead, her face in painful concentration and her arms down at her sides, fists clenched as though she were carrying two buckets filled with concrete. She appeared to be listening for something.

A moment later the kids returned shouting, "The horses and all the barn animals are OK. You just have a few trees down. Everything is fine except for the corn crib. It blew over onto the burn pile!"

"Well, that's everyone accounted for. You know this has to be a miracle!" said Carly.

With that Lillian relaxed. Her face softened and she let out a sigh. She gave me a knowing look like a teacher admonishing a foolish student, turned and walked down the path toward her home looking as though the weight of the world had just been lifted from her shoulders.

I borrowed a pair of sneakers from Carly and made my way though the fallen trees. I passed a tree with a trunk over two feet in diameter. It had been uprooted and swept across the road. It missed hitting the hoghouse roof by less than a foot and had landed harmlessly by the rear door. The roots of the tree left tracks that looked like a large and muddy broom had just swept across the road. The tornado followed the tree line along the edge of the property. It was clear where it lifted above the ground and twisted the tops off the trees like a spoiled child ruining flowers in a garden out of spite.

I was greeted by a loud whinny from Gracie, the prima donna broodmare. Although she was clearly distressed by the situation, I couldn't help noticing that she was dry and sleek without a drop of water or mud on her. The geldings that shared the field with her, on the other hand, were not so lucky. They were caked in mud, but only on one side of their bodies. It was in their ears and eyes, and plastered into their coats, manes and tails. It appeared as though Gracie, fully embracing her role as Lead Brood Mare, had positioned herself in the back of the three-sided walk-in shelter and used the geldings as a shield against the flying mud and pounding rain. It takes a Diva.

I completed a brief survey of the damage. It had been a very powerful and localized twister, so the carnage was limited to a few felled trees, none of which had hit any buildings or fences. The corn crib was totaled, but had indeed landed squarely on the burn pile. Luckily, the house was untouched. Nothing was disturbed, not even the rockers or hanging planters on the front porch.

As I finished my inspection and my breathing began to return to normal, I heard the sound of chainsaws biting into the fallen trees. I quickly changed out of my mud-splattered suit and tattered stockings into jeans and a t-shirt. A chain saw! I finally had an opportunity to contribute to the farming community in a big way.

I've accepted my fear of power tools with some degree of grace, learning instead to compensate by optimizing my sledge hammer and crow bar skills. I am not ashamed to admit that I manipulate others who have a comfort level with power equipment into doing work requiring a circular saw or an electric drill. My family hasn't come to the same level of understanding. They believe that I am not only crazy but that I am in possession of super-human skills that deem me capable of doing anything.

The previous Christmas, my sister from North Jersey had given me a chainsaw. Not an ordinary chainsaw, mind you, but the largest, most vicious tool ever made by the John Deere company. It could have (or actually may have) starred in a B-grade horror movie. "Oh, the salesman suggested a smaller one," said sis proudly, "But I told him, my sister would consider anything less than this one to be merely kitchenware!" The thing came in a huge black plastic case that looked like something one of the members of the Corleone family would have used to carry a dead body. The dire warnings from the "Have a Healthy Respect for Your Chainsaw" segment in the Cooperative Extension Service Farm and Home Safety course taught by "Lefty" Miller echoed in my mind. I accepted the gift with a vague but sincere smile and murmured "Just what I always wanted" with as much enthusiasm as I could muster. When I returned from the holiday, I asked one of the Groundhog Hunters to move the chainsaw from the car to the house and down to the basement, where it had remained, untouched, unopened, and hidden from view ever since.

Until now. I ran to the basement to locate the chainsaw, and then it took twenty minutes to wrestle it up the coal cellar stairs. By sitting on my butt and bracing my feet against the door jamb I got enough leverage to move it up the first few steps and roll it end-over-end up the final steps. I finally dragged it across the porch to a waiting wheelbarrow.

Word of the tornado had traveled quickly. Farmers riding tractors came across the back fields to see if they could help. Others brought log chains to help drag the trees out of the road. Charlie from the dairy farm sent a work crew over to Bootleg Road. I offered the chainsaw to a couple of robust looking fellows who arrived without tractor or power equipment. They were thrilled to the point of giddy and seemed to have no trouble figuring out how to open the case or fill it with the oil and gas fuel mixture. They also had the upper body strength to pull the damn cord to start it. Happy to both contribute and spread joy, I backed off a safe distance from the tree cutting operation.

I located the women and children's section, where everyone was using their pent-up adrenaline to gather up sticks and smaller branches. When the Leopold brothers showed up with a chipper the size of a semi-truck, the mothers grabbed their small children and headed for higher ground. By 7:30 p.m. the last of the trees had been cut up into logs ready for splitting. It had been graciously divided among families with wood-burning stoves. Mulch piles were delivered to whoever needed them and the road was 'broom swept clean." All problems had been solved without argument, scandal or hurt feelings. The road was clear, debris was gone, and lawns were cleaned up.. Some had even been raked, and looked better than they did before the tornado passed through.

My thoughts wandered to a similar evening in a much "nicer" suburban neighborhood where I'd lived before moving here. A hurricane had blown down half-a-dozen trees which had landed in several backyards. The property owners all came out and took pictures of the fallen trees and called insurance companies who sent people out to take more pictures of the fallen trees. Because no one could agree on how the trees fell or where the trees were when they started to fall versus when they finished falling, the pictures were sent to Lawyers who had their Paralegals take more pictures and write letters to each other about the pictures that they had already taken. The Lawyers hired Surveyors to confirm whose property was where and what trees went with which property line. In the process they discovered that one man's fence was too close to another woman's shed and that someone else had planted Pampas grass on land that they just didn't own and it takes Some Nerve to do something like that. Six months later, the Paralegals were still writing letters for the Lawyers, none of the neighbors were speaking to each other and the trees were rotting on the ground with large fungi growing out of the sides of them. Not so on Bootleg Road where practicality wins over pride every time. The contrast was remarkable.

As the final cord of firewood was being loaded into the last pickup truck, the police showed up. No one had thought to call them since everybody was busy getting the trees off the road. The officers happened to stumble on the tornado scene while taking a shortcut over Skull Hill. They put on their flashing lights, set out a few cones and a couple dozen flares and called for backup, but by that time it was pretty much all over but the shouting. Everyone agreed it was a good idea to file a police report about the Peterson's trailer, and it gave all the participants a good chance to "debrief" and get it out of their system how the tornado sounded like a freight train and all.

"Any other property damage?" the one officer asked after he had finished his report on the Peterson's trailer. "It's best to get these things documented for the insurance company."

"The corn crib on the Shock's place," replied one of the farmers.

Suddenly I became the center of attention. The corn crib was covered under my farm insurance, I was sure of that. I could legitimately claim the replacement value which was well over my deductible. It would be a little extra cash in my pocket, a little shot in the arm. I thought of Lillian, the eagles, the feathers, the timing of the school bus, Sherry Peterson's trip to the store, Gracie tucked safely in the walk-in and the corn crib sitting on the burn pile.

"Nothing to claim, it landed on the burn pile, which is exactly where it belongs," I said as I picked up the handles of the wheelbarrow and escorted my well-used chainsaw home.

Beware the Song of the Lorelei

Raising the two foals was surprisingly uneventful. Their mother took care of them for the first five months and then I turned them out to pasture with New Shot, the thirty-year-old former show horse who took it upon himself to keep them in line. Emily was a sweet filly, somewhat spoiled by too many carrots, but affectionate. Bootleg Jack was a handful, but no match for the veteran New Shot who put more than one bite mark on his hide.

But society expects that horses will eventually have to be ridden. Oddly, society doesn't do the dirty work when it comes to breaking them. When that time arrived, I added a fourth rule to my "Principles for a Good Life": 1. Always pay what you owe (including taxes); 2. Never sleep with a married man; 3. Don't drink and date; and now, 4. Don't ride a horse under the age of five.

From this point forward breaking the babies was going to be contracted out to experts. When Emily came of age, she was shipped to the Strausstown Equestrian Center for the Potentially Gifted to be started under saddle. I put Emily in training and scheduled lessons for myself on well-schooled lesson horses so that when Emily turned five, I would be back in practice and able to ride her.

My lesson time was 8:00 a.m. on Saturday. An unusual new customer at the stable—Gary—had a lesson scheduled for nine. It was December, and I was in jeans, with three layers of clothes covering my dirty blue ski jacket/barn coat with hay sticking out of all the pockets. Gary was in the tack room whipping up some lattes. He wore black riding britches with black paddock boots, a black long sleeve shirt with a red and gold threaded paisley vest. Over the vest he wore a black velvet bolero jacket. He had shoulder length hair and a small diamond piercing the side of his nose. A so completely un-Bernville, Bernville resident. He was clearly not of this world. Turns out that he was a master plumber who had spent a lifetime meeting New York City codes for Manhattan hospitals and skyscrapers. Somehow he had landed in Bernville.

Gary was a novice in the world of horses. He was considering purchasing the trainer's best lesson horse and had that optimistic blush of new horse ridership. "Horses are so completely Zen!" he said joyfully. "I'm just hoping that I can get my girlfriend, Susan, to be interested in them."

"What does she do?" I asked politely, still digesting the Zen comment.

"She's a flautist," Gary replied with a sense of pride. "We used to have a band in New York City. We bought a fixer-upper place on thirty-five acres about five years ago. Still working on it. Would you like some carrots for your horse? We grow organic vegetables."

I stared at the man in disbelief. He was happily sipping away on his latte while slicing up organic vegetables into horse bite-sized pieces. Everything he did and said was purposeful and *interesting*. There was also something fragile about him. When first meeting Gary it was like walking through a crowded porcelain shop carrying an oversized shoulder bag. You didn't want to be clumsy or common or most of all unkind or maybe the spell would break.

With each passing week, we talked over tack room-made lattes while waiting for our riding lessons. We learned that we had been living parallel lives in the tiny town of Bernville.

Gary was a second generation Italian-American. His grandfather had come over from the old country and carried his farming tradition to what was then the rural community of Yonkers. The old man grew his prized figs and red-ripe tomatoes in a small plot in the backyard.

In 2000, the new millennium, Gary and Sue decided to leave the safety of the New York City suburbs and purchase a thirty-two acre fixer-upper farm with a small, late 1800s farmhouse on it in need of repair. In exactly the same year that I bought my farm, Gary dug up his grandfather's fig tree from the backyard in Yonkers and transplanted it, along with Sue, onto Moby Grape Farm in Bernville, Pennsylvania. Like me, they fell in love with the land and barn and the cheap real estate prices more than the house. They then spent the next four years in a sort of rural purgatory tearing their home down to the bare studs in an effort to eliminate embedded odors. They also upgraded all systems and generally make a silk purse out of a sow's ear. Their house was in the same state of disrepair and they came with the same wide-eyed optimism and lack of understanding of rudimentary farming skills that marked Flower Hill Farm's early years. Gary's plumbing skills did give him a leg up in the construction arena. He was also wise enough to choose Sue, a life partner with no fear of power tools and fairly refined cabinet making abilities.

For four of the last five years, Gary and Sue had made the daily commute from Bernville, Pennsylvania to New York City, the Big Apple. They woke up at 2:00 a.m., were on the road by three, into the city by six and home again by seven to maybe get an hour or two of either demolition or construction done before heading to bed to repeat the cycle again. This year, Gary turned fifty-five and, thanks to a lifetime of membership in the New York plumbers union, was able to retire to a life in the country. Upon his retirement, Sue convinced her Manhattan-based company to allow her to telecommute, and thus ended four years of the Commute from Hell. Gary was tasting his first breath of freedom.

"Now that the house is in reasonable shape, I thought we'd get a couple of horses."

The horse-loving gene sits on the extra leg of the X-chromosome, the one reserved for females only. That is why all little girls get teary-eyed when reading tales of Flicka, Stormy and Black Beauty. They have a natural affinity for the beasts and starting around eight years of age tend to harass their parents endlessly to buy a pony. I never progressed beyond that eight-year-old stage. But now, instead of nagging Mom and Dad, I just buy my own ponies. This has been the joy of my life as well as my downfall, since ponies, like cars, are far easier to buy than they are to sell. I accept this fact, and wouldn't change a thing.

Gary, on the other hand, has a mutated Y-gene that expresses itself in pony-loving. This gene had not manifested itself until his manhood and recent retirement, but nonetheless, it was always there. Like adult onset diabetes, it lay dormant, and suddenly, with few tell-tale signs, it appeared as a full blown obsession. I confess that I did little to save him from the addiction. Our chance meeting at the riding stable did not help matters. At that time his plan was simply to take lessons, learn how to handle a horse, and maybe purchase one to ride on his thirty-five acres later on.

A natural born enabler, instigator, kibitzer, and cheerleader, I egged him on past the safe point with tales of a fulfilling horse-enriched lifestyle. Gary sat on the slippery slope of near equine ownership, poised on the edge of that financial and emotional abyss that is the horse world. The only thing that stood between him and eternal damnation was Sue, his significant other. Not being able to imagine anyone who didn't want a horse and wouldn't buy several if they were in the enviable position of having a few acres and a husband who wasn't opposed to it, I must admit I was a little prejudiced about Sue.

She, I reasoned, has a defective female X-chromosome, since she was not born with the horse-loving gene. To her, horses are large vicious creatures with sharp hooves with which to slice you on a whim or Stomp You To Death. Steam gushes from their nostrils, flames burn in their eyes, hatred kindles in their hearts. In her world they are not to be messed with under any circumstances.

The challenge was to lure Sue into the trap of horse ownership. This would be difficult to do since Sue refused to come out to the barn or have anything to do with the whole horse scene.

Gary, ever trying to manipulate Sue into doing what she has emphatically said she will not do, approached her one day with a sly maneuver: practicality. "I'm thinking of buying a work horse," he said, "Something that can pull a plow. We'll save on gas and diesel, and it's *so* organic. It won't contribute to global warming and will produce all the fertilizer we need. It'll carry the picnic basket when we have lunches in the woods" he mused.

Sue shot back, "When have we ever stopped to take a meal sitting down, much less loaded up a picnic basket? We don't even own a picnic basket. Do they even make them anymore?"

"Actually, yes," Gary said while reaching under the couch cushion where he had stashed the Windy Ridge Farm Horse Accessory catalog I had given him the week before. He flipped through the dog-eared pages to the "outing" section that featured picnic saddle bags, pocket-sized grills, and inflatable gazebos. "These would be perfect for the woods behind the lower ten, don't you think?"

"Sure," she sighed. "Let him have his little dream," she no doubt thought to herself. She was certain that the fantasy would end the first time he got bucked off the lesson horse. After that he'd lose interest and his thoughts would quickly return to his previous obsession: his tractors.

But Gary did not get bucked off, kicked, or bitten by the lesson horse. In fact, his enthusiasm mounted in response to the trainer's constant regaling on the subject of jumping and competing and winning, all egged on by my similar tales. Not that I actually DID a lot of jumping, competing and winning, but I can talk a good game when needed. Like a novice gambler in Las Vegas, he was slowly being sucked into the horsey world, and he didn't even realize it.

Sue had no intention of becoming a horse junkie, even as Gary became thoroughly hooked and started planning vacations to Colorado or Montana or wherever it is that horse people congregate. His nose continuously ran from riding in the cold. His hands quivered from overstrain at the reins. He nodded his head during the day from lack of sleep because he spent his nights lying awake scheming of how to buy a horse and still make their mortgage payments. He had the classic symptoms of heroin addiction, but it was only the ponies.

Sue watched his downward spiral with trepidation and hardened her heart while bracing for tough love. She refused to share this new aspect of his life or encourage him in any way. "I'm not interested in horses," she insisted. "It's your thing, not mine."

A crimp was put in her resolution in the form of a longing clinic held at the stable. Sue had no intention of going, of course, but it was in the middle of January, and there was no field or garden work to otherwise draw her attention. A run on "chestnut mocha" wood stain due to both Oprah and Martha featuring it in the December issues of their respective magazines left Sue with no materials for her current project. This was a dividing wall in the kitchen to separate the "mud" area where jackets, boots and gardening gloves were dumped at days end from the more civilized and sanitary cooking and eating areas. An ambitious design, it was four feet high and had coat hooks, boot storage boxes and a pet feed bins on one side and beveled-glass-doored china cabinets on the other.

The stain shortage crisis had left her with a few hours with nothing to do. Gary mentioned the clinic and suggested that she go along. She wouldn't have to do a thing and it would be a great way to spend a small portion of her precious time with him. The guilt, lack of work, and cabin fever took their toll.. As she put on another layer of clothing to keep warm, she muttered about it all being a waste of time. Oddly, she found herself sitting next to me, most likely because Gary purposely guided her there.

Not being enamoured with horses, Sue began our relationship in the customary way. She asked about basic employment background and college level, general health, political belief system, which church I attended, and what brand of Chardonnay I drank. After those first light-hearted minutes, though, I got down to business. I grilled Sue on her horse history, or lack thereof, and anything that could remotely be construed as being "horshish" in her life. Did she ride as a child? What kind of horses did she own? Did she jump, compete, or trail ride? On all counts Sue came up sadly and completely empty.

Early on in that first conversation, I fully admit that I became tired of speaking with someone who had no experience at all with horses. I rudely leaned behind Sue's back and began comparing notes with Gary on the big chestnut mare that was longing in the arena in front of us.

"She's tracking quite well," I said, "but there's a problem with…."

I went on and on and Sue's eyes soon glazed over. She left the seating area and wandered to the tack room, where she was soon nursing a cup of hot chocolate.

"She knows…," I thought to myself as I watched Sue walk away.

The Trainer was a tall, handsome man, in his late thirties who spoke with a British accent. He was raised in Wales, trained with the Germans in stadium jumping and dressage, and claimed Canadian citizenship.

Somehow, in some misdirection of life currents, he too found himself in Bernville. His passion for horses was apparent. It was his lot in life to bring the *haute couture* of European sport horses to the wilds of Pennsylvania where most of the horses were either rejects from the racetrack or had been picked up for a few hundred dollars at the local auction. He cut a distinguished figure in beige jodhpurs, high black riding boots complete with spurs, and a brown tweed riding jacket. He stood in the middle of the arena holding one end of a thirty-foot longe line, with the chestnut mare trotting obediently in a circle around him at the other end.

The clinic attendees consisted mostly of thin, fit, and energetic teenage and pre-teen girls from the local pony club mixed with fifty-something overweight, well, maybe more husky, women with ruddy complexions and bad hair from spending too many hours outside mucking the barnyard. The young girls dreamed of great moments in the jumper ring, sure of eliciting the same beauty and obedience from their horses that the trainer commanded from this mare. The older women, whose dreams of Olympic competition were long gone, were asking long-winded questions, anecdotes, really. They were not designed to gain information, but rather to let others know that they still retained their edge, and were still in the game. Questions like:

"You remember my gelding, the seventeen-hand bay horse with the white socks and the wonderful movement? Remember how difficult he was to start on the longe line? It wasn't until we started showing him at the A circuit level that he really started to settle down. Now if we hadn't sold him as a Grand Prix prospect, what would we be doing to get him to longe to the left?"

Then there was Sue. She stood out as someone who had planned to fit in, had dressed to fit in, but was clearly from another world. For one thing, she did not have any straw stuck on any part of her shoes or clothing. She was wearing black jeans and a black leather jacket. Her long black hair was tied up neatly under a fleece hair band. Her petite flautist hands were sheathed in tiny leopard print gloves. Her eyes shone with a mixture of intelligence mingled with a good dose of skepticism.

"She knows," I thought. "Poor Gary. She sees. She sees through the whole thing. The trainer is not a horse whisperer, not an especially gifted human or near deity with the ability to look deep into a horse's soul. He's just a guy wearing stretch pants and black leather boots. The horse is just an animal moving around at the end of a string. Nothing special, nothing that a dog couldn't do with a little training and a lot less fuss. She doesn't think it's magical or even extraordinary. She sees that horses are a large, expensive extension of the human ego. They are high maintenance, impractical, and break easily. She doesn't have the gene; she won't get her heart broken. She is never going to pay twenty-one dollars and ninety-seven cents for ten ounces of horse hair care product. She even has a chance of keeping her retirement savings intact."

In spite of the big beautiful mare longing in the arena, free-jumping, snorting, stopping on a dime, and coming instantly as her trainer quietly called her, I could see that Sue remained steadfastly unimpressed. The chestnut horse had a way of almost prancing as it trotted, gracefully bouncing on its sculpted long legs. She had a breathtaking canter composed of huge strides and perfect balance. Sue saw the poetry, but fought back with the heart of a Puritan. She could not succumb to the lure of the horse world with its egomaniac trainers, high-strung owners, and over bred animals. It all seemed a supreme waste of good time and energy to her. She did concede that horses were indeed impressive and beautiful; she would give us that. From then on she stopped calling Gary a lunatic behind his back.

Gary bought Ricci, one of the trainer's best lesson horses. Ricci had been there, done that, and was just about as bombproof as a horse can get. Gary dipped a little too far into his life savings to pay for the horse and the myriad of horse sheets, blankets, leg wraps and other accessories deemed necessary by the first time horse owner.

Sue's conversion happened suddenly and with little warning. Her "road to Emmaus" experience struck one day when she agreed to go with Gary and myself to a "going out of business" sale at a local tack shop.

Tack shops are the horse owner's equivalent of a Willy Wonka Chocolate Factory, only much more expensive. In a tack shop sane and conservative people will max out their credit cards on mane and tail créme rinse, paddock boots, sparkly hoof polish, or apple-flavored horse cookies all the while forgetting what they came to buy in the first place. A "going out of business" sale is better than great. The possibilities are endless. It's amazing what you can't live without at such a sale. Sue had come along to insure that Gary, who really just needed a riding helmet, stuck to their agreed upon budget. She escorted him directly to the helmet area where a woman in tight jeans and a red flannel shirt was ready to help them. I headed over to the "Final Sale—Clearance" rack of hunt coats to try to find a great bargain should I ever actually find myself at a horse show.

The sales woman had measured Gary's head and was looking for the correct-sized helmet with all the necessary safety features.

"What kind of covering are you looking for?" she asked.

"Covering?" questioned Gary.

"Yes, if you just want something for around the barn you can go with a plastic helmet, but if you are going to hunt or show you will probably want a velvet cover."

"Velvet?" asked Sue, clearly intrigued. "They come in velvet? Maybe I'll try one on."

I was watching with interest from my position behind the hunt coats. Textiles! Of course, why hadn't I thought of it before? I sidled down the twenty feet of hunt coats that separated my size from Sue's and found a classic navy blue model trimmed with a velvet collar and velvet-covered buttons.

I approached Sue with the coat in my left hand, trying to appear casual as I caressed the velvet collar between my right thumb and forefinger.

"You should try on a jacket to go with the hat, just for fun. The prices are unbelievably good for a jacket of this quality."

Sue put on the hat, the hunt coat and a pair of black calfskin gloves. For a moment, everyone in the shop stood still. The folks over in the whips and spurs area stared gobsmacked. Her dark hair was tucked neatly under the velvet hunt cap, and the blue jacket, cut perfectly to her size four figure, showed off her flawless ivory skin and her shining dark eyes. She looked the picture of an age gone by, like a part of the American Aristocracy. She was Jacqueline Kennedy Onassis at the Far Hills Hunt. Gary stared at her at first with admiration, then with awe and finally, with lust. I turned back to the hunt coat rack in an attempt to hide my grin as I sang the Song of the Loreli quietly to myself, "Somebody's getting a PO-NY, Somebody's getting a PO-NY."

It's Not the Cost It's the Upkeep

Most people thought Pogo was a big mistake. In times of lucidity, Sue and Gary agreed, but they would never let on. One evening, after sharing a magnum of Chardonnay, Sue confessed the full story of how they acquired Pogo.

The most appealing thing about the ad for the horse in *Lancaster Farming* was the modest fee. "Modest" being the operative term here. Gary had no interest in purchasing an expensive horse. Pogo was advertised as being a full-blooded Peruvian Paso, but was suspiciously priced at a very reasonable price. This should have been clue number one.

"Well, the horse has never been trained and we're trying to cut the herd down," Ted, the horse's owner, said on the phone when Gary asked why the horse was so inexpensive. "But he's got papers."

It all sounded great. He and Sue made the trip over to Ted's with a borrowed trailer. Due to their extreme ignorance, Gary had hired Sid, his trainer, to assist with the purchase and help transport the little horse to where he would be broken and made ridable for two people who knew next to nothing about ponies and horses.

For some strange reason, Sid, the multi-talented Olympic-hopeful, trainer and breeder of champion horses, had few comments when the trio turned into the drive to Ted's place. The operation spread out before their eyes, and it should have been obvious to all that the best thing for them to do would be to turn around and leave without disturbing the occupants of the "farm." Wild bay-colored horses were everywhere. Mares were mixed with stallions, and half-grown babies ran rampant. Three stomping something-or-others were cordoned off in an area that included an old oil tank, a bathtub, and a corn crib. Two mares were grazing in another area that consisted of a 1950s motor home, a broken horse trailer, and an old kitchen sink.

Eyeing the big pen with the incestuous family of fifteen or so Pasos running around happily procreating and eating oats, the only thing Sid said was, "Looks like a creative breeding program going on here. You might check about the horse's papers before doing anything else." That was the sum total of Sid's advice which, had Gary and Sue known a little bit more, was clearly code for, "Run away, run away fast!"

Ted came ambling down the steps of his three-bedroom rancher opposite the pen to meet his prospective customers. "Wanna see the new baby?" he asked, knowing that everybody, even those who know nothing of ponies and horses, love babies, and is soon lulled into a buying mood once they see them.

He led them into the pen with the fifteen or so Pasos and, as the yearlings followed along sniffing and nipping the strangers, he showed them the foaling stall, one of four stalls in the barn. Ted wasn't quite sure which one held the foal, however. There were no lights in the barn and he couldn't remember which of the mares it was that had had the baby.

"I didn't even know she was pregnant," Ted said, chuckling.

"Not surprised," Sid muttered under his breath.

"What was that?" Ted asked.

"Nice looking baby," Sid answered.

Everyone agreed and oohed and aahed for the requisite amount of time until Gary finally moved things along, saying "So which of the horses is for sale?"

"Well," Ted replied. "All of them, actually. You can have your pick."

"Well, which ones were advertised for the modest price?" Gary asked.

Ted proceeded to show us two mares in a separate pen and three stallions in another.

"They look funny," Sue said, not having a clue about ponies and horses and so not knowing what they were supposed to look like. "Are they part Shetland Pony?"

Ted laughed. "No, no, they just have their winter coats on. Wait 'til springtime. They'll be sleeker'n a waxed floor."

Not really wanting a waxed floor-looking horse, but doubting that Ted was capable of an honest homegrown metaphor, they accepted his answer. Everyone nodded in understanding.

The mares seemed angry, the stallions scared, so Gary gravitated to the stallion pen. He watched the three of them for awhile and honed in on the one that seemed to have the fewest knots in his mane.

A Peruvian Paso, when properly groomed, has a mane to die for. They are reminiscent of Tina Turner during her big hair days. The Paso mane is black with strong hues of red that make it look like it had a Hollywood henna job. The tail and mane both are three times thicker than a regular horse's, giving them a hands-down win in any beauty contest. They look at you with eyes peeking through a thick forelock that hangs down on their face. You cannot help but love these horses; when they have been properly taken care of, that is.

The Pasos in Ted's herd had never been groomed. In fact they had never even seen a curry comb or horse brush. Their manes and tails were so knotted up that the group looked like a rasta band high on ganga sporting powerful dreadlocks. Any minute they'd burst into hoof-beat reggae while singing about jammin' man.

Ever interested in the superficial details, Sue pointed to the one Gary was interested in. "So what's this one's name?" she asked.

The ever-gregarious Ted laughed once again. "Why, we don't name 'em. We just grow 'em."

Sid coughed and looked far into the distance as if wishing he were a thousand miles away. Not wanting to insult Gary, his client, though, he remained silent.

Everyone nodded in understanding.

"So how is he under halter?" Sid asked, not wanting to hear the answer.

"Well, I guess we'll find out," Ted answered.

Sid coughed again.

Surprisingly, the halter went on quite easily. The new horse, having never been out of his pen since the day he was born, had no idea what a halter was and so stood passively as Ted slipped a bit of moth-eaten rope around his head and behind his ears.

The trainer attached a longe line and pretended to longe the confused horse that, instead of going in a circle, merely ran away quickly while his head snapped back when the end of the line was reached. He then moved just as quickly in the opposite direction until reaching the end of the line there. Sid watched the action, not really expecting much more than what he was seeing.

"He's not lame," Sid concluded, retrieving the line.

Everyone nodded in understanding.

"How old is he?" Sid asked.

"Well, I'm not real sure how to age horses because January 1 is every horse's birthday. This one was born in May, but it's only March, so I guess he'd be three."

"As per standard January 1 birthdate or actual birthdate?"

"Yup," Ted answered.

"What difference does it make?" Gary asked.

"Well, the younger he is, the more he'll grow. He's pretty small," Sid answered. "And the older he is, the harder it will be to train him."

"Well, at three, he's still got a ways to go," Ted assured him.

Everyone nodded in agreement.

"Well, I guess I'll take him," Gary said.

"What about the papers?" Sid asked.

"Come on in the house and we'll get the papers and everything else," Ted laughed again.

Sid and Sue stayed back while Gary went in to carry out the transaction. Sue petted the new horse that stood by the fence where the bathtub held some of last week's unmelted snow. Without a source of water, the little guy was eating the snow to quench his thirst. Due to his confinement in the pen for most of his life, he'd never experienced quite so much exercise as he did during Sid's longing test, and he was thirsty.

Soon Sue grew tired of petting the horse and moved on to the other horses in the area. She cooed over the young ones and returned to the foaling pen and even visited the two angry mares to make faces at them which set them off, neighing and kicking. Sid spent most of his time kicking the ground, shaking his head, and looking at Ted's operation in disbelief.

An hour-and-a-half later, Gary and Ted emerged from the house. Gary's face was dark and his eyes seemed to be moving in opposite directions. He carried a bundle in his hands.

"They couldn't find the papers," he said, "so they gave me these."

He handed Sue two magazines in Spanish with the title *Caballo*. They were the Marzo [March], 1965 and Maio {May] 1967, issues. Included in the pile was a sheet of Holiday Inn letterhead on which was written in pencil, "This horse was born May 31, 2002." This made the horse four years old in chronological years, five using the standard horse birthdating system.

"Oh we'll keep looking for those papers," Ted said quickly. "We'll find them just as soon as we clean up the files. But that birthdate is accurate, we got it off the calendar."

Sid fired a questionable look at Gary., but he just shook his head and said, "Let's get outta here."

The lead line was hooked up to the little pony-sized-not-gonna-get-much-bigger horse and after half-an-hour of cajoling, pushing, kicking, swearing, and other frightening maneuvers, they were able to get him into the horse wagon.

Then, after the drive to Sid's stable, where he would be trained, and another half-hour of cajoling, pushing, kicking, swearing, and other frightening maneuvers, they were able to get him off the truck. The same set of maneuvers was required to ease him into a stall.

Imagine how you would feel if you had been ripped out of the only home you'd ever known, a field filled with all the necessary comforts: sisters, cousins, aunts, and various discarded home appliances. Then you're stuffed into a small black box that moves along the highway at high speeds, and dumped into another small black box where you are expected to behave like My Friend Flicka.

They tried to calm the little guy down, but he was inconsolable. He sweated and snorted, kicked and cried, and refused grain, carrots, and water, and threatening to die of apoplexy any moment. After the disappointing purchase and the life-threatening transport, Gary and Sue felt they now knew a single truth about ponies and horses: They should stay as far away from them and the people that breed them as possible.

Resolute, however, they moved forward within their given situation.

An unbroken, untouched five-year-old is the horse equivalent of a real estate money pit. First off, since he was a stallion, and not much of a breeding prospect, the little horse had to be gelded so that he could live in peace with Riccie. Then he needed eight hundred dollars in shots, worming, dental work and farrier services, all done under sedation since Pogo was not especially keen of his new-found domestication. This all in preparation for the months of training and thousands of dollars in training fees (or as Sid described it, "danger pay") it would take before the little fellow was even approachable, much less rideable. Gary and Sue were hooked, hog tied and damned to a life of horse-induced poverty.

You Get By With a Little Help From Your Friends

I suppose I felt a little guilty about the part I played in enabling Gary and Sue's horse addiction. But the truth was that I needed them. They were a part of a small band of pioneers who crossed the great divide from the suburbs to the country. They, too, had once led normal and successful lives.

Gary and Sue met through a mutual love of music. For years they played in a jazz/blues band, produced a few good CDs and had some prestigious gigs before giving it up for their day jobs.

The topic of a jam session came up at the Blue Marsh Canteen on "Open Mike, Talent Scout" night, which was on a Thursday. A night when all the local wanna' be's and coulda' beens show up wearing a lot of makeup and clothes that might be just a smitch too tight. They hook their guitars into a community amplifier, make use of the "house" keyboard and microphones and produce music of vastly varying quality.

That night, as is typical, someone at the bar had had a little too much to drink and fancied herself the next American Idol. Weeping, and wiping her tears with the back of her hand, she swayed toward the microphone and, with a nod to the keyboard player *du jour*, asked him to play "Somewhere Over the Rainbow."

"Do you miss the band?" I asked Gary as the singer began her best Judy Garland interpretation.

"I don't miss the gigs." Gary said carefully. "What I miss is the Music, when sometimes on a good night the band was tight and everything was working right and the crowd was sending us their energy. Sometimes when the Music took over and passed from band member to band member and into the crowd until there wasn't a band or a bar or an owner or a guitar player, vocals, flute or keyboard, but just Music taking over and giving everyone a sense of what it is to be alive. That's what I miss."

The singer, meanwhile, was stuck somewhere between the first and third verse and kept returning to the chorus sounding very much like the siren at the local fire house every time she sang the line "Somewhere over the rainbow."

"How about a jam session tomorrow at your house?" Gary proposed. "You can play the piano, I'll play bass guitar and Sue will bring her flute."

I am not musical by nature. I had sort of backed into taking a year of piano lessons after I had accidentally bought a baby grand piano on e-Bay. In my defense, I thought I was only buying the piano bench. It was the perfect size to fit under the window in the bathroom and well worth the fifty dollars. I put in the bid and went to bed.

When I received my "Congratulations, you are high bidder" e-mail in the cold light of morning, I realized that I bought both the bench and its matching piano, along with the six-hundred dollar fee to ship it to Flower Hill Farm.

Not wanting to endure the stigma of NEGATIVE FEEDBACK, I decided to go along with the deal. After a year of piano lessons and with a lot of practice and a robust warm up I can play "The First Noel," "Rock of Ages" and "Way Down Upon the Suwannee River" But I am still vague about the names of the notes and which chord is which. I steadfastly refuse to use the black keys as they are not really notes in their own right and only tend to complicate matters. The dogs only let me practice for twenty minutes at a time. After that, Vinnie walks under the piano, sticks his head under my hands and gently nudges them off the keyboard. Now here I was at the Blue Marsh with my greatest fear being realized, the request to play for witnesses (even if it was only two witnesses, and in the privacy of my own home).

The bar had grown quiet as the singer had inadvertently tangled the microphone up in her hair extensions and the waitress was trying to free her without cutting them off.

"You only need to know three chords: C, G and F," said Gary, sensing my latent fear. During their band days, Gary and Sue were used to having to make do when a "regular" band member didn't show up at the last minute and you had to go with what the Talent Gods sent you. They became good at training whoever was available. The show must go on after all. Sue could teach a Cro-Magnon the cords C, G and F on the keyboard in twenty minutes, ten if he was sober. Not sure if I was up to the task, I started to move my fingers trying to see if I remembered where the chords were. In my silent concentration I failed to notice that the folks at the Blue Marsh thought I was a deaf-mute and was "signing." They felt sorry for me, and began casting sidelong pity-filled glances in my direction. Looks generally reserved for deaf mutes that show up at "Open Mike, Talent Scout" nights.

"Lets call it a night," said the ever-observant Gary as he escorted me to the door. "We'll see you tomorrow."

Gary and Sue arrived at Flower Hill Farm the next day with instruments, amplifiers, sheet music and CDs. Sue briefed me on the required chords. Miraculously, Gary found some music in his collection that did not require any black keys ("C is the key of the common man," he said by way of explanation). They worked out a system where I could play the chords on Sue's signal. Soon we were all jamming in fine style. As the afternoon went by, our little impromptu band got better and better. Sue alternated between the flute and a full range of well-schooled vocals and Gary took off on a series of inspired guitar solos. I stayed focused on playing F, C and G chords on demand and, for the first time ever, I didn't irritate the Doberman.

As the afternoon wore on, something happened. It was during a rendition of "House of the Rising Sun." Sue and Gary started playing off of each other, switching between melody and harmony, passing the music back and forth, letting the music take over. Low tech, high touch. Just making music with our friends. Good times, and something to do during the long, dark days of winter as residents of this house have done for over two hundred years.

Winter is a challenge in the country. Life is hard. It's dark most of the time and gray the rest of the time. It's also unpredictable. Travel is dangerous. Any plan made more than seventy-two hours in advance is sure to be fouled up by an ice storm. It's a long stretch between Christmas and Easter. Sure, there's the farm show in January at the Agricultural Hall, but after you've marveled at the life-sized butter sculpture of *Washington Crossing the Delaware*, crowned the winner of the "Sheep to Shawl" contest, and the Draft Horse and Mule Princess congratulates Barney and Clyde, the two-horse team able to pull eleven-thousand-eight-hundred pounds of cinder blocks twenty-seven feet, what else is there to life?.

It's February. Mercifully designated as the shortest month by the powers that be. But far too long for those of us who have been leading energetic yearling colts over compacted ice fields since November. We need all the Holidays we can get. None of this celebrating President's Day as one consolidated holiday. In the country you unbundle President's Day. It's Lincoln's Birthday, and Washington's Birthday, thank you very much, with a celebratory nod to Ronald Regan and William Henry Harrison born on the sixth and the ninth respectively. Then to fill in the rest of the spaces you need to make up holidays. Everybody does it.

February starts with Groundhog Day. As tradition has it groundhogs come out of their burrows every February second and check to see their shadows. If a shadow appears, it means six more weeks of winter. If not, it means an early spring. Either way, the groundhog goes back to bed and forgets about the whole thing. As most of us know, the Official Groundhog hails from Gobbler's knob in Punxatawny, Pennsylvania. Any good travel agent can put together a deluxe three-day package there, which includes two nights in a moderately-priced hotel in Dubois (Which means "the Woods." But forget the French; the locals pronounce it as Dew Boys), tickets to the Groundhog's Ball and the crowning of the King and Queen, bus transportation to Gobblers Knob for the festivities (including the marching bands, proclamation ceremony, full-screen TV views of Punxatawny Phil seeing his shadow (or not), fireworks and a scrapple breakfast at one of the local fire halls).

I figured that Gary and Sue were new to the local customs so I could pretty much design a "traditional Groundhog's Day" anyway I wanted.

Sue is an awesome cook and canner. She spends the better part of August in cutoff shorts, a halter top and a bandanna around her head blanching vegetables, pickling cucumbers, shredding cabbage for sauerkraut and putting up tomato sauce, tomato juice, stewed tomatoes and salsa, not to mention jams, jellies, chutney, apple sauce and peaches. Picture, if you will, the hottest dog days of August. Three canners have been boiling away on the stove for the past five days in a little, low-ceilinged house with no air conditioning. Sue's hands are chafed from the acid of the tomatoes and peppers, both arms and a few of her flautist fingers bear second degree burns from filling hot jars with boiling produce and moving them, eight at a time, in and out of the boiling water bath. All this sacrifice, pain and suffering become worthwhile if only one can experience the taste of home-canned peaches on the second day of February.

The bright sunshine-yellow peaches gently nestled in the clear nectar of light syrup, each peach half round, succulent, and seductive behind the glass Mason jar, tempting and voluptuous, like prostitutes in the windows of Amsterdam's red light district. The faint hiss and clink of the vacuum-packed can lid as it is gently pried off the jar gives promise to the flavor lying beneath. Close your eyes, inhale deeply, and tenderly spoon out one of the peach halves with its attendant juices. Suddenly, in the deepest, darkest recesses of winter, like a dream or a miracle, it's mid-August again. Laughing children are playing Frisbee on the lawn with a black and white dog wearing a blue bandana tied around his neck, steaks are cooking on the grill, the bees are droning over in the garden and four guys with beer bellies covered by denim overalls are laughing and playing horseshoes. This is the power of home-canned peaches on the second of February.

The objective was to get at the canned goods. I carefully explained that Groundhog's Day is a time for taking stock of things. "If you have half your wood and half your hay on Groundhog's Day it means that you will make it through the winter. It's a time to celebrate. Most people invite friends to get together and eat canned goods. Especially if they have any canned peaches left."

They bit hook, line and sinker. The Groundhog Day dinner menu was salsa, peach and apple chutney, pickled beets, squash lasagna, home baked bread, dandelion wine and the sweetest golden canned peaches you ever tasted. I would have gotten away with the peach coveting ruse if Gary hadn't stopped down at the Dove Song Dairy Goat Farm and Cheese Factory.

"How was your Groundhog Day dinner?" Gary cheerfully asked the woman behind the counter as he picked up his order of goat yoghurt, goat mozzarella and goat cheddar cheese.

"Our what?" asked the Goat Lady.

"You know, the tradition where you celebrate having half your hay and half your wood by eating your home-canned goods."

"I've heard about having half your wood and half your hay on Groundhog's Day, but there is nothing about canned goods in the tradition." She paused and looked directly at Gary. "Sue didn't by any chance can peaches last summer, did she?"

What Doesn't Kill Us Makes Us Stronger

Sometimes life can take an unexpected turn after creeping up on you just one little bit at a time.

My country abode was a perfect place to live. I delighted in waking up every morning to the joyful singing of birds. I experienced a feeling of glee as I fed the horses, mucked the stalls, broke up disagreements between the pony and the pig, and then went about my day. This was as close to blissful as I had ever been in my life. I became almost fit and even lost a little weight. Ribs and pelvic bones that had been comfortably encased in mid-forties flab were making an encore after an absence of ten years. I ate garden fresh vegetables, canned food for the winter, and grew my own herbs for both cooking and medicinal uses. I had never been closer to the land and the simple life; Helen and Scott Nearing had nothing on me. I hadn't fallen off a horse, broken an arm or stepped on a nail in over a year.

I had never felt better. So what was that nagging, niggling little doubt that seemed to creep into my subconscious from time to time? Slight bouts of irritable bowel (too much good food, combined with a stressful job), irregular periods and weird mood swings (probably perimenopause, every grocery checkout I stood before had at least three magazines touting how to deal with the latest symptoms), or maybe a little depression as my beloved father had passed away suddenly just a few months previous. I reaffirmed to myself that everything was fine, just the inevitable changes that come with age.

Nothing to worry about. I was always very good about going for my annual exam, getting mammograms, and the like, and always passed with flying colors.

Nothing to worry about. Heart disease ran in the family. None of the symptoms fit.

Sometimes the Fates provide respite from the relentless battle that is farming: the mid-winter thaw. It manifests itself by a week or so of temperatures in the 50s, which helps melt some of the snow and ice before the start of the planting season. Yes, there are still stalls to muck, neurotic dogs, demanding pigs and horses coated in mud. But you can breathe in deeply without your nostrils sticking together, and walk an energetic yearling across the barnyard without losing your balance on several layers of ice. For fleeting moments your feet are even warm. During the thaw, people look out beyond their parka hoods and start to realize that there is life around them. They take a momentary break from the necessity of just trying to stay warm and keep the buckets from freezing to think about other matters. They pull out their seed catalogs and, forgetting that they swore to limit gardening to a few tomato plants, proceed to fill out an order for melons, cucumbers, peppers, radishes, broccoli and pumpkins. They take a mid-winter respite to stop, breathe and pay attention to other things beside mere survival.

It was during the mid-winter thaw that I felt the lump. At first I simply pretended that it wasn't there. I rationalized that it must be a bit of leftover fluff from too much fattening holiday food. It was just my imagination playing tricks on me. But I could feel the thing when I lay on my stomach and turned just the right way. It was indeed real, and I had to deal with it.

I called on Monday to make an appointment with my doctor. Surely there was nothing to worry about; I just need a check up. He could see me on Friday morning, so no rush. That was fine, since my doctor conveniently worked at the same hospital where I worked. I had known him for years and we got along well. During the course of infrequent (non-trauma related) visits we would chat about the latest farm project, what the ghosts were up to, or the politics of the health system. This visit was no different. We talked about the management changes at the hospital, the new clinical information system, and the newest additions to the Flower Hill Farm menagerie. When it came time to get down to business, I said, "I've got a lump."

"Where?" he asked.

"In my abdomen. You can feel it pretty easily."

He put one hand on my stomach and pressed gently. Then he turned away and reached into a drawer for the CT scan order form. I saw his face as he turned away and knew the situation wasn't good. After retrieving the form he said, "We're just going to order a test and see what's going on here," but his voice was a little too cheerful, his lips a little too tight.

By noon I was sitting in the radiology waiting area drinking the Hawaiian Punch-flavored dye to prepare for my cat scan. Forty-five minutes later I was lying on a table in a hospital gown.

Ever the change agent, I looked around for opportunities for improvement. I might as well get some work done while waiting, I reasoned. I'd been working with this radiology group on some major modifications to their area. They had not been very keen on this, so the project had been long and difficult, but was now starting to show some signs of success. The group joked and talked shop as they injected some dye into my arm. They were still joking through the microphone as they ran the first set of images. "Just lie still for a minute. For once you won't be making changes!"

"On the contrary, this is giving me a chance to be a Secret Shopper!" I shot back.

Then there was silence. No sound came from the glass observation booth. Finally, a slightly quivering voice said, "You can get dressed now."

"What does it show?" I asked, even though I knew they wouldn't tell me.

"The radiologist has to read the results and then he'll call your doctor," came the pat response.

"Compassionate liars," I thought. I'd seen the radiologist in the booth during the entire test. They already knew. My family doctor called me at my office at 7:30 on Monday morning.

"Stop down at my office at 9:30 this morning so that we can talk about what you've got."

The visit was short and to the point. "What you have is unusual in a woman your age. In fact, it's almost exclusively seen in children under the age of twelve. Stem cells in your body can start to reproduce and grow tissue. In your case it appears to be a tooth. It's called a teratoma and yours is growing rapidly. They are almost never malignant, but it has to come out. Do you have any questions?"

"Questions," I thought slowly. I had a tooth growing in my stomach? What questions could one possibly ask? Let's see...is it a molar or an incisor? Perhaps a wisdom tooth? Should I schedule a visit with a surgeon or a dentist? Will this be covered under major medical or the dental plan? I shook my head. No questions.

The doctor continued: "I was able to get a consult with the GYN surgeon at 4:00 this afternoon so you'll have to clear your schedule."

No negotiating, no "by your leave," no choices. My job was simply to shut up and show up.

"Serves me right," I thought. I've gone all these years ignoring my biological clock and when it finally starts to look like I'm never going to get around to marrying or having children, some rogue stem cells in a fit of reproductive indignation take it upon themselves to start dividing away and making things indiscriminately.

Instead of an immaculate conception, I get unauthorized mastication. Isn't that just something?

I liked the surgeon immediately. A tall, older woman, she had an air of confidence and decisiveness that I respected despite my unbelievable diagnosis. She explained that the surgery that was required was a complete hysterectomy and abdominal exploration, and that it should be done right away. There was time on the OR schedule this Friday. Pre-op testing could be done on Wednesday. I would not be able to lift anything at all for six weeks after surgery and it would be three months before I could lift more than twenty pounds. My first thought was "How can I possibly run a farm with those kinds of restrictions?"

I left the doctor's office and returned to work. I should have been upset, worried, concerned, something. But I wasn't. Instead, I did what I had been doing since I first set foot on the farm, when I took on that first insurmountable task of throwing the gross carpet right through the upstairs window. I made a list and went directly to tasks. Instead of *dealing*, I absorbed myself in *doing*. It was the purist pure form of denial, the "denial of doing." Carrying on my regular duties and maintaining control.

What easier way to maintain control than to go it alone? My experience with the CT scan led me to that conclusion. Or maybe my first brush with cancer when I had the face surgery helped in my decision. I recalled friends who remained aloof and when contact was so overdue that something had to be said responded with, "I just felt so bad I didn't know what to say."

Then there were the well-meaning people, more acquaintances than friends, who had stared at my face, squinting and cocking their heads like they were looking at a new paint job on a car, finally announcing in a satisfied tone, "The plastic surgeon did a pretty good job."

I had no desire to deal with the explanations, the worry, the concern, the anecdotes of aunt so and so who had such and such an operation/malady/disease and either lived or died. In addition, I was and am part of the support system for several friends dealing with cancer. No sense in putting people through this. Until I was sure, I could stay on the outside and deal with the tasks at hand. And the tasks were legion. I worked at a fever pitch to get things done at the office. I hired full-time barn help. I bought grain, cat food, dog food, ten pounds of vermicelli and an electric broom; I cleaned out the refrigerator, organized my underwear drawer, cleaned out the trunk of the car, polished the silver, crocheted an afghan, put photos in the family album. Granted, not all this was entirely necessary, but the chores kept me occupied.

On Friday morning, I packed a bag for my hospital stay and caught a ride to work with a coworker. I put in a full morning at my job in an effort to save as much of my sick leave as possible. I finalized some contracts and sat in on couple of project meetings. At 11:30 I walked from my office over to the pre-op area. I was in the 1:00 p.m. surgery slot.

I changed into a hospital gown and the nurse took my bag and all my other possessions. Then I met with the anesthesiologist. I had made sure that he was a good one. Several years in healthcare taught me that if you're going to have surgery, a competent anesthesiologist was as important as an experienced surgeon. He confirmed my identity by asking my name and birth date, even though we'd worked together for the last six years. He asked for the thousandth time whether or not I had any allergies. No problems, no questions. Then he said," It will be a little over an hour before your surgery, do you want a little something for anxiety?"

"ANXIETY, hell yes I want something for anxiety," I thought to myself, the prospect of an hour with nothing to do finally triggering a full-blown panic attack. "And not a 'little something' thank you very much, I want a lot of something. I want to go in search of Elvis, I want to visit Pluto and chat with the aliens to find out how they feel about losing their planet status, and I want to get as far away from here as chemically possible."

The changed and somewhat shocked expression on the anesthesiologist's face hinted to me that I was actually using my "out loud" voice instead of my "inner voice." He gave me a generous dose of Ativan, wished me luck and slowly and gently backed out of the room. No problem. Nothing to worry about.

My next recollection was a hazy flurry of activity as I was transferred from the PACU (Post Anesthesia Care Unit) to my room in the OB/GYN unit. It was dark outside. I remembered asking if I could get up and feed the horses. They gave me a shot of something and I fell back into a drug-induced haze. I woke up a couple hours later with the surgeon standing at the foot of my bed.

"She looks tired," I thought, as the fog lifted and I came to my senses enough to understand that the surgeon was speaking to me.

"The mass was larger than we thought, it weighed two kilos. It appeared to be still encapsulated and I think we got it all. But, I'm sorry, it's so rare in these cases, I'm so sorry, we found cancer." Her voice broke, she was crying.

I tried so hard to think of something encouraging to say to this woman who had been working since early that morning in clinic, had a full afternoon of surgeries, and was now ending her day telling a forty-six-year-old woman that she had cancer.

"Do we have to do anything right now?" I asked, hoping in all honesty that I could get a good night's sleep before having to start battling cancer.

"The oncologist happened to be in the OR, so we did a complete staging and took lymph nodes and tissue for testing. The lab results won't be final for a few days. Then we'll come up with a plan."

"So there's nothing we have to do now, like right now?" I asked.

The surgeon looked around the room and realized, for the first time, that we were totally alone. "Is there someone that you want to call, someone that you want me to help you explain this to?" she asked.

"What time is it?" I asked.

"Nine o'clock. Friday night."

"No, all the farmers are in bed and nobody else is sober."

I woke the next morning around 5:30 a.m. to find my newly designated oncologist seated in a chair next to my bed. He wore thick glasses, a white lab coat and sneakers. His age wasn't betrayed by his face or his voice. Like the Metal Man, you could not tell how old he was. "You have a very unusual form of cancer," he said, apparently an oncologist's way of introducing themselves. "The odds of seeing this type of cancer in a person your age are very, very remote."

"From where I'm sitting the odds seem to be about one point zero," I responded. I couldn't help myself. This man invited bantering.

He laughed, "True enough."

"Where do we go from here?" I asked.

"We don't know much about it. Depending on the lab results we may have to do radiation or chemotherapy, or we may just keep a watch and see. In any case, you will have to be followed by an oncologist for the rest of your life."

Still foggy from THE ORDEAL, some part of my brain had confused *oncologist* with *ornithologist*.

"That will spook the horses," I said, picturing white-coated men with green field vests, binoculars and sneakers lurking in the multiflora rose bushes taking notes on stainless steel clip boards.

"We're pretty careful about things like that," the oncologist replied without missing a beat.

"Is there anything I have to do right now?"

"You can't go home until someone documents flatulence."

"Flatulence?"

"You have to fart."

"I'll get right on it."

Two days later, having farted to the apparent satisfaction of the medical community, I was home stretched out on the couch in my living room. The discharge instructions clearly stated that I was only allowed two trips up and down the stairs each day. As I had already used up seven days' worth I was planning to do fewer trips later on in the week to average it all out. The Jack Russell terrier was lying on the couch next to me with her head between her paws. The Labrador, my permanent shadow, was on the floor beside the couch. Every once in a while he looked at me with his kind brown eyes and let out a deep sigh.

Vinnie, the Doberman, was outside patrolling the perimeter of the house for the umpteenth millionth time. When I slowly and painfully got up to let him in, he trotted purposefully from room to room, looking in all the closets and under the furniture. The slightest noise from outside sent him charging around the house barking until I let him out on patrol again. Vinnie didn't like this new situation at all. It was clear to him that in spite of his constant vigilance Something got in. Alpha Bitch was down. Somehow the perimeter had been broken, and Vinnie was hell-bent that it wasn't going to happen again. As a result, he was driving all occupants of the house pretty much insane.

The Groundhog Hunters stopped by to see if I needed anything. As everything, with the exception of Vinnie, was pretty much under control, they helped themselves to a couple Yeunglings and sat down by the fireplace. I gave them some sketchy details about the cancer, leaving out the part about the tooth, since I did not want to give them too much fuel for future chop-busting. I stressed that the surgeons were confident that they got it all and we were just waiting for confirmation from the lab. No big deal. Just a hysterectomy with a slight hiccough. At the word "cancer" Scott got up and started pacing back and forth across the room, running one hand through his hair while holding the Yeungling in the other.

"Oh, God. Jeeze, Liz. Oh God. Are you OK? Of course you're not OK. Who would be OK? Oh jeeze." Rick, on the other hand, had been sitting quietly, taking it all in. He suddenly keyed in on the word "hysterectomy," and brightened considerably.

"Ah, a hysterectomy!" he began. "My sister-in-law had one of them when she was your age. I know just what will happen. You should start getting hot flashes within the next week or so if you haven't already. You'll probably wake up with night sweats most nights. You have to watch getting too emotional about things so that you don't start crying all the time. You are going to start forgetting things like your car keys and whether or not you left the water running in the barn. No matter what you eat or how careful you are, YOU WILL GET FAT. That's just the way it is." Perhaps thinking that he had overdone it a bit, he paused and said, "You should start thinking about taking hormones."

I stared at this man, the Groundhog Hunter. He was wearing faded jeans, sneakers with white socks and a red flannel shirt. He was a burly looking sort of guy with a full beard and a beer belly. He sat on the stone hearth of the fireplace, with his beer in his right hand resting on one knee and his left elbow resting in the other, his index finger extending to punch at the air every time he described a new symptom of pre- peri- or post-menopause.

"With such fine medical guidance, who needs an Academic Medical Center?" I thought.

There was, however, something I did need. I wanted to see my friend and first riding instructor, Naomi. She and her husband Jack had moved to Kentucky a few years ago, ostensibly to retire, build a home, and "just have brood mares." But there is nothing "retired" about running a fifty-acre Thoroughbred breeding farm.

Naomi had been battling ovarian cancer for eight years. It was one of the few battles in her life this feisty little woman was going to lose. Naomi had had yet another surgery a few weeks before mine, but unfortunately, in her case, the doctors couldn't get at the tumor, and her prognosis was poor. The horse business does not stop for cancer and Jack was scheduled to be away on business. He didn't want to leave Naomi alone, so it was a perfect time for me to visit.

I broached the topic carefully with my surgeon. She understood the situation and okayed it for me to fly even though this was less than two weeks after surgery. The only limitation was that I had to make sure someone could carry my luggage *every step of the way*. Raised by frugal parents who stressed the value of hard work and personal independence, no one, in the history of my life thus far, has ever carried my luggage. Not sure how the whole thing worked or how exactly to value this service, I figured I'd better smile sweetly and tip like my horse just won the Preakness. The shuttle driver who drove me to the airport took a look at the bill I gave him and asked for my return flight, then he changed his schedule so that he would be sure to be the one picking me up. He handed me and my bag off to the curbside baggage handler who also seemed quite pleased to escort me and my luggage to the gate. Word must have gotten out because by the time my flight landed in Kentucky there were five baggage handlers waiting in readiness.

Naomi was parked in the "No Parking" zone in front of the airport in her "arrest me" red jaguar. The baggage handler guided my belongings into the trunk, gave them a loving tap, smiled and saluted as I gave him his well-earned tip. I gave Naomi a big "Hello" hug. She was a lot thinner than the last time I had seen her, and I calculated that she couldn't weigh more than ninety pounds. Her skin had taken on a pale yellow color. Her eyes, however, were as bright and sparkly as ever. It was good to see her.

As we got in the car and drove toward the farm, it felt like Naomi had never moved away. She was my trainer, mentor and friend, who believed fiercely in just a few things. She believed in her horses, her husband and her friends. She had come out to look at my farm all those years ago and was the only person that shared my vision. Where others saw Devastation and Decay, Naomi saw Potential. She told me to go for it. Nothing was ever impossible for Naomi.

She didn't believe in limitations, but she did believe in persistence, a quality that had pushed her to the top of the game. Show Jumper Champion, "A" circuit horse show judge, show horse and race horse breeder, she had done it all. Despite a body ravaged with cancer she was still in the hunt.

"How about lunch at the Thoroughbred Club?" Naomi suggested.

The Thoroughbred Club is a stone's throw from Keeneland racetrack. It's the local hangout for members of the horse industry in Kentucky and the food is very good. If there was a breath left in my body, I would make it to lunch at the Thoroughbred Club.

We arrived about mid-afternoon. The entrance hall was a tasteful blend of rich green and burgundy with portraits of the Big Horses of racing: Man O' War, Secretariat, Alydar, Ruffian. A bronze lamp of a racehorse and jockey sat on a mahogany antique table. The dining room itself had white wainscot paneling with green-tinted textured wallpaper. Flat panel television screens were mounted from the ceiling such that every table has a clear view of a minimum of two of them. They were tuned into racetracks from around the country. The entire atmosphere reeked of racing, rib eyed steaks and martinis, and, of course, Mint Juleps for the tourists.

The Moby Grape and Flower Hill Farmers of the world love our little pieces of paradise and are dedicated to doing everything possible to make our horses happy. The Horsemen of racing are in an entirely different world of their own. They've quit their day jobs (if they ever had them) and their dedication manifests itself in their lifestyles. It's horses from 3:00 a.m., when the horses-in-training eat their breakfast, until 10 p.m. when the last bed check is over. During the foaling and breeding season (from January until roughly the end of May) no one sleeps at all in the whole state of Kentucky.

In between all this work, the Horsemen have to figure out how to make a living. It's said that to make a little money in horses, you have to start out with a lot of money. The Thoroughbred Club is where Horsemen go about the business of trying to make their living.

The Maître D' sat us at a table situated a polite distance from the others. We were clearly out for a "Ladies Lunch" and it was obvious that there was "Men's Business" going on in other parts of the room. Some tables held wealthy farm owners and their trainers, while others had stallion owners meeting customers with well-bred mares, blood stock agents, real estate agents, and jockey's agents.

In February in Kentucky everyone's dreams are in full flower in hopes that this year will bring the Big One: the perfect foal, the highest priced yearling for the sale, the two-year-old race prospect, the three-year-old Derby prospect, or the next Breeders Cup champion.

The dining room was alive with the business of this unbridled and unfounded optimism, the upbeat tone that perennially makes up horse racing this time of the year.

Suddenly all activity ceased. Plates stopped clattering, conversations halted in mid-sentence, waitresses stood still, diners sat frozen with forks halfway to their mouths. "And they're OFF!" the announcer on the television shouted. The activity in the room was suspended for one minute and forty eight seconds as the stakes race on the TV screens came to conclusion. This was a "road to the Derby" race, the winning colt just one step closer to the Run for the Roses. A twist of fate, a turn of fortune, this was the foundation of the horse business.

"Hot Dog!" exclaimed Naomi, her face lighting up with delight. The winning colt was a half-brother to a colt she and Jack bought at the yearling sale to pinhook at the Keenland sale the coming fall. Pinhooking is the business of buying a horse as a weanling or yearling in the hopes of selling it at a profit six months to a year later. All this provided that the bloodlines are still "hot," the animal stays alive and doesn't run through a fence or step in a groundhog hole, and it grows up the way you hope it will.

Naomi was grinning ear to ear. If this colt made it to the Kentucky Derby, the value on her colt would go through the roof! Then she started to cough. She held a napkin over her mouth with one hand and held her chest with the other. "It's in my lungs," she said simply.

We acknowledged in the silence between us that Naomi wasn't going to be at the fall Keenland sale. Cancer is a bitch. In the Great Paddock of Life, Cancer is the lead brood mare.

"Do you have enough energy to stop by Karen's farm on the way home?" asked Naomi. "I'd like to see if the Big Mare had her foal yet. You should see her, she's one of the best."

This was indeed a beautifully bred mare in a state where the top bloodlines are made. Her second foal had won over a million dollars so far and had placed second in last year's Kentucky Derby. She was now in foal to one of the leading sires. The mare's owner had turned down several offers to sell her, all well within seven figures.

"Wouldn't pass this one up!" I said.

We drove over to Karen's Westgate Stud Farm. Karen had spent most of her life building a first class broodmare operation. The farm was the temporary home for over one-hundred-fifty mares, a few of which were hers, but most of which belonged to customers. I liked Karen and admired her. She had made her way in the world with her tremendous energy and a commitment to doing things right.

Naomi drove the Jaguar up to the imposing steel gates, pressed the intercom, and waved at the closed-circuit camera. The gate slowly opened inward and we drove through two massive stone pillars. Karen met us at the top of the drive, next to foaling barn number one of five. After a few minutes of casual conversation Naomi asked, "How's the mare?"

"The vet was out this morning and I had him check on her. She should go tonight," Karen replied.

Karen continued. "This foal should be something. The mare's just coming in from the field, would you like to see her?"

We walked into the foaling barn, a long structure with an asphalt aisle and stalls on either side. One groom was sweeping the aisle where the mare had walked, and the other was in the stall with her. The place was immaculate. The eighteen-foot by eighteen-foot stall was bedded in at least two feet of straw. Typical of well-run Kentucky barns, it was fluffed up and level as a pillow top mattress with two carved out half-moon areas, one for the feed area and one at the door. The groom had removed the mare's leather halter and cleaned it before hanging it on a nearby hook.

Having never been close to a horse of this quality, and being more than a little intimidated by the efficiency of Karen's operation, especially as compared to my little pig-donkey-horse-duck-turkey farm, I kept quiet, just taking it all in. The mare was a little taller than sixteen hands, and had perfect confirmation, a broad chest and a beautiful sloping shoulder. She didn't care that she was a million dollar investment; she just knew dinner was on its way, and hopefully this foal would be too. Karen stroked the mare, checked her udder with a flashlight and lifted her tail. The mare nuzzled her pockets looking for treats.

"She looks good," Karen said."The cameras are on so I can keep an eye on her from the house, but we have someone in the barn all night during foaling season."

Excited for Karen and the prospect of the new foal and potential Derby winner, we said our goodbyes. As we drove to Naomi's farm we passed the pristine white fences and trademark red gates of Calumet Farm, then the rustic stone walls and perfectly-maintained fences that surround Gainsway Farms. I thought, "What drives some people to this level? What makes their dreams bigger than everyone else's? If they're so smart, why would they ever own horses?" And, since I was pretty much done in by the day's activities I asked myself "Where do they get the energy to do all this?"

When we arrived at the house, I flopped down on the couch, too exhausted to move. Naomi sat in the leather recliner to return the day's phone calls. I soon fell asleep to the sound of Naomi happily chatting away with her husband, going over the events of the day, plans for the horses, and next year's breeding selections.

The next day we went shopping at Keenland and visited a couple of tack shops. Inspired by the near-perfection of Karen's and Naomi's farms, I bought leather halters with "Flower Hill Farm" engraved on brass plates riveted onto them. "Have to start somewhere," I thought happily. When I got back to Pennsylvania I would get my farm shipshape, up to standard, dust free, everything freshly painted, all tack cleaned every day, blankets, legwraps, towels all in their respective places. None of this malingering, no more pigs or ponies in the house. Get the goats out of the kitchen and turkeys out of the road. I would ride every day two, no, four hours a day. Nothing is impossible! The sky's the limit!

The phone was ringing as we walked through the door into Naomi's kitchen after our shopping spree. As soon as Naomi answered, I could tell it was bad news. Listening to half a conversation I braced for the worst.

"Oh no."

"Was the vet there?"

"She did? I'm so sorry."

"There isn't anything you could have done. It's a tough business."

"Have you told the owner?"

"Let me know if there's anything I can do. Hang in there, Karen."

The Big Mare was dead. Her water broke late last night, but Karen and the experienced attendant knew something was wrong within ten minutes and quickly called the vet. He was at a nearby farm and got there in no time, but there was nothing they could do. The mare had a massive hemorrhage, and she was gone within minutes. Her foal died in the early morning hours. A big, beautiful chestnut colt. Twist of fate, turn of fortune. A busted dream.

We sat in silence in the living room and cried. It's never easy when something beautiful dies. Then we talked about the great horses we'd known. Not million dollar broodmares, but Gracie and New Shot, Naomi's jumper, TJ, who used to follow her around the showground without benefit of bridle or halter, Duncan the miserable pony, and Petey, Naomi's retired stakes horse. Horses that shared our lives as friends and partners. The really great ones. We also talked about cancer and how much time Naomi had left.

I've stopped the chemo, so now the doctor doesn't want anything to do with me. Keeps referring me back to the Bugboys."

"Bugboys" in the racing world are apprentice jockeys. It was Naomi's term for the young medical residents at the cancer center.

"They're figuring less than six months. I'm going to miss this."

"I'm going to miss you, my friend" I said. It was enough. Nothing more needed to be added.

Early the next morning Naomi dropped me off at the airport. "What's up for the rest of your day?" I asked, mostly to avoid dealing with the growing lump of emotion in my throat.

"I'm off to the training track. Our Gone West filly is going to work this morning. She's put in a couple of good works already and may be racing in a couple of weeks. She's the real deal. She can run a hole in the wind!"

I smiled and waved as the red Jaguar growled down the road. Somewhere through the weekend all my questions were answered. Loss was sad. Death was sad. Cancer was sad. Sad, but I wouldn't let it be tragic. Tragedy would be letting something other than my own dreams define my life and dictate my future. Eyes up, look straight ahead. Keep going. Life will throw out every kind of calamity. That's life's business. My business is to keep dreaming and keep working as long as there is work to do on Flower Hill Farm. "Move over cancer, you're not the lead brood mare in my paddock!"

The Hoghouse

Fixing up the house and the barn was time consuming, expensive and life affirming. At every step of the way, I was guided by a clear mental blueprint which had remained unchanged since that Elvis night years ago at the Auction Gallery when I bought a pitchfork and made the commitment to farming. I worked the plan right down to the wave petunias, herb garden, four-board fence painted white and stone-walled kitchen. From the time I first looked at the deteriorating manure-filled buildings, the end vision was clear.

I even knew from day one what colors to paint each room in the farmhouse. On an eerie note, without knowing or planning it, my chosen colors matched to the shade each room's original colors, discovered while I was scraping the walls to remove half-a-dozen layers of paint.

I had great advice from great mentors. Naomi taught me the secret of laying out the stables. "Count the steps you take to do the barn chores, feeding, mucking, watering," she had said. "Whatever changes you decide on, make sure to minimize your steps because you will be walking the distance twice a day for the rest of your life. Spend a little extra money to relocate the feed room door or move the water hydrant. An extra twenty feet is a long way to carry a water bucket at 4:00 a.m. on an icy winter morning." The carefully-planned barn restoration considered water hydrant placement, feed room location, arrangement of the tack room, wash stall and location of the pitchforks to maximize efficiency. In the end it all worked in synchrony.

For all this clarity of vision and focused determination that had been directed at the house and the barn, I drew a blank when it came to the Hoghouse, a structure located at the corner of the property near the road, about a hundred yards away from the house and the barn. In all fairness, it was never part of the initial Fantasy Farm, but rather an extra that came along for the ride. For the first couple of years, it was used as a woodshop, since a cabinetmaker had rented it from the previous owners and I had decided to keep the arrangement since it provided a little income each month. He kept to himself and was at the shop mostly during the hours when I was at work. Both the cabinetmaker and the hoghouse were out of sight and out of mind while I focused on other things. Eventually, he retired and moved his machinery and wares out.

I didn't have any further plans for the Hoghouse. Not for myself, anyway. Mostly what Flower Hill Farm's Hoghouse does is provide work for the unemployed. When things got slow after the barn restoration, Brian offered to use the leftover paint from the barn roof. Just a couple of days pay, and it needed to be done anyway.

As I was writing out the check for his work, Brian mentioned, "By the way, there are squirrels living in the Hoghouse. You should patch up the boards under the eaves so that they can't get in. They'll chew up the wires and start a fire."

I'm a sucker for fire safety. I had come to grips with the bat infestation in the house, but wasn't up to dealing with a family of Hoghouse squirrels.

"Would you be able to do it?" I asked.

"Sure, won't be more than a couple days pay, plus materials."

True to his word, Brian had the work done. The Hog House was now safe and secure from wire-chewing rodents.

"What are you going to use it for?" asked Brian as he picked up his check.

"I'm not sure. It would make a great little potting shop for growing herbs or even selling them." I said offhandedly, not really giving it much thought.

"You know, whoever did the wiring in there really didn't know what he was doing. It's a two-twenty amp line and the gauge on the internal wiring isn't high enough. You should disconnect some of those circuits and replace some of that wiring, especially if you plan to put grow lights in there."

"How much would that be?"

"Just a couple days pay, plus materials."

Two days and a couple hundred more bucks later, the Hoghouse was free of roof leaks and squirrel families, and was "grow light ready." Brian found his next painting gig over in Lehigh County and work on the Hoghouse was suspended for a time. Two years in fact.

This was, coincidentally, when one of the Groundhog Hunters got laid off. Scott was a good worker, showed up every day and gave his company his all for about sixty salaried hours each week. But then a new factory opened in China, oil prices went up, consumer spending went down, and somebody hiccoughed on Wall Street. The Groundhog Hunter had lost his job.

Given the situation, he was handling it well. Scott asked me to help him rewrite his resume and put together some cover letters. We also did some goal planning. I did "life coaching" on the side and was having fun helping my good friend. The subject of the Hoghouse came up.

"What are you going to do with it?" asked Scott.

"I don't have a clue. What I'd love to do is quit my job and turn the Hoghouse into a classroom where I could teach motivational thinking and goal setting, getting people on the path to finding their dreams. Or maybe teach computer skills, like Excel, PowerPoint, that sort of thing. Then I'd feed them homemade soup and canned peaches for lunch and they could shop for herbs afterwards."

"You'd be working with a bit of a niche market, there." Scott commented, scratching his head.

We finished the resume and the letters and headed down to the Hoghouse to take a look.

"What needs to be done?" Scott asked.

"Well, the roof doesn't leak, there are no squirrels living in it and it's wired for a grow light," I said while opening the padlock on the door. The Hoghouse is a cinder block building about thirty feet wide by sixty feet long. The right hand side of the building, the one closest to the road, had no windows, the other side had five windows of various sizes, makes and models, probably selected because they were left over from the cabinetmaker's remodeling projects. When it housed hogs, all that was really necessary were block walls, a concrete floor with floor drains, a source of electricity and a frost-free pump. To convert it to the woodworking shop, the man had framed in a couple of closets and then run electrical wires over the rafters to some ceiling lights. A half-dozen outlet boxes dangled on wires from the ceiling to various locations around the building where he had placed lathes, turning machines and sanders. With the exception of the outlet box for the grow light, it didn't appear in any sense to be "up to code."

"The first thing we need to do is frame the inside walls and put in insulation, then run some outlets. That way it's ready to drywall," said Scott, fully embracing the vision.

"Who is the 'We'?" I asked, wondering if this was really such a great idea. The girl-like giddiness from celebrating barn and house re-construction completion hadn't faded. I hadn't taken a sledge hammer to a wall, torn down a ceiling or repaired plumbing in weeks. I was even starting to grow fingernails again.

"My buddy, Rick, of course. We can do anything. That's our motto: 'No job too big, no job too small.'"

"Have you ever done anything like this?" I asked, hearing a faint sucking sound both in the back of my mind and in my bank account. Scott looked at me over his wire-rimmed glasses. "Now Liz, we built the tree house didn't we?"

"How much will it cost?" I asked.

"Just a couple days pay for the both of us, plus materials.

I let go and let God. It was only the Hoghouse after all, not the Taj Mahal. Besides, Scott needed the money and the sense of accomplishment that the project would bring. I wouldn't even have to get involved, and the building was far enough from the house to keep the dust away. From my front porch, I could hear the sounds of men at work: circular saws, hammers and the occasional expletive when a Groundhog Hunter struck himself with a hammer.

The work continued. Soon a couple of days had stretched into a couple of weeks. I watched from my front porch as pickup truck loads of wiring, insulation, Tyvek and various sizes of lumber were hauled through the front door. And watched again as empty cases of Yeungling bottles were carried out the back door. I continued my regular routine, getting up early to feed the animals, going to work, tending the gardens, canning peaches and trying to ignore the flurry of activity taking place in the Hoghouse. The only thing that drew my attention there were the sounds of gunshots, a particularly long string of expletives, or the occasional chainsaw motor.

At the end of the second week, I came home from work to find two tired and dejected Groundhog Hunters drinking Yeunglings on my front porch, farm dogs lolling happily at their feet.

"We changed our motto," began Scott. "It's now 'No job too small, some jobs too big.'" I think we got in a little over our heads. Also, I got a job. It starts tomorrow."

"Congrats on the new job. How far did you get in the Hoghouse?" I asked.

"We had a little trouble nailing the framing into the concrete floor," started Scott.

"But then we found this cool hammer at the Home Depot," added Rick, his enthusiasm welling up. "It's really a nail gun that works using .22 shells!" That explained the gunshots.

"We ran all twenty-four outlets and most of the fiber optic cable," continued Rick.

"Twenty-four outlets? Fiber optic cable?" I said, stunned. "Why does a Hoghouse need twenty-four electrical outlets and fiber optic cable?"

"For the computer classes."

"Couldn't we have just gone with wireless?" I asked, vaguely recalling that I had once said something hazy and non-specific about computer classes.

"Wireless doesn't work in Bernville," chorused the Groundhog Hunters in unison.

"We framed out a space for the kitchen and ran into a little trouble with the circuit box for the hot tub."

"WHAT HOT TUB?!"

Rick looked over at Scott. It was obvious that they had been anticipating a little resistance in this department.

"Liz," began Scott, "We got to thinking that the Hoghouse would make an awesome party room, a place to go to after the Eagle's games in the tree house to relax, play some pool, and use the hot tub. Only on weekends, of course, when you weren't teaching computer skills, motivational leadership or how to grow herbs or make soup."

"I don't need a party room," I said with my head in my hands. "I should have given you a specification!"

"Not to worry, we used a specification!" said Scott.

"Yepper, a dart board shall be placed exactly nine-feet-seven-and-one-quarter inches from the throw line" quoted Rick proudly.

"And the center of the bulls eye shall be exactly sixty-four inches from the floor and the throw line shall be exactly three inches wide," Scott chimed in. "Wait till you see the spot we picked out for the throw line. It's right next to the square we chalked in for the keg master and martini bar"

"What, no cappuccino machine?"

"We added an outlet right next to the line for an ice maker."

"It's a HOG HOUSE; it has windows on one side, limited ventilation and I haven't been in it more than half-a-dozen times since I moved here."

"You just need a little vision, Liz. This building has endless potential!" said Scott.

"Just how much of its potential has been realized over the past two weeks?" I asked, fumbling in my purse for my checkbook.

"Well, we did most of the framing, put in a lot of insulation, rough-wired most of the outlets and chalked squares on the floor for the dart board, pool table and major appliance locations. We also tacked up a couple dozen sheets of drywall. We've got one heck of a start for the next guys."

Scott gave me a figure that was more than reasonable for two weeks worth of work plus materials and a forty percent complete journey toward somewhere.

I tried hard to forget about the Hoghouse. I took a brief tour about a week after the Groundhog Hunters left and nothing came to me as far as a vision for a thirty-by-sixty-foot squirrel-free cinder block building with windows on one side wired for a grow light, fiber optic cable, twenty-four outlets, and chalk marks where a dart board, pool table cappuccino machine, major appliances and hot tub ought to go. I toyed with a few ideas. For instance, it might make a great guesthouse except that it is too close to the road and too close to the swamp to ever get a septic system (let alone occupancy) permit. It would be great as a tack room, only it's too far from the barn. Maybe an antique shop, tack shop or farrier supply store?

What was really bothering me? The farm was finished, the dream fulfilled. I had finally achieved some level of comfort and contentment. All major construction was completed. Heck, I'd even hung curtains.

I had also made peace with the ghosts for the most part. Weird things still occasionally happened, like coming in from gardening all day and finding a freshly-drawn bath steaming in the claw footed tub in the upstairs bathroom. I've learned to adjust, and make some accommodations. A nightlight in the "little boy's room" seems to comfort my spirit resident. When it is left on it quiets the footsteps on the stairs and the knocking on the closet wall in the wee hours of the morning.

The seasons waxed on, starting with a bumper crop of strawberries and asparagus in spring, bulging bushes of ripe and juicy wild blackberries in June, tomatoes to die for all summer long and fruit trees groaning with peaches, pears and apples in the early fall. The generosity of the universe was being manifested at Flower Hill Farm. The horses were content, fat and dappled under the rich ample pasture, the pig reveled in leftover scraps from the garden and daily trips to the orchard to see what Mother Nature had dropped off for him. I canned peaches, dried herbs, blanched and froze vegetables and filled the root cellar with summer's gifts.

One of my last tasks of the canning season was to bury a batch of Backyard Peach Brandy (a Ladies of the Grange recipe: fill quart size jars with layers of sugar, peaches, sugar, peaches, and so on to the top, press out as much air as possible and seal, then wrap the jars in brown paper and bury them at least eighteen inches deep in the garden. Dig up in ninety days and freeze the juice, take off the ice and pour off the brandy, serve fermented peaches over ice cream). I'd just finished tamping down the soil and marking each jar with little white, blue and red French flags left over from July's Bastille day party when Lillian came by.

"I see you've got your peach brandy going," she said. "Are you making any Silo Whiskey?"

"Silo Whiskey?"

"My, yes, you put apples and sugar and apples and sugar and apples and sugar layered in quart sized jars, press out all the air and seal them. Then wrap them in brown paper and put them in the bottom of the silo, and fill the silo with silage. When the cows eat down to the jars the whiskey should be ready." She paused for a moment and then added "Oh, you need a forty cow herd."

"I'm at a slight disadvantage there." I said sadly, not having ready access to such a herd. I briefly thought of Craigslist or eBay, but quickly dispelled the idea.

"Pity," she said.

"Pity," I agreed.

"What are you going to do with the Hoghouse?" Lillian continued, getting right to the heart of things as she always did.

"I don't know," I said, a little defensively. "I guess it can just sit there for awhile."

"And burn a hole in your heart." Lillian simply replied.

The Hoghouse was painted on the outside. Who cares if it is a mess on the inside? I did! It bothered me like an unpaid bill, an overdue trip to the dentist, or income tax forms still remaining untouched in late March. I was ignoring it, hoping that it would go away, but knowing that it wouldn't.

"I don't know what to do with it. I've dumped a lot of money into it, and good friends have put a lot of time into it. It's a costly investment, and is still less than half finished. All in all, it's just been a big waste of time and effort." I said.

"When did you put yourself into it?" Lillian asked.

It was a good point, as usual. "I have to mull that one over," I replied. She smiled and left me to my thoughts.

I spent some time on the subject. What was it about the Hoghouse that made me so unsettled, so unsure of myself? Was there some existential meaning here? Suddenly it became clear. The Hoghouse was the unspoken part of the vision which represented the commitment to Flower Hill Farm.

It was the crossing of the great chasm between the safe, secure, comfortable and paralyzing environment of everywoman's corporate environment to the unknown of creating a life based on passion and fulfillment of a dream, along with the belief that the Dream can nurture and sustain you for as long as you live. The Hoghouse had the potential for sustenance, but at the same time demanded my commitment and my vision.

With a leap of faith, I toured the Hoghouse again,, this time with a tablet and a pen. I knew I couldn't do it all, but I could get started, I could clean it out. I could tape and spackle the drywall and I could even hang the dart board if that fit the vision. I headed to Home Depot with a list and bought two five-gallon buckets of spackling compound. It was an initial down payment on a dream. The next weekend found me tottering on makeshift scaffolding (a board placed between two step ladders), taping and spackling with a zest I hadn't felt since the first Flower Hill Farm demolition days.

Suddenly, a shadow appeared in the doorway, it was Lillian, draped in a blue green cape, same gray braided hair and same gray-green eyes. She asked, "Have you decided what it is going to be?"

"Not yet. " I replied, "But it is going to be wonderful."

About the Author

Elizabeth Clark has had an eclectic career in nuclear engineering, construction project management, strategic planning, organizational development, leadership and career consulting, process redesign and healthcare quality management. The day job supports her passions for raising horses, writing poetry and whipping up the occasional garlic poultice or ironweed tea. *Lessons From the Hoghouse* is her first book. She lives in her beloved village of Bernville, Pennsylvania with five horses, two dogs, a pig, donkey, cats and an increasing number of groundhogs.

CPSIA information can be obtained at www.ICGtesting.com
Printed in the USA
BVOW02s1447080913

330383BV00001B/7/P